Visual Culture in Organizations

Routledge Studies in Management, Organizations, and Society

This series presents innovative work grounded in new realities, addressing issues crucial to an understanding of the contemporary world. This is the world of organised societies, where boundaries between formal and informal, public and private, local and global organizations have been displaced or have vanished, along with other nineteenth century dichotomies and oppositions. Management, apart from becoming a specialized profession for a growing number of people, is an everyday activity for most members of modern societies.

Similarly, at the level of enquiry, culture and technology, and literature and economics, can no longer be conceived as isolated intellectual fields; conventional canons and established mainstreams are contested. **Management, Organisation and Society** addresses these contemporary dynamics of transformation in a manner that transcends disciplinary boundaries, with books that will appeal to researchers, student and practitioners alike.

Breaking Through the Glass Ceiling
Women, Power and Leadership in
Agricultural Organizations
Margaret Alston

The Poetic Logic of Administration
Styles and Changes of Style in the Art
of Organizing
Kaj Sköldberg

Casting the Other
Maintaining Gender Inequalities in
the Workplace
Edited by Barbara Czarniawska and
Heather Höpfl

**Gender, Identity and the Culture of
Organizations**
Edited by Iiris Aaltio and Albert J. Mills

Text/Work
Representing Organization and
Organizing Representation
Edited by Stephen Linstead

**The Social Construction of
Management**
Texts and Identities
Nancy Harding

Management Theory
A Critical and Reflexive Reading
Nanette Monin

Visual Culture in Organizations

Theory and Cases

Alexander Styhre

Routledge
Taylor & Francis Group

LONDON AND NEW YORK

First published 2010 by Routledge
2 Park Square, Milton Park, Abingdon, Oxon OX14 4RN

52 Vanderbilt Avenue, New York, NY 10017

First published in paperback 2012

Routledge is an imprint of the Taylor & Francis Group, an informa business

© 2010 Taylor & Francis

Typeset in Sabon by IBT Global.

Library of Congress Cataloging-in-Publication Data
Styhre, Alexander.
   Visual culture in organizations : theory and cases / by Alexander Styhre.
     p. cm. — (Routledge studies in management, organizations, and society ; 9)
   Includes bibliographical references and index.
   1. Visual perception—Social aspects.   2. Visual sociology.   3. Organizational sociology.   I. Title.
   HM500.S79 2010
   302.3'5—dc22
   2009052884

ISBN13: 978-0-415-65314-5 (pbk)
ISBN13: 978-0-415-87190-7 (hbk)
ISBN13: 978-0-203-84868-5 (ebk)

Contents

Figures

Preface

One of the first things I did as a doctoral student at Lund University in the mid-1990s was to be send out to do a consulting/research work at Tetra Laval in Malmö. Tetra Laval is part of the food packaging industry in the Malmö—Lund region in southern Sweden and the unit I and my colleague from the Faculty of Engineering, Lund University, were studying was producing printed circuit boards that served in process control technologies used in the packaging industry and elsewhere. The components were mounted on the printed circuit boards through using advanced manufacturing technology and robotics and demanded little human intervention besides the surveillance of the operations. At the very end of the production line, a number of persons were working to visually inspect all the printed circuit boards. These operators were sitting by a desk visually inspecting each and every unit to detect any production error. When asking the managing director what kind of competencies that this rather specific procedure demanded, he responded that the company had trained a number of persons that were regarded as specifically apt for this work but that he could not really tell why some people were better than others to do the work. I was fascinated about the central role that the human vision played in this huge system of advanced manufacturing technologies, robotics, and microelectronic components; the whole manufacturing system seemed so vulnerable, ultimately being dependent on the very gaze of some specialized operator determining the outcome. No matter how much technologies are brought in, by the end of the day it is still the human look and human attention that makes a difference between a properly functioning and a default unit. I also remember being intrigued by the degree of concentration and attention needed to excel in the work. Spending week after week sitting by the desk, visually inspecting one printed circuit board after the other, sounded like a real challenge for any person. How did these operators cope with these working conditions? Since I never had the chance to talk to them, such questions were never answered. What has been a lingering concern, however, was the role and importance of the capacity of seeing, looking, inspecting, glancing, and so on as part of a professional skills and training. The gaze of the expert is then what ultimately determines the quality of the outcome in a variety of professions. This book is addressing vision and visuality as a form of professional activity and is therefore for me a form of return to this topic of interest, now more than fifteen years old.

This work has been possible to accomplish through the contributions of a number of persons. Pernilla Gluch has been collaborating with me in the studies of the two architect bureaus reported in the book, and Fredrik Nilsson helped me and Pernilla to organize the interviews and provided insightful comments on the architect profession. Mats Sundgren has been very helpful when organizing a number of research activities in the pharmaceutical industry and has also dedicated a significant amount of work to explain all the intricacies of all new drug development. Finally, I would like to thank my family, Sara, Simon, and Max for being such delightful persons.

"There is no such thing as just looking."

James Elkins (1996: 31)

Foreword

Pierre Bourdieu, the great French sociologist, is offering a most critical view of the role of management theory, that is, the bulk of theory formulated in business schools:

> Management theory, a literature produced by business schools for business schools, fulfils a function identical to that of the writings of the European jurists of the sixteenth and seventeenth centuries who, in the guise of describing the state, contributed to building it: being directed at current and potential managers, that theory oscillates continually between the positive and the normative, and depends fundamentally on an overestimation of the degree to which conscious strategies play a role in business, as opposed to the structural constraints upon, and the dispositions, of managers. (Bourdieu, 2005: 200)

Are the theories and models provided in the business school research only a thinly veiled politics, beneficial solely for the emerging and still growing administrative and executive classes, or is there a domain of thinking that Bourdieu is ignorant of? The first thing to notice is that Bourdieu is by no means the only researcher critical of business school research; a number of intramural writers are equally critical of the business school research agenda (Pfeffer, 1993, 2008; Fournier and Grey, 2000; Starkey and Madan, 2001; Pfeffer and Fong, 2002; Grey, 2004). Even insiders are critical of the discipline, both mainstream researchers such as Jeffrey Pfeffer and Robert Sutton (2006) and so-called critical management scholars, conceiving of much management theory as being overtly instrumental and functionalist (Silverman, 1970; Deetz, 1992; Alvesson and Willmott, 1996). One of the key questions derived from such harsh criticism is what a proper theory is and what such a proper theory is expected to contribute with (for some debate in the field of organization theory, see Weick, 1989, 1999; Sutton and Staw, 1995; Locke and Golden-Biddle, 1997; Czarniawska, 2001; Gabriel and Willman, 2005; Locke, Golden-Biddle, and Feldman, 2008). One of the more radical suggestions is that one can put into question the value of theory altogether and instead recognize the value of what in a philosophical discourse is called "thinking" (Lotringer, 2001). While theory is an entity, an outcome, and a statement of relationships between identified components, thinking is a process wherein a number of possibilities and relations are accounted for and brought together. In German, the concept of *Denken* is used—a central term for Heidegger (1966, 1968)—and in French thought the term *Pensé* denotes thinking. However, in the continental tradition, there is arguably a higher degree of acceptance for the processual view of thinking, and consequently the concept of thinking is subsumed under the concept of theory in Anglo-American thought, giving us the handy term *theorizing*.

Thinking of academic work and writing as a process of theorizing is to get rid of a range of thorny epistemological issues regarding truth, objectivity, and validity without abandoning the idea of paying tribute to what other researchers have previously argued. It is, as suggested by Karl Weick, a form of process, a practice, bridging the past, the present, and the future:

> Theorizing involves continuously resetting the boundaries of the phenomenon and continuously rejustifying what has newly been included and excluded. In theorizing, as in everyday life, meanings always seem to become clear a little too late. Accounts, cognitions, and categories all lie in the path of earlier action, which means that definitions and theories tend to be retrospective summaries of ongoing inquiring rather than definitive constraints on future inquiring. (Weick, 2005: 395)

No academic writing subsists in a vacuum or is the outcome from individual thinking in isolation (Latour, 1987). Originality is a rare gift. Instead, the theoretical language employed by academic writers is, to use the vocabulary of Mikhail Bakhtin, in essence heteroglot and dialogic; it is based on the reiteration of what has always already been said but what may deserve to be said again. Thinking takes place in a field of what Julia Kristeva (1980), heavily indebted to Bakhtin, calls *intertextuality*—the "literary word" is no longer "a point" but an "intersection of textual surfaces" (Kristeva, 1980: 67). Theorizing recognizes this dialogic nature of language and faithfully quotes and references other writers. In addition, theorizing as concept is an attempt at separating theory and (in its conventional meaning) truth. Theories are not of necessity "true" in some ontological sense but are instead true if we find the theory useful. Simmel (1978: 107) emphasizes this performative quality of truth: "We dignify with the name 'truth' those representations that, active within us as real forces or motions, incite us to useful actions." This is what one may call a pragmatist view of truth as "what actually works"—the truth of an idea is not a stagnant property inherent in it. "Truth *happens* to an idea," William James (1975: 97) claimed. Richard Rorty, the most prominent contemporary representative of pragmatist philosophy and a pragmatist view of truth, is following James's position: "My slogan is that if you take care of freedom, truth will take care of itself. A true statement is just one that a free community can agree to be true. If we take care of political freedom, we get truth as a bonus" (Rorty, 2006: 58). "A free community" is thus what sanctions truth in Rorty's view. Thus it is complicated for an individual researcher to hope to formulate theory qua truth prior to any recognition in the broader research community. Instead, he or she may hope to formulate what is interesting, intriguing, or, if nothing else, reasonably truthful to empirical observations. Such a perspective encourages researchers to formulate daring conjectures and to think in new terms rather than merely rephrasing what authorities of the field have already stated. A most intriguing thinker such as Gilles Deleuze is providing some encouragement for anyone more interested in theorizing than in theory:

> Method alone does not exclusively govern our thought, especially when there is a more or less explicit image of thought, tacit or presupposed, which determines our ends and means whatever we try to think ... Error is the enemy to be defeated—the only enemy—and we presuppose that truth has to do with solutions, propositions capable of serving as answers. Such is the classic image of thought. As long as this image remains untouched by a critique, how will we bring thought to consider problems which surpass the propositional mode, to have such encounters as escape recognition, to confront enemies other than error, to reach into the heart of what necessitates thought, or wrests it from its usual torpor, its notorious bad faith? (Deleuze, 2006: 300)

If we hope that we can allow for ourselves a little bit of theorizing amid the vast sea of theory, then we need to find an adequate model for such a project.

The first thing to learn when engaging in theorizing is to relax from the usual pressure for formulate unified and coherent theories. We may here make a reference to Alfred North Whitehead (1929: 64): "Now there are two kinds of intellectual enjoyment: the enjoyment of creation and the enjoyment of relaxation. They are not necessarily separated." The French sociologist Gabriel Tarde offers the useful term *conversation* to denote such a less constrained discussion within a particular field. For Tarde, conversation is what is in opposition to utility as the only legitimate benchmark for academic value: "By conversation I mean not only dialogue without directs and immediate utility, in which one talks primarily to talk, for pleasure, as a game, out of politeness. This definition excludes juridical inquiries, diplomatic or commercial negotiations, and even scientific congresses, although the latter abound in superfluous chatter" (Tarde, 1969: 308). Tarde speaks of "nonessential discussions" (a somewhat bland translation of Tarde's more intriguing original French term *entretien de luxe*) as what is capable of advancing new thinking and proceeding along new pathways. Tarde (1969: 308) concludes: "It [nonessential discussions] is ... the strongest agent of invention, of the propagation of sentiments, ideas and modes of action." Thus, nonessential discussions are where theorizing may take place; it is attempting at thinking along new categories and modes of though while still recognizing the contributions of others. If theorizing is not primarily aiming at producing some immediately practical effects—it does not reside in utility—it is by no means an entirely frivolous activity. Using the Freudian term *Dürcharbeitung,* the psychoanalyst and his or her patients "working through" the entire psychological baggage to eventually reach a point of reconciliation, this method of working through (in fact, a term suggested by Elliott Jaques [1951: 306] in his classic study of a cultural change in a British factory) is what the nonessential discussion is aiming at, that is, to if not exhaust a topic of discussion so at least seek to unfold the topic in many ways and in many direction. In the following, the concepts of vision and visuality are examined within an organization theory framework not with the intention of *primarily* providing tools and techniques for how to manage visual practices (which is not to say that the discussion is devoid of practical implications altogether) but in order to discuss vision and visuality from many different and complementary angles and perspectives. This working through is also conducted with Whitehead's suggestion that the "enjoyment of creation" and the "enjoyment of relaxation" are not of necessity mutually excluding. Not all insights and scholarly work are the outcome of strenuous efforts, but they may also derive from the ability to take a step back and think in new terms. That is the value of the nonessential discussion, a potentially fruitful venture combining the two modes of intellectual enjoyments.

Part I
Epistemologies of Vision

1   Introduction
From the Lexical to the Visual

ORPHEUS'S GAZE AND THE MYTHOLOGY OF VISION

"One learns by looking. That's what you must do, look."

Francis Bacon (cited in Archimbaud, 1993: 153)

The perhaps most widely known and also most intriguing myth on the power of vision is that of Orpheus and Eurydice. Orpheus is a masterful musician, playing the lyre and singing beautifully. When his wife Eurydice dies after being poisoned by a snake, Orpheus is consulting the gods and nymphs on how to bring Eurydice back to life. After traveling to the underworlds, into Hades's territories, the home of the dead, Orpheus's music is so compelling and beautiful that he manages to convince Hades and Persephone to let Eurydice return to the "upper world," the world of the living. The one condition is that Orpheus must walk ahead of Eurydice and that he cannot turn around to look at his wife before they depart from the realm of the dead. At one moment, when approaching their destination, Orpheus is failing to keep his promise and turn around to look at Eurydice and at that very moment she disappears forever into the subterranean domains. Orpheus's gaze is what is preventing the bringing of Eurydice back to life; he is guilty of impatience and his very look is what ultimately separated himself from his beloved wife for the rest of his life.

In this Greek tragic myth, vision is what is capable of separating life from death; seeing is what is associated with the restlessness and the impatience of the human being and failing to control and restrict one's vision is what is even potentially dangerous. In the Foucaultian tradition of thinking, derived from Jeremy Bentham's writing on the *panopticon* (discussed later on in the book), vision is associated with omnipresent power and discipline. On the contrary, Slavoj Žižek (1995) has emphasized the helplessness of the look, a seeing that is capable of observing but not intervening into the acts being committed. His illustrative example is Alfred Hitchcock's *Rear Window* (1954), wherein the main character, played by James Stewart, stuck in his wheelchair, is witnessing a murder on the next building but is incapable of intervening in the act:

> *Rear Window* reads like an ironic reversal of Bentham's 'Panopticon' as exploited by Foucault. For Bentham, the horrifying efficacy of the Panopticon is due to the fact that the subjects (prisoners, patients, schoolboys, factory workers) can never know for sure if they are actually observed from the all-seeing central control tower—this very uncertainty intensifies the feeling of menace, of the impossibility of escape from the gaze of the Other. In *Rear Window*, the inhabitants of the apartment across the yard are actually observed all the time by Stewart's watchful eyes, but far from being terrorized, they simply ignore it and go on with their daily business. On the contrary, it is Stewart himself, the center of the panopticon, its all-pervasive eye, who is terrorized, constantly looking out of the window, anxious not to miss some crucial detail. (Žižek, 1992: 92)

In the Foucaultian view, vision is unified and universal; in the Žižekian version, it is fragile and vulnerable. In Stanley Kubrik's *A Clockwork Orange* (1971), based on Anthony Burgess's novel, the adolescent delinquent Alex is being treated by a new therapeutic method, structured around the practice of witnessing the brutality of the criminal acts committed. To prevent Alex from looking away, specific mechanical tools are used to keep his eyes wide open. In Kubrik's/Burgess's understanding, vision is neither part or power nor subsumed under power but instead vision is a means for acquiring an understanding and even strong dislike of one's own and others' violent crimes; vision is a form of pathway for acquiring information about the external world. At the same time, vision, or rather the absence of vision, could be used as a form of denial or retreat from the world. "Looking away shall be my only negation," Nietzsche writes in *The Gay Science*. The absence of look, the complete blank ignorance, is perhaps the most significant use of power through the visual apparatus. The drunkard singing and waving his hands in a public place, and especially a confined place (say, a bus or an elevator), is often mindfully ignored by other individuals present. A form of "nonseeing" is executed with tact and skill and is demonstrating the unwillingness to take part in the uncomfortable situation. The great French anthropologist Marcel Mauss (1992) once published an essay entitled "The Techniques of the Body," examining the various uses of the human body to accomplish a variety of social practices. For Mauss, the body is not only a tool for each and every human being but it is also serving a symbolic function coordinating the relationship between human beings. The same would be relevant for the faculty of vision; vision comes in many forms and serves a variety of roles and functions. For instance, staring (Garland-Thomson, 2006) is in many cases an act of indiscretion and is often regarded as a being impolite or (at best) rather indicative of the staring person's inability to cope with a specific situation. For instance, celebrities of the highest ranks are probably used to dealing with people staring and pointing at them while for the most of us exposure to such forms of vision would be, one is inclined to think, rather negative experiences.

In the following, vision and visuality are not examined as being used to play these various social roles. Instead, vision is used as a form of professional skill or competence, the ability to detect and identify interesting observations through visual inspection. As will be pointed out, vision is by no means strictly an individual, subjective, and professional skill that is innate; instead, to execute what is called *professional vision* is the outcome from long-term formal training and education, work experience, and collaborations with peers and other relevant social groups over time and under a variety of conditions. Unlike in the mythologies, vision is not per se capable of accomplishing very much, and yet it is playing a very important, indeed a *central*, role in a great number of human activities and domains of expertise. This ability to transform one's capacity of registering visual sense impressions into a systematic procedure adhering to a set of professional standards and enacted routines will be discussed in some details in this book. In everyday work life in the contemporary period, there is no Orpheus's gaze capable of destroying or ruining a social condition just through the very act of looking, but vision is always more fragmented, fluid, multiple, and diverse to serve such a devastating role. In Elskins's (1996) account, vision, "seeing," is what is relatively autonomous from our agency:

> Seeing is irrational, inconsistent, and undependable. It is immensely troubled, cousin to blindness and sexuality, and caught up in the threads of the unconscious. Our eyes are not ours to command: they roam where they will and then tell us they have only been where we have sent them. No matter how hard we look, we see very little of what we look at. If we imagine the eyes as navigational devices, we do so in order not to come to terms with what seeing really is . . . Ultimately, seeing alters the thing that is seen and transforms the seer. Seeing is metamorphism, not mechanism. (Elkins, 1996: 11–12)

At the same time, vision is what is potentially operating as a powerful means for coordinating action and social relations. "Being seen" at the wrong place at the wrong time is, for instance, what is potentially threatening careers and reputation. This double nature of vision—on the one hand fragile, uncertain, and beyond our full control, on the other, what is serving as the ultimate evidence, the witnessing of an actual condition—is interesting for organization researchers. Vision can be many things and serve many functions and its capacity to be coordinated with organizational action and objectives is what is intriguing to understand for students of organizations. Therefore, the intersection of vision and organization is here further examined.

THE FIVE MODALITIES OF PERCEPTION

Undoubtedly, vision plays a central role in informing the human mind about the outside world, thereby helping humans directs themselves in the world (for an introduction and overview of the terms *vision* and its accompanying and more general concept, *perception*, see Gregory, 2004a, 2004b; Ratey, 2002: 97–109):

> [A]lthough little is known with relative certainty about thought processes and their mechanisms, neurobiologists assume that around 60% of all information that reaches the brain is of visual provenance and that the brain uses a considerable proportion of its capacity (about 30 percent) to process this information. Further, the physiological basis of vision is by no means fully understood, especially since vision is regarded now as a complex neurophysiological process and no longer primarily as an optomechanical one (a view precipitated by George Berkeley's theory of vision, formulated in the early seventeenth century). (Zielinski, 2006: 84)

However, this does not suggest that vision is the sense exclusively guiding human activities. Vision is in many cases accompanied and complemented by the use of other senses (Grasseni, 2004). In Douglas Harper's (1987) ethnography on the work in Willie's repair shop in upstate New York, there is a strong emphasis on Willie's "kinaesthetic sense" for the materials worked on. For Harper, Willie's work over decades has taught him a certain "feel" for the materials, a contact with the artefacts, and the tools, and the object being repaired that is not easily accomplished. Harper writes:

> The kinesthetic sense influences all of the work. Married to the knowledge of materials, it procures a working knowledge that stands in stark contrast to the working knowledge produced in formal education. The kinesthetic quality of Willie's working method shows how his shop is premodern, a multidimensional dialectic of the theoretical and the empirical. Willie's training has been informal and years-long, and it has trained the hand and the eye as well as the mind. The result is more than the sum of the parts . . . Gaining the kinesthetic sense, however, reduces the gap between the subject—the worker—and the object—the work. (Harper, 1987: 132–133)

It would not be unfair to say that Harper is quite impressed by the ingenuity and dexterity of Willie; he is more or less capable of repairing all sorts of tools and machinery. Harper's ethnographic work of the handyman Willie is in passages reminding of Martin Heidegger's emphasis on the philosophical significance of the hand, both as what is directing humans in their everyday undertakings in the social world and as a metaphor for human existence. In addition, Heidegger's fascination with the mundane, the vernacular, and the quotidian—expressed in, for instance, the analysis of Vincent van Gogh's painting of a peasant's worn-out shoes (Heidegger, 1977)—comes to mind when reading Harper's ethnography. What both Harper and Heidegger share is the interest for tactile sense perception; the touching, weighting, stroking, and so forth, of the material in order to acquire some relevant information of the object to be worked on (Pallasmaa, 1996). Harper is here talking about a "kinaesthetic sense," while Prentice (2005: 857), examining surgery simulation training technologies, is favouring the term "somato-conceptual intelligence" (see also Johnson, 2007). Surgery is not solely a matter of having detailed medical and anatomical knowledge but also a matter of being able to hold the scalpels and other tools straight and interpreting the "somatic impressions" when operating (see also Cook and Yanow's 1993 study of flute-makers' capacity to detect faults when examining the instruments). The empirical research of Harper (1987) and Prentice (2005) suggests that knowledge—which we here use as a rather general term denoting an intimate understanding of a specific field—is not solely residing in the cognitive capacities of the human being but that knowledge is a distributed, indeed embodied, capacity or skill. Knowledge is a term that transgresses the Cartesian body–mind divide.

In the Western tradition of thinking, knowledge has always been closely associated with intelligence. As being a most complex and highly contested scientific term, intelligence may be defined in various ways. Piaget (2001) speaks of intelligence not as a single unified entity or system but as a texture of interrelated and collaborating systems.

> [I]ntelligence itself does not consist of an isolated and sharply differentiated class of cognitive processes. It is not, properly speaking, one form of structuring among others; it is the form of equilibrium towards which all the structures arising out of perception, habit, and elementary sensori-motor mechanisms tend. It must be understood that if intelligence is not a faculty this denial involves a radical functional continuity between the higher forms of thought and the whole mass of lower types of cognitive and motor and adaptation; so intelligence can only be the form of equilibrium towards which these things tend. (Piaget, 2001: 7)

Intelligence is then not located in one single center of the brain but is instead the capacity to combine and bridge a number of interrelated cerebral systems into an operative function guiding and directing thoughtful action. "Intelligence is thus only a generic term to indicate the superior forms of organization or equilibrium of cognitive structurings," Piaget (2001: 7) contends. Speaking of the intelligence of Willie or of surgeons, in a Piagetian perspective they share the ability to combine cognitive, tactile, and sensorimotor capacities in one single moment, in the act of tinkering with materials and using surgery instruments and tools. One of the most important implications from Piaget's theory is that perception is always at the very heart of intelligence and the acquisition of knowledge. Perception is here used broadly to denote the active use of the five senses to construct operative knowledge of practical or theoretical use. Piaget (2001) emphasizes that there is a certain proximity between perception and the object, whereas knowledge is acquired when the object of inquiry is examined from some distance: "Perception is the knowledge we have of objects or of their movements by direct and immediate contact, while intelligence is a form of knowledge obtaining when detours are involved and when spatio-temporal distances between subject and objects increase" (Piaget, 2001: 59). In a Bergsonian tradition of thinking, perception is not a passive act of registering impressions but is instead an active construction, a "synthesis," of the perceived external world (Lazzarato, 2007: 102). In other words, we do not first perceive the world and then categorize what is seen; on the contrary, we start with our memory, which enables us to see what we actually register through our senses—we move from ourselves to the object of perception (Bergson, 1988). In other words, intelligence, knowledge, in short what Bergson calls *memory*, and perception have a rather complicated relationship. Perception is always constituted by "mixed impressions" (sight, sound, touch, etc.) and it is always embedded—if we adhere to the Bergsonian view—in what is previously experienced or perceived. As a consequence, from both a philosophical or theoretical perspective and from a practical point of view, it is most complicated to separate and sort out different kind or perceptions. If intelligence is a bundle of entangled structures and perception is accomplished through such cognitive capacities, then sight, sound, smell, touch, and taste are always part of the same material substratum, that of the perceiving human body. In everyday life, many impressions are naturally belonging to either category of sense impressions: I look out of the window when having breakfast and notice a bird sitting on the fence in the garden. I only see it, nothing more. In other cases, sense impressions may be mixed and blended. When drinking my coffee, I can feel the warmth of the coffee mug in my hands and the taste and the smell are central to the agreeable experience of having one's first sip of coffee. I look at the coffee to determine whether I have poured the right amount of milk into it—it should be neither too dark nor to "milky." As philosophers such as Henri Bergson and eventually Maurice Merleau-Ponty emphasize, one sense impression may produce other embodied effect: when looking at an image of some tasty food, memories may produce a sense of smell and taste that recalls past experiences. In the discourse on aesthetics, theorists may claim that great works of art are capable of producing this kind of "transperceptual" effects. Beautiful music creates other forms of sense impressions and great visual art is enabling a hearing of sounds or a particular smell. Elizabeth Grosz says:

> Painting aims to enable us to see sounds, as music aims to make us hear colors, shapes, forms. Each of the arts is concerned with a transmutation of bodily organs as much as it is with the whole of the sensing body, capturing elements in a co-composition that carries within the vibrations and resonances, the underlying rhythms, of the other arts and the residual effects of each of the senses. (Grosz, 2008: 82)

Again, art is what is effectively exploring the intricate relationships between forms of sense impression. The five senses are not part of different and inherently separated human faculties but are instead part of one single register being part of the structure that we may call intelligence. To summarize the argument, the work of the handyman Willie in his rural upstate workshop is by no means a human endeavour residing solely on the basis of one single perceptual capacity (that of tactile capacities), but it is instead based on the ability to combine forms of sense impression, perception through the senses, with cognitive skills and previous experiences and entrenched skills. Willie's work is the effective and thoughtful blending of touch, sight, smell, and listening, and a great variety of skills enabling a tinkering with the materiality. The same goes for surgeons, musicians, engineers, or virtually all professional and occupational groups working with reasonably complex material resources in their day-to-day work.

Even though this book is aiming at examining and discussing the concepts of vision and visuality, sense impression through looking, staring, glancing, and in other ways using the eyes to acquire data and information about the external world, the idea here is that it is epistemologically and practically complicated to conceive of vision wholly devoid of other embodied capacities. Therefore, when speaking of the "epistemologies of eye" and "practices of seeing," this is to some extent a simplification of how human perception operates in practice. There is no "pure gaze" or "unmediated eye" but all these practices of seeing are always embodied experiences, bound up with other senses and previous experiences. "*My experience is what I agree to attend to*, William James (1950: 402, emphasis in the original) declares. This is one of the consequences of regarding perception as what is derived from memory rather than the other way around. Being attentive is therefore not only a responding to one's perceptions of the external world but to actively seek to identify and "understand" the impressions from the senses. As a being in the world, a Heideggerian *Dasein*, humans have recourse to their sense impressions and their previous experiences. The concern is, however, that analytical projects aiming at understanding the role of, e.g., vision and visuality, are often reducing the complexity of the senses to five essentially separated modalities operating and being executed relatively autonomously. This is no warrant that this book will perform better than other attempts at theorizing the senses, but at least there has been a formal announcement of the epistemological fallacy of misplaced concreteness (Whitehead, 1925) related to conceiving of vision as being compartmentalized and isolated from the other senses.

VISION AND VISUALITY IN MANAGEMENT STUDIES

The social sciences and organization theory have over the last years been preoccupied with what has been labelled "the linguistic turn," a theoretico-practical framework underlining the constitutive nature of language in all social undertakings and endeavours. The linguistic turn has brought a variety of new and intriguing perspectives on organization, ranging from discourse analysis methodologies to literature theory–oriented approaches such as narrative studies. Notwithstanding all the strengths with such language-oriented perspectives, they are still adhering to a strong Cartesian tradition of thinking, assuming that the rational and the sensuous or emotional are ontologically and epistemologically separated. Language as a constitutive component of reason, the human rational faculties, is here located in opposition to what is sensual and embodied, thereby subsuming the sensual human faculties under the authority of reason. "We are still spellbound by a tradition that arranged psychological faculties hierarchically, relegating 'sensuousness'—that is, perception—to a lower position in comparison to higher, reflective functions of reason and understanding," Niklas Luhmann (2000: 5) remarks in his *Art as a Social System*. Reason is commonly regarded as what regulates human thinking and perception and therefore visual, auditory, olfactory, and tactile capacities are subsumed under cognition. The senses help guide us in the day-to-day work, but it is at the bottom line the faculty of reason that arranges, structures, and coordinates the sense impressions. However, a variety of social scientists and scholars in the diverse fields of the humanities are pointing at the increased emphasis on what has been called the "visual turn," "the pictorial turn," or the "iconic turn" in social theory (Mitzroeff, 2006; Moxey, 2008). For instance, the historian Martin Jay has in a number of places (e.g., Jay, 1988, 1996, 2002a, 2002b) defended a visual turn in the social sciences and the humanities. Jay is also contrasting the linguistic turn perspective and what he refers to as the pictorial turn:

> The new fascination with modes of seeing and the enigmas of visual experience in a wide variety of fields may well betoken a paradigm shift in the cultural imaginary of our age. What has been called 'the pictorial turn' bids fair to succeed the earlier 'linguistic turn' so loudly trumpeted by twentieth-century philosophers. The model of 'reading

texts,' which served productively as the master metaphor for postobjectivist interpretations in many different phenomena, is now giving way to models of spectatorship and visuality, which refuse to be described in entirely linguistic terms. The figural is resisting subsumption under the rubric of discursivity; the image is demanding its own unique mode of analysis. (Jay, 1996: 1)

The pictorial turn is by no means representing a unified or coherent epistemological or methodological position but is instead what is diverse and includes a variety of analytical models and approaches. Jay (1996) is instead speaking about "culturally specific forms of visuality" as—using a term employed by French film critic Christian Metz—"scopic regimes." Seen in this view, vision and attention are always contingent on cultural conditions and are a situated and local practice determined by a variety of contextual practices. The pictorial turn is not a recent shift in focus in Western epistemology but is instead a long-standing tradition privileging vision as a source of true knowledge, beginning at least as early as Plato and continuing into modern times (Warneke, 1993: 287). Pre-Socratic thinkers such as Empedocles did not create a hierarchy of the senses: instead, everything exists side by side and "seeing is not privileged over hearing, not taste over touch and smell" (Zielinski, 2006: 47). However, what Daston and Galison (2007) call "the epistemology of the eye" is a strong undercurrent in the Western tradition of thinking, adhering to the Platonist line of thought.

More recently, a variety of scholars have emphasized the shift in focus in Western culture and indeed the emergent global culture to move from the written text as the principal mode of communication to the increased use of images and pictures to communicate meaning. While the printed book, invented in the second half of the fifteenth century in Europe and many centuries earlier in China, served as the most credible medium in the early modern, modern, and late modern periods, we are today witnessing a gradual erosion of the authority of the written and printed word. Instead, a new regime that American film theorist Jonathan Beller (2006) has called the "cinematic mode of production" is being established. The emergence of computer-based technologies, the Internet, and a long series of technologies, techniques, and social practices related to these overarching changes has brought a new generation that perhaps for the first time is better equipped to handle images and film clips than written texts. Book reading is going down in the Western world but the new generation is instead visually literate; they are capable of interpreting, interacting, and collaborating in a milieu constructed predominantly out of images, photos, and film clips. The emergent regime of communication, no longer bounded by the linearity of the written text and the authority of book as the principal medium for communication, is posing new challenges for the social sciences and organization theory more specifically. During the influence of the linguistic turn, organizations were examined as "linguistic communities,"

communities that collectively engaged in storytelling, document making, policy writing, and a variety of social practices drawing on the authority of the written and spoken word. However, organizations are no longer solely enabled or restrained by the language in written or oral form. The visual turn and its emphasis on images, models, computer-aided simulations, cinematic representations, and so forth are not really moving beyond the written and spoken word but are certainly complementing existing forms of communication with new modes of representation. This book is an attempt at properly theorizing the visual and visual practices in organizations. Rather than assuming that vision and visuality are uncomplicated social practices, the use of visual representations is opening up for new ontological, epistemological, and methodological choices and opportunities. No longer bounded by written texts or spoken words, organizational practices become determined by coworkers' various sensual capacities and especially the faculty of vision. Images and pictures may not communicate more things or offer more accurate accounts of perceived social reality, but they certainly offer new opportunities for theorizing organizations and organizational practice. Thinking about organizations in a regime of visual representations demands perhaps new analytical models and procedures. The aim of this book is to think in such new terms.

THE POLITICS OF VISION: VISION AND VISUALITY IN ORGANIZATION THEORY

From the very outset, vision and visuality have been subject to manipulation, political endeavours, and other forms of manifestations of power. For instance, Goody (1997) shows that after the French revolution, the art of the *ancien régime* became subject to criticism because of the supposedly antiquated values it represented:

> The arts were also a problem because they were seen as necessarily political; there was no question of art for art's sake. In his article on painting in the *Encyclopédie*, Diderot had announced that 'the governors of man have always made use of painting and sculpture in order to inspire in their subjects the religious or political sentiments they desire them to hold'. With the revolution, art of the old order was held to carry the wrong message, but it was at first agreed that the Commission de monuments should preserve the best. As early as 1790, however, one group of artists requested the king to 'order the destruction of all monuments created during the feudal regime.' The collapse of the monarchy in 1792 saw the beginning of a torrent of iconoclasm that lasted three years. Statues came crashing down; pictures at Fountainbleau were burnt to appease the spirit of the murdered Marat. (Goody, 1997: 120–121)

If arts and monuments are a tool in the hands of the power elites and the *nomenclatura* (Riegl, 2004), then vision and visuality per se are what are of necessity laden with power and interests. As Jacques Lacan—to be discussed in greater details in the next chapter—points out in his fourth seminar, speaking of the concept of "the Gaze," vision is always already interpenetrated by the vision of "the Other." The commonplace framework for understanding such vision infested by power is to claim that vision is always already a social practice and social practices are of necessity shaped and formed by "collective consciousness," justified true beliefs, and other forms of commonly held knowledge. Seeing is therefore to adhere to collectively established principles. Seen in this view, vision is already what is a collective procedure and practice; it is not what is the starting point for social practices but rather the outcome from collective accomplishments. The ability to see in a certain manner is a form of expertise, an entrenched skill, a professional capability.

Besides the more theoretical views of the politics of vision and visuality, in a historical view of vision, the concept of *perception management* offers an intriguing trajectory for the bundling of visuality and management and organization. Developed within a military setting, the concept can be defined in a various ways. Terranova (2004) uses the following definition:

> Perception management includes public relations work, knowledge of local conditions, information warfare and media manipulation, but in ways that explicitly recognize that what needs to be managed is not simply the knowledge that surrounds a certain event, but its 'perception.' Perception management is thus not mainly addressed to what we might recognize as a 'public opinion.' (Terranova, 2004: 140)

Elsbach (2006: 12), a management professor at University of California at Davis, uses a similar definition:

> Organizational perception management is designed to influence audience perception of the organization as an entity or a whole. Such perception includes organizational images (e.g., organizational legitimacy or trustworthiness), reputation (e.g., being known as a tough competitor), and identities (i.e., organizational categorizations, such as being top tier). (Elsbach, 2006: 12)

Perception management is thus a term that advances a variety of perceptual manipulations and elaborations to produce the desirable effect in a market, market segment, or the public more generally (in the military use of the term). Rather than engaging in actual, underlying changes in policy or practice, perception management is used to produce desirable effects beneficial for the focal organization. While the political nature of perception management is never explicitly addressed, it is a helpful term from an analytical perspective because it is underlining the intersection between perception, or more specifically visuality, and organization, that is, the active constitution and manipulation of vision and visuality in organizational settings. Perception management is thus a tool in the hands of decision makers and executives enacting policies and strategies for firms and organizations.

In summary, from an analytical perspective, vision and visuality are grounded in social relations that in themselves are constituted by tightly knit webs of power and authority. In a practical or methodological perspective, vision and visuality are again what have been used to actively produce desirable images of social reality. In the most conspicuous cases, such manipulation is referred to as propaganda—Grigory Potemkin's fake settlements is perhaps the most telling example—while in the less explicit cases, the more unobtrusive manipulation of visuality is part of everyday life, ranging from carefully arranged office spaces to promote a sense of harmony and creativity, to the manipulation of photos of models in the commercials featured in television programs. The contemporary environment is saturated with images and pictures that in various ways are shaping, forming, and actively influencing the way we look at and perceive social reality.

SEEING AND BEING SEEN IN ORGANIZATIONS

There are great number of papers and research monographs that implicitly investigate practices of seeing and procedures for being seen and rendered visible in organizations. This literature is most diverse and includes a number of perspectives and theoretical frameworks. Already Charles Babbage, one of the pioneering authors in the new genre of management writing (see Babbage, 1833), claimed that "[o]f all our senses, that of sight conveys intelligence most rapidly to the mind" (cited in Bloomfield and Vurdubakis, 1997: 643). From the very outset, management has been highly oriented towards a specific form of vision, a vision that aims at achieving what Bloomfield and Vurdubakis (1997) call "functionalist transparency":

> This privilege of vision implies a corresponding preoccupation with functionalist transparency. For example, a large part of set of activities subsumed by the term organization are concerned with methods, conventions and techniques for dis-aggregating, encoding and representing of objects and acts on paper and on screen. (Bloomfield and Vurdubakis, 1997: 643)

Managerial practices such as accounting and operations management established procedures for monitoring either relevant performance parameters or the ongoing processes. Management is a specific form of vision anchored in instrumental interests.

In terms of studies of vision in organizations—to start somewhere—there is a number of papers that examine the dress code and the codes regulating the uses of the human body in organizations. For instance, feminist theory–inspired researchers have showed that female service workers are expected to conform to cultural and organizational standards for what counts as an adequate appearance both in terms of attire and embodied features. Rafaeli et al. (1997) show that the business attire is a major issue for female administrative employees seeking to navigate between being dressed all too extravagantly feminine and thereby risking being regarded as someone exploiting one's sexuality, and being regarded as someone dressing too "unwomanly." Female administrators were then always balancing between being too visible and too invisible, seeking to strike a balance between these two end positions. In the same vein, Trethewey (1999) has shown that embodiment is a contested terrain for most women, being trained and disciplined on how to carefully restrict and control one's movement and bodily postures in organizational spaces. A number of studies of, for instance, flight attendants, beginning with Hochschild's (1983) seminal work, show that this specific category of service workers, historically associated with the privileged upper tiers of society and with the glamour of international business travel, are serving two functions in organizations: on the one hand, they are service workers comforting and helping the customers; on the other hand, they play a decorative function in terms of being embodiments of aesthetic norms and values the organization wants to convey. Like perhaps no other category of service workers, flight attendants are supposed to serve as what is aesthetically enhancing the experience of consuming air travel services (Tyler and Abbott, 1998; Tyler and Taylor, 1998). "Women [flight attendants trainees] were deemed to be capable of caring for 'other' bodies, but also for their own. In other words, women flight attendants were also thought to be inherently capable of presenting their female bodies as 'feminine,' as aesthetically pleasing, not only by their employers, but also by customers and by themselves," Tyler and Taylor (1998: 168) argue. Consequently, female flight attendants are in many cases expected to demonstrate a servile attitude towards customers and in, for instance, Hochschild's (1983) account of the work, there are significant individual costs for maintaining a neat and friendly appearance no matter what events unfold.

In the case of female flight attendants, their role is both to handle a series of practical activities on board but also to be visible, to conform to cultural and social standards on attractiveness that in turn are part of the branding strategy of the firm. Especially younger female coworkers are exposed to this kind of what may be called *visual labour* demanding a close attention of one's bodily appearance and attire. This visual labour, which of course also men are taking part in, for instance, traditional male occupations such as the police force or various forms of bodyguards demand that men are capable of demonstrating certain embodied features, is part of what has been called *impression management* (Alvesson, 1994), the use of symbol-ism, body language, gestures, and other resources to underline or reinforce a set of values that the organizations embrace. Feminist theory–oriented organization researchers have shown that organizations are primary sites for the deployment of gendered beliefs and ideologies (Gherardi, 1995). For instance, Benschop and Heihuizen (2000) show that annual reports are in fact featuring pictures of primarily male managers and when women appear on the pages they are regularly dressed in a manner that will separate them from their male peers. Annual reports are formal documents aimed at positioning the organization as a modern, reliable, and credible institu-tion, and therefore a close scrutiny of what is published in these documents may reveal underlying beliefs and ideologies. Gustavsson and Czarniawska (2004) show that avatars on the Internet, animated figures serving to help and guide newcomers on an Internet home page, are commonly female characters. Since there may be a general belief in society that most Internet users would feel more comfortable being helped by a female than a male character, ultimately embedded in the idea that women are more suitable for caring and nurturing activities than men are and that women have a "natural capacity" for such undertakings, gendered beliefs are transformed into the computer code producing the avatars on the computer screen. In this case, vision and visuality are mingling with the use of media but the gaze of both the computer code programmer and the Internet end-user is nevertheless a sexualized gaze positioning women in a certain manner. More generally, there is a growing literature on the so-called "creative industries" in, e.g., film, TV, and media production, that is strongly ori-ented towards various visual media and forms of visuality (Caldwell, 2008; Caves, 2000; Christopherson, 2008; Dempsey, 2006; Elsbach, 2009; Gill and Pratt, 2008; Hesmondhalgh and Baker, 2008; Jeffcut, 2000; Townley, Beech, and McKinlay, 2009). In this work, the output of various visual artefacts (films, images, etc.) and the work as such, characterized by a con-stant oversupply of workers, is largely a matter of being visible and to make an impression. Only in the Los Angeles area, the center for film production in the Western Hemisphere, 250,000 creative workers are employed in this specific form of production (Caldwell, 2008).

Other forms of vision and visuality in organizations are executed in the formal ceremonies and rituals of organizations (Meyer and Rowan, 1977). For instance, in two ethnographic studies of such ceremonies, Rosen and Astley (1988) and Rosen (1985) have examined the intricate social symbol-ism and rituals in, first, an annual Christmas party in one company and a business breakfast in another company. In Rosen and Astley's (1988) and Rosen's (1985) view, such events are providing a dense ethnographic mate-rial for understanding a set of generic social procedures and mechanisms in contemporary life. For instance, the reciprocity between the employee's loyalty and the company's offering of an extravagant experience in a down-town New York City hotel is reminding of the reciprocal social relations first identified by the anthropologist Bronislaw Malinowski in his studies in Micronesia and reported in his *Argonauts of the Pacific*. The two studies of Rosen and Astley (1988) and Rosen (1985) suggest, in this setting, that the cultural and social orders of the particular organizations are possible to read like an open book during these kinds of events. Just like political analysts and commentators—the field of Kremlinology, perhaps defunct today, comes to mind—have over centuries been capable of decoding the hierarchical structure of a social community, ethnographies of formal organizational events are offering a similar opportunity for understanding how organizations are reproducing their formal and informal hierarchy and authority through the use of certain forms of visuality. In the same manner, Ropo and Parviainen (2001) suggests that leadership work is largely a matter of embodied performances, that is, the capacity to exploit forms of visuality and one's visual capacities in order to position oneself as a credible and trustworthy actor. In leadership work, and especially in the more executive layers of organizations, visuality is never far away. Symbolism and body language are playing an important part of any effective leadership work.

Another field of research where vision and visuality are playing a decisive role is the organization of space. Social space is by no means devoid of politics and interests, and examining the influence of social space is an important part of organization studies. Edenius and Yakhlef (2007) underline the importance of space:

> Most previous research assumes that spatial orderings of things and people are merely part of the background that does not intervene in the learning process. Rather, the concern has been with the relation between learning and processes of interacting, working together, sharing tools, story-telling and narrating (Lave and Wenger, 1991). This relationship is framed in ideological terms, overlooking the centrality of the (prediscursive) visual, perceptual, bodily incorporations, and how discursive and cognitive practices are contingent upon incorporating practices. (Edenius and Yakhlef, 2007: 207)

In her study of a start-up IT company in Stockholm, Miriam Salzer-Mörling is emphasizing the role of shared social spaces in companies being increasingly "virtual" in their outline. While most of these new firms are what is called *professional service firms* (PSF) or *knowledge-intensive firms* (KIFs), treating know-how and intellectual capital as their principal production factor, the lifeworld of the coworkers cannot remain totally abstract but must be anchored in some tangible physical setting: "Paradoxically, it seems that the more virtual or intangible the organization is, the more that place matters," Salzer-Mörling (2002: 129) contends. She continues: "[C]reating and shaping the knowledge of the network require the physical presence of being in the room; of taking part in the embodied practices of the group" (Salzer-Mörling, 2002: 130). Speaking in terms of vision and visuality, the study suggests that firms cannot survive for some time unless there are actual arenas where coworkers can meet, exchange ideas, and socialize. This conclusion is consonant with Richard Florida's (2002) much-cited study of the emerging creative class, being attracted by the possibility of meeting not just representatives of same profession or field but also encountering creative individuals working in other domains having ideas and thoughts that could be appropriated and used elsewhere. That is, for Florida, the creative class, flocking in places like Austin, Texas, Seattle Washington, or the San Francisco Bay Area in California, is demanding interesting ideas and inspiration in order to thrive. Another example of the role of shared social space is Arnoldi's (2006) study of how the "floor trading" in the financial markets in, e.g., the New York Stock Exchange, was displaced by forms of electronic trading based on computer-based media. In the old regime, when the stock trader was "working on the floor," "[t]he body language and look of a given trader make it possible to know which state of mind the trader is in, information which the counterpart will seek to exploit," Arnoldi (2006: 387) suggests. By looking at the other financial analysts and traders, the acting trader could get a "feel for the market" (Arnoldi, 2006: 389), a sense of what is going on and what to do about it. However, with the implementation of the new electronic trading system, experiences from such "practices of seeing" were no longer useful. One of the market traders explained how this created a sense of being "cut off from the information flow":

> It is like suddenly being blind and deaf. It is a complete cut-off from the information flow. Being a focal point, centre of all market activity, is suddenly gone. Instead of being in the centre I suddenly found myself outside. (Market trader, cited in Arnoldi, 2006: 388)

Financial market trading is today no longer based on the direct visuality of the financial traders but is instead mediated by software, mathematical models, and mass media, which, Arnoldi (2006: 391–392) suggests, represent a "more formal and more abstract forms of framing, which are disembedded from local contexts and networks." Direct vision is thus displaced by *mediated vision*, in many cases in the form of graphs and ratios and other forms of "mathematized vision" (see also Hassoun, 2005; Knorr Cetina and Bruegger, 2001, 2002).

Also time per se may be visualized through the use of various management techniques and tools such as the much-used Gantt chart or software like Microsoft Project is providing means for visualizing time. Yakura (2002) is examining the use of what she calls *temporal boundary objects* in engineering project work, that is, tools like Gantt charts and toll-gate models to temporally structure large projects. Since there is a difference between "lived time," what Henri Bergson calls *duration*, the direct experience of time—in some cases, "time flies" while in other it barely moves but slowly proceeds second by second—and mechanical clock time, carefully separated into equally long time units and sequentially leading from one moment of time to the next, there is a need for establishing shared procedures for structuring and visualizing time. Yakura (2002) claims there is a "pluritemporalism" in organizations, many different experiences of time coexisting and therefore in a need for coordination. The Gantt chart, structuring a sequential time line and separating different key activities, is playing the role of imposing a sense of order and control over what is inherently dynamic and changing. "Timelines gives participants an illusion of 'management' or 'control' of a project," Yakura (2002: 968–969) argues.[1] In addition, Yakura (2002) suggests that the very use of the Gantt-chart, besides providing a shared map over how the available time should be used to accomplish the task assigned, also imposes a "narrative logic" implied in the chart. Yakura (2002) suggests that as soon as time is portrayed as a timeline and outlined as a set of activities that needs to be accomplished, the viewer of a visual model is getting a sense of being assured that the ends will finally meet and that the project will be terminated as planned: "The narrative logic of the timeline suggests that once you start, you will finish; tasks and milestones are portrayed as flowing linearly and progressively" (Yakura, 2002: 958–959). However, many complex projects, for instance in the field of civil engineering and large-scale construction work, timelines are regularly broken and the costs may be soaring (see e.g., Cicmil and Hodgson, 2006: 7). Still the timelines has some fascinating innate capacity to create a sense of security—as if by magic, the project leader is capable of mastering the flow of time as soon as it is visualized, tamed by means of graphic illustrations. "[A] timeline creates an impression of concreteness that belies the inherent uncertainty underneath. This allows the chart to be both useful and credible," Yakura (2002: 969) says (see also Roth and Bowen [2003] and Roth [2003] for a discussion of the relationship between semiotics and rhetoric and the use of visual representations).

Vision and visuality are emerging in many forms and is arguable playing a central role in the functioning of organization. Since human vision is to some extent always already present, it is somewhat paradoxically also what is somewhat taken for granted and overlooked (no pun intended); it is an "absent present" in organization theory. Always all-too-mundane to be noticed, yet largely theoretically unexplored, vision is what deserves a proper analysis and a proper theory.

OUTLINE OF THE BOOK

This book is an attempt at introducing and discussing the concepts of vision and visuality and to address theories pertaining to this objective. Rather than discussing these terms strictly from an organization theory framework, the approach here is perhaps best described as being syncretic, bringing together a range of theories, models, and concepts from the social sciences, organization theory, the humanities, and from philosophy.

The book is structured into two parts and a final chapter. In the first part of the book, including this introductory chapter and the second chapter, theories of vision and visuality are examined, suggesting that modern theories of vision are offering radical new ideas on how vision is constituted and what vision is in comparison to classic (i.e., Greek) thinking or early modern thinking. Modern theories of vision have their roots in the first half of the nineteenth century, fundamentally propelled by new scientific procedures and philosophical thinking. While the classic view held the faculty of vision to be shared between individuals, the modern theories conceived of subjective forms of vision. As a consequence, vision became a social and psychological practice subject to individual differences, skills, and interests. These new theories of vision also called for novel research problems such as the capacity to pay attention to things in the social environment. Since attention became a scarce resource in the increasingly urbanized metropolitan areas in Europe and North America, psychologists and researchers were increasingly examining the human capacity of paying attention. Eventually, attention became part of the central concerns for managers, how to accomplish as much output as possible given a limited stock of resources. There is thus a certain linearity between novel theories of vision and the emerging discipline of management studies of organization theory.

In the second part of the book, empirical studies of vision and visuality in the workplace are reported. In the first empirical chapter, Chapter 3, vision and visuality in science-based innovation work are examined. Drawing on a heterogeneous body of literature including science and technology studies (STS), anthropology, and innovation management literature, it is suggested that vision and visuality are of central importance for the production of "scientific facts" and the collective analysis of the variety of graphs, images, diagrams, and so forth, produced in scientific work. Examining the case of new drug development (NDP) in a major pharmaceutical company, it is shown that one of the most distinguished competencies among the researchers is the ability to identify and isolate interesting visual representations in their work. Seen in this view, science-based innovation work is ultimately a matter of combining theoretical know-how with visual competencies.

In the next chapter, Chapter 4, vision and visuality in architect's work are accounted for. While science-based innovation work such as new drug development work is often regarded as what is inherently theoretical and visual practices are merely substituting for theories or other forms of knowledge proper, architects inhabit a world wherein vision and visuality are fully recognized and rendered legitimate sources of know-how and expertise, perhaps to the point wherein the very notions of vision and visuality are overstated. The study reported shows that architects use a variety of visual tools including photographs, CAD images, and full-scale models to articulate ideas, capture certain features of the imagined building, and to convey meaning. Seen in this way, both pharmaceutical researchers and architects have developed their own forms of what will be called "professional vision," forms of structured ways of perceiving social reality and the capacity of inspecting a variety of visual representations mobilized in the work.

In the fifth and final chapter, some of the main arguments and the lingering concerns addressed in the previous chapters will be revisited. The chapter also aims at addressing some methodological issues pertaining to the study of vision and visuality in organizations. Finally, the chapter is proposing some topics of discussion in forthcoming research in the field.

2 The Visual Turn in Social Science and Organization Theory

INTRODUCTION

> "The very fact of perceiving, of paying attention, is selective; all attention, all focusing of our consciousness, involves a deliberate omission of what is not interesting. We see and hear through memories, fears, expectations. In bodily terms, unconsciousness is a necessary condition of physical acts. Our bodies knows how to articulate this difficult paragraph, how to contend with stairways, knots, overpasses, cities, fast-running rivers, dogs, how to cross a street without being run down by traffic, how to procreate, how to breathe, how to sleep, and perhaps how to kill."
>
> Jorge Luis Borges (1999: 61)

In this chapter, the concepts of vision and visuality will be introduced and examined in some detail. Before we proceed to the discussion of the historical development of a modern theory of vision, a few central terms needs to be defined. Following Natharius (2004: 239), we speak of *vision* as "the mechanical process of receiving visible light waves through the retina." That is, vision is primarily a chemico-physical somatic response to external stimuli. On the other hand, *visuality* is denoting "the social/psychological process of socially constructing the meaning of our perceived visual data" (Natharius, 2004: 239). Similarly, Elkins (1996: 19) uses the term *vision* to denote "the anatomical actions of the eyes" while *sight* "refers to all the wider senses of seeing, from suspicion to unconscious desires." Elkins is, however, suggesting that recent neurological research shows that practically separating these two terms is problematic. Still, vision provides input that is cognitively and emotionally processed in order to produce coherent meaning and make sense out of what is seen. Since vision is perhaps the sense most widely used by human beings in everyday life, there is a tendency to assume that vision is capable of offering accurate images of social life (Natharius, 2004: 241). However, in comparison to, for instance, olfactory capacities, vision is less closely tied to memory; a certain smell almost immediately provokes responses like no other sense. In addition, in comparison to taste, vision is vague and imprecise. When tasting something you dislike, you do not need to be too uncertain whether you like the taste or not—you know straightaway—but when looking at something there are no such direct responses. Still, as argued in this chapter, vision has served as the dominant paradigm for truthfulness and accuracy in the Western episteme and there are many reasons for critically examining this tradition of thinking and to examine its organizational practices and implications.

This chapter is structured as follows: First, cultural theories of vision will be addressed. Then the concept of vision as a specific trait of modernity and the intersection between science and vision are examined. Third, what here is called technology-laden vision and philosophical and sociological theories of vision are subject to analysis. In the remainder of the chapter, the concept of professional vision, vision in the domain of organizations, is elaborated upon.

CULTURAL THEORIES OF VISION

In the Western tradition of thinking, vision has been a guiding metaphor for truthfulness and certainty, for a variety of credible and desirable qualities (Blumenberg, 1993; Levin, 1993). Given this baggage of history of ideas, it is little wonder that the anthropologist Margaret Lock (2001), studying the practice of organ donations, strongly reacted during a participative observation of the procurement of organs from a patient just recently passed away. When the eyes are removed from the body to be used for transplantations on another patient, Lock cannot help but feel this is a form of transgression that the procurement of the internal organs did not represent: "For me, it seems, removal of the eyes represents more of a violation than does procurement of internal organs" (Lock, 2002: 22). The eyes are what culturally define both humanity and individual personalities, and the removal of the eyes from the patient is playing a symbolic function in once and for all establishing a definite line of demarcation between the former (living) patient and the dead body from which a range of organs may be procured. This strong emphasis on seeing, inspecting, reviewing, examining, and so forth, is a historical, cultural, and sociological trait of the Western world that in itself needs to be theorized. For anthropologists like Timothy Ingold (2000), perception *qua* vision is not a universally privileged road to truth and certainty but is instead what is contingent on the conditions of living in a certain culture: "The very idea that the world is known by representing it in the mind is bound up with assumptions about the pre-eminence of vision that are not applicable cross-culturally," Ingold (2000: 250) claims. He continues, emphasizing the fickle nature of vision: "The visual path to objective truth, it seems, is paved by illusions. Precisely because vision yields a knowledge that is indirect, based upon conjecture from the limited data available in the light, it can never be more then provisional, open to further testing and the possibility of empirical refutation" (Ingold, 2000: 246). When engaging in what Ingold (2000: 250) speaks of as "an anthropology of the senses," an analysis of the various uses of the senses in different cultures, vision is not universally privileged as the most important source of knowledge of external reality. For instance, for the Umeda, living in the jungles in Papua New Guinea, sight is restricted to "close-range, eye-to-eye contact" and is regarded as being dangerous because sorcerers may attack through the eyes, inflicting damage on the victim. In addition, Umeda live in a thick, almost impenetrable jungle where sight is only of limited value; instead, it is the faculty of hearing that is serving as the principal sense guiding and directing the activities, for instance, during hunting. Consequently, for the people living in environments (i.e., biotopes) giving priority to hearing, the language is not filled with metaphors and metonymies emphasizing the faculty of vision as a credible source of truth. For instance, the word *ku-umba*, in Sayá language, a people living in Mato Grosso in Brazi, translates not only "to hear" but also as "to understand" and "to know" (Ingold, 2000: 251). Hearing is here what is regarded the principal means for acquiring knowledge proper. Anthropologists like Ingold (2000) show that the Western experience is by no means the only possible tradition of thinking. While vision has served as a "root metaphor" for a variety of experiences in the European tradition, in other parts of the world other senses have played a significantly different role and, as a consequence, their language, their mode of thinking are not as *ocularocentric* as in the West. Listening may in many cases be a more useful capacity when living in environments where sight is restricted. Learning to see these differences in tradition is one of the major gifts of anthropological contributions.

THE EMERGENCE OF THE MODERN
THEORY OF PERCEPTION

The history of the philosophy of vision is a long-term tradition, beginning naturally with Greek thinking (Foster, 1988) and continuing into modern times with the radical reformulation of theories of vision in the first half of the nineteenth century. In the ancient period, Pliny did, for instance, insist on regarding the eye as some kind of passage point between the mind, the ultimate source of vision, and the outside world: "The mind is the real instrument of sight and observations, the eyes acts as a sort of vessel receiving and transmitting the visible portions of the consciousness" (Pliny, cited in Leppert, 1996: 6). However, for Plato, Neiva (1999: 22) argues, perspective in painting was immoral because the painter is then aiming at "correcting" the proportions of reality and adapting them to the conditions of eyesight. Plato rejects such perspective because since it is "sheer appearance," a mere illusion resulting from painters, sculptors, and architects' conscious intention of deceiving the viewer, it is in conflict with the true formal matter beyond the shallow appearances. In the Platonist tradition of thinking, eyesight is no reliable source of knowledge and consequently he advocated a mathematization of research methods to avoid the exposure to the fallacies of vision. Contrary to this view, the Aristotelian tradition of thinking is more empiricist and emphasizes taxonomies as valid epistemological categories (Koyré, 1968).

Gombrich (1960) list a few major works such as Ptolemy's *Optics* (c. AD 15) and the great Arab scholar Alhazen (965–1040), who formulated a number of principles and ideas regarding the nature of vision and vision's role in securing solid knowledge in his *Book of Optics* (published in three volumes). Alhazen was a prolific scholar and produced 92 works whereof more than 60 have survived (Howard, 1996: 1205). Alhazen is most widely known for his work that influenced Johannes Kepler, but he produced a great number of research results and propositions that in many cases did not get any more elaborate scientific evidence until more than eight centuries later, in the latter half of the nineteenth century. Alhazen taught the medieval West, for instance, the difference between sense, knowledge, and inference, all of which came into play in perception: "Nothing visible is understood by the sense of sight alone," he says, "save light and colors" (cited in Gombrich, 1960: 15). Much writings on vision in the medieval period, such as that of Roger Bacon (c. 1220–1292)—generally credited for the invention of eyeglasses—the Polish scholar Vitello (1230–1270), writing the first European treatise on optics with the title *Perspectiva* (1270), and John of Peckham (1240–1291), archbishop of Canterbury, were essentially commentaries on Alhazen's work (Howard, 1996: 1206). Speaking in less scholarly term, in the medieval period, vision was among the broad social strata something completely different than it is for the contemporary human being. "Their [medieval humans] sight was different than ours in kind; accepting a more inclusive concept of reality, they saw more than we do," Erickson (1976: 29) suggests. Seeing angels and having "visions" or otherwise encountering unknown creatures (the Scandinavian folklore is, for instance, filled with trolls and unicorns and similar fairy-tale figures, representing an intricate symbolic system and embodying both collective fears and hopes) was part of the folklore, and many hagiographies—a popular literary genre of the medieval period (Stock, 1983)—accounted for how various saints had visions of God or the archangels in their dreams or when being awake (Gurevich, 1988). For the medieval man, vision was not simply restricted by the human anatomical visual system but stretched into the realm of the mystical or the mythological. Alhazen's and other scholars' insights on vision had a minimal influence on popular ways of seeing.

Barry (1997: 29) says that Johannes Kepler was the first, in 1604, to envision a model of the eye as a camera capable of accurately recording the outside world with the lens as optic and the retina as the receptor. Eventually, John Locke, the great British empiricist philosopher, claimed that all knowledge derived from the senses and questioned how the third dimension could be perceived when the eye only registered light and colour. The Irish bishop and philosopher George Berkeley reached the conclusion in his *New Theory of Vision* (1709) that all our knowledge of space and solidity "[m]ust be acquired through the sense of touch and movement" (Gombrich, 1960: 15). In classic and medieval thinking, vision remained unquestioned in terms of being regarded a widely shared human faculty. It was not until the modern period that vision was reconsidered and given its proper theoretization. Jonathan Crary (1990: 27) points out that during the the seventeenth and eighteenth centuries, the *camera obscura* "was without question the most widely used model for explaining human vision, and for representing the relation of a perceiver and the position of a knowing subject to an external world" (Crary, 1990: 27). The Chinese work *Mo Ching*, published as early as in the fourth century BC, describes the camera obscura (Howard, 1996: 1206), and in medieval Europe it was a well-known technical device. The camera obscura enables an image to be reproduced on the walls of the camera when light is let in through a small hole in the wall of the otherwise dark chamber. Kofman (1999: 3) argues that the medieval model of the camera obscura was itself an invention in order to break with ancient thinking, and more specifically the predominant Euclidean idea of vision: "The history of sciences shows us that the camera obscura imposes itself as a model for vision in order to do away with the Euclidean conception according to which it is from the eye that emanates the luminous ray. The model of the camera obscura thus implies the existence of a 'given' which would offer itself as already inverted." Numerous artists used the camera obscura to accurately portray external social reality. For instance, for Leonardo da Vinci, who thought of direct observation and experience to be "the gateway to discovery" and thus spoke of visualization as *saper vedere*, "knowing to see" (Trumbo, 2006), the camera obscura was "[a] means for accurately reproducing objects situated at a certain distance; a tool for copying, even if the object given in the camera obscura appears inverted, in accordance with the laws of perspective," Kofman (1999: 30–31) suggests. Leonardo did otherwise adhere to the idea that the eye operates on basis of sense impressions penetrating the retina in the form of images: "If you look at the sun of some other luminous body and then shut your eyes you will see it again inside your eye for a long time. This is evidence that images enter into the eye" (Leonardo da Vinci, cited in Kofman, 1999: 31). Vision is, in other words, largely given by what is entering the eye; vision is not a fabrication or an outcome from subjective or psychological processes.

MODERN THEORIES OF VISION

In general, until the first decades of the nineteenth century, vision was conceived in terms of analogies to the sense of touch by most early modern philosophers, including Descartes, Berkeley, and Diderot (Crary, 1990: 59).

Since vision was treated largely as a mechanical procedure in the human body, there was little attention paid to the subjective differences in vision. For Crary (1995), the emergence of "subjective theories of vision" represents a major change in focus in modern thinking:

> One of the most important developments in the history of visuality in the nineteenth century was the relatively sudden emergence of models of subjective vision in a wide range of disciplines during the period from 1810 to 1840. Dominant discourses and practices of vision, within the space of a few decades, effectively broke with a classical regime of visuality and grounded the truth of vision in the density and materiality of the body. (Crary, 1995: 46)

For Crary (1995), the modern subjective theories of vision—"the notion that the quality of our sensations depends less on the nature of the stimulus and more on the makeup and functioning of our sensory apparatus" (Crary, 1995: 46)—are by no means a scientific curiosity in the history of ideas but are instead a prerequisite for a variety of social practices that are used in modern society, including surveillance techniques, managerial practices, modern marketing activities, and so forth. Crary (1995: 47) writes: "The rapid accumulation of knowledge about the workings of a fully embodied observer made vision open to procedures of normalization, of quantification, of discipline. Once the empirical truth of vision was determined to lie in the body, the senses—and vision in particular—were able to be annexed and controlled by external techniques of manipulation and stimulation." Crary (1995) lists a number of social and scientific changes that brought the new theories of vision. First, in the second half of the nineteenth century, the perceived differences between the *biosphere* and the *mechanosphere* began to evaporate and the previously indisputable distinction between the interior of the body and the exterior was gradually disintegrated. For instance, in her analysis of the emergence of medical visualization technologies, Cartwright (2005) argues that much of the technologies used in the cinematic apparatus were initially used in medical practices: "It is by now commonplace of film history that many of the techniques and instruments that contributed to the emergence of the cinema were designed and used by scientists, and that they were developed as a means of investigation into optics and physiology," Cartwright (1995: 3) writes. For Cartwright (1995: 3), new medical technologies such as the myograph, the kymograph, and the electrocardiograph—some of which are in use still today—can be seen as components in a "cinematic apparatus," a "cultural technology" ultimately designed to improve the discipline and management of the human body. Following Marie François Xavier Bichat's famous definition of life in his *Recherches physiologiques sur la vie et la mort* (published in May 1800; Haigh, 1984: 10), as "an ensemble of functions deployed to resist death" (cited in Rabinow, 1996b: 80),[1] the new medical visual techniques reduced the human body to a set of individual functions that could be rendered subject to visual inspection.

Second, in the late nineteenth century, Crary (1995) suggests, in the emerging field of psychology, the concept of *attention* became a central issue. This problem was formulated on the basis of the *Lebenswelt* of the urban subject, characterized by an overwhelming amount of sensory input. Crary (1995: 47) suggests that this concern regarding attentiveness was both triggered by and further propelled the new theories of vision formulated in the first half of the century. In fact, the concept of attention became one of the central issues in modern society: "It is possible to see one crucial aspect of modernity as a continual crisis of attentiveness, to see the changing configurations of capitalism pushing attention and distraction to new limits and thresholds, with unending introduction of new products, new sources of stimulation, and streams of information, and then responding with new methods of managing and regulating perception," Crary (1995: 47) says. Third, perhaps seemingly peripheral, philosophers contributed with new theories of vision. For instance, in his *The World as Will and Idea*, Arthur Schopenhauer formulated a distinction between vision and visuality similar to that of Natharius (2004), cited earlier:

> What the eye, the ear, or the hands feel, is not perception; it is merely data. Only when understanding passes from the effects to the cause does the world lie before us as perception extends in space, varying in respect of form, persistent through all time in respect of matter . . . perception is not merely of the senses, but is intellectual: that is, *pure knowledge through the understanding of the cause from the effect.* (Schopenhauer, 1995: 9. Emphasis in the original)

Schopenhauer (1995) suggests that vision is not a matter of merely registering changes in light and colour but that all vision is the *active construction* of meaning on basis of visual stimuli. For Crary (1995), all these interrelated changes brought the possibilities for the new subjective theories of vision. While prominent scientists such as Hermann von Helmholtz (to be discussed shortly) made significant contributions to the theory of vision, Crary also points to the social, cultural, and economic changes during the nineteenth century as important drivers for change in the theories of vision. For instance, Crary suggests that the emphasis on attention is representative of an economic regime relying on a swift circulation of capital:

> Part of the cultural logic of capitalism demands that we accept as *natural* the rapid switching of our attention from one thing to another. Capital, as accelerated exchange and circulation, necessarily produces this kind of human perceptual adaptability and becomes a regime of reciprocal attentiveness and distraction. (Crary, 1995: 48)

Elsewhere, Crary (1999: 13) continues:

> At the moment when the dynamic logic of capital began to dramati-
> cally undermine any stable or enduring structure of perception, this
> logic simultaneously attempted to impose a disciplinary regime of at-
> tentiveness. For it is in the late nineteenth century, within the human
> sciences and particularly the nascent field of scientific psychology, that
> the problem of *attention* becomes a fundamental issue. It was a prob-
> lem whose centrality was directly related to the emergence of a social
> urban, psychic, and industrial field increasingly saturated with sen-
> sory input. Inattention, especially within the context of new forms of
> large-scale industrialized production, began to be treated as a danger
> and a serious problem, even though it was often the very modern-
> ized arrangements of labor that produced as an ongoing inattention.
> (Crary, 1999: 13. Emphasis in the original)

For Crary (1999), modern theories of vision are intimately connected to
changing socioeconomic conditions in the nineteenth century.

In the emerging discipline of management and organization studies, the
question of attention was of fundamental importance. Fredrick W. Taylor's
scientific management principles made the inattentiveness and ignorance of
the workers a major challenge for the modern corporation and the modern
managers. Taylor's perhaps most notorious and widely spread dictum, first
published in his *Shop Management* (1903) prescribing that "all possible
brain work should be removed from the shop and centered in the planning
and laying-out department (Taylor, 1911: 36), is suggesting that attentiveness is not equally distributed in the population but is what demands discipline and above all engineering training.[2] However, as many studies of the
application of Taylor's principles have demonstrated, the principal objective
for these concerns was not primarily the highly praised quality of *efficiency*
but *control* of the work force. Margery Davies (1982) reports in her study
of the Taylorization of office work:

> The vast majority of scientific office management were determined to
> exert increasing control over the work process. Their efforts were of-
> ten cloaked in terms such as 'eliminating waste motion', 'increasing
> productivity', and 'improving efficiency'. Such terms were invariably
> invoked in the struggle over reassigning tasks to the lowest-paid worker
> possible. Put differently, this involved fitting the worker to the job. (Da-
> vies, 1982: 118–119)

Somewhat paradoxically and at least in conflict with the official rhetoric
of the scientific management proponents, the alleged "lack of attention" on
part of the worker was replaced by a work situation where the work process
was scattered into its components and thereby prevented any coherent and

meaningful view of the office work whatsoever. Taylor and his disciples fought inattentive workers and produced a work situation where attention was not even possible to accomplish:

> For many office workers, the minute division of labor meant that the scope of their work was reduced to the repeated performance of limited tasks . . . Because their activities were so restricted in scope, they did not have the opportunity to grasp other office procedures and to see how their particular task fit into the work flow. Thus deprived, they could not determine whether their particular task had been organized in the most practical way. Denied through their ignorance the possibility of changing the design or scope of their work, they were forced to work as their superiors prescribed. (Davies, 1982: 127)

The scientific management program, perhaps the single most influential contribution to managerial practice, is thus relying on the concept of vision as what is of necessity problematic or sub-optimized as long as it is not handled properly by trained and dedicated engineers. Given the ambition of Taylor and his followers to render the world a better place, it is somewhat tragi-comical to see how much monotonous and static work assignments the scientific management program produced; concerning vision, the concern regarding lack of attention was gradually transformed into a range of problems derived from the loss of possibilities for attention altogether.

SCIENTIFIC ELABORATIONS ON VISION

Modern theories of vision are, to use Louis Althusser's (1984) term, *overdetermined* by a variety of social, cultural, economic changes, and changes in philosophical and scientific doctrines and beliefs. Among the most central agents in this pervasive change was the German scientist Hermann von Helmholtz, whose work on visual perception was groundbreaking. Helmholtz showed that preceding theories of vision, assuming that the eye was transparent and essentially an organ capable of objectively registering external reality, were fallacious and that the eye is not a perfect apparatus but one "[w]ith built-in aberrations, proneness to error, and inconsistencies in its processing of visual information" (Crary, 1999: 215). In addition, Helmholtz embedded the eye in the thickness of the body, rendering it an organ determined by subjective capacities. Helmholtz (1968: 180) starts to distinguish a few central terms in his theoretical model. First the term *perception* (*Perzeption*) denotes the "pure perception" devoid of previous experience. Apperception (*Anschauung*) is perception that is accompanied by some idea of belief (*Vorstellung*) that helps creating a sense of meaning regarding what is observed. Apperception is thus perception that is mingling with preconceived ideas and previous experiences. Helmholtz (1968) suggests that rather than being an innate and essentially unproblematic procedure, vision is always subject to training, previous experience, interest, beliefs, and so forth. In other words, vision is for Helmholtz a subjective experience and a subjective capacity. Helmholtz (1968: 185) exemplifies: "Steady fixation of a point for a long time while observations are being made in indirect vision; controlling the attention; taking the mind away from sense-impression; estimation of difference of colour and of difference of space in the visual field—all those things take much practice." As a consequence, Helmholtz is suggesting that his scientific work is not a strictly scientific matter but a matter for the emerging behavioural sciences, and especially psychology. "The theory of perception belongs properly to the domain of psychology," Helmholtz (2004: 43) declares. Helmholtz also accounts for the entire procedure that connects the eye, the visual apparatus, and the faculties of reason residing in the human brain:

> *Physiological Optics* is the science of the visual perception by the sense of sight. The objects around us are made visible through the agency of light proceeding thence and falling on our eyes. The light, reaching the retina, which is a sensitive portion of the nervous system, stimulates certain sensation therein. These are conveyed to the brain by the optic nerve, the result being that the mind becomes conscious of the perception of certain objects disposed in space. (von Helmholtz, 2004: 42)

Helmholtz's seminal work was followed by a variety of contributions, for instance, Wilhelm Wundt's *Grundzüge der physiologischen Psychologie* (1874), wherein the concepts of *Blickfeld* and *Blickpunkt* were introduced. The *Blickfeld* was the "field of consciousness, of conscious awareness" and the *Blickpunkt* was the very "[f]ocus of consciousness where apperception occurred, effectively synonymous with attention" (Crary, 1999: 292). Wundt thus further advanced Helmholtz's ideas that vision is subjective and underlined the very act of choosing, deliberately or not, the site of the *Blickpunkt*. The concept of attention is again closely associated with human vision.

More recent scientific research on vision emphasizes the unique features of human vision. In fact, one of the principal challenges for artificial intelligence (AI) research is to handle the complexities of vision enabled by the perceptual apparatus. Barry (1997) stresses the qualities of human vision:

> The eye, unlike the camera, is not a mechanism for capturing images as much as it is a complex processing unit to detect range, form, and features, and which selectively prepares data that the brain must then interpret. As we survey the three-dimensional ambient optical array of the environment, properties such as contour, texture, and regularity, which are invariant under perspective transformations, allows us to

discriminate objects and to see them as constant and external to ourselves. (Barry, 1997: 33)

That is, rather than being a passive recipient of sensory data, the perceptual
apparatus is a dynamic relationship between the eye, the brain, and the
cognitive capacities and the perceived outside world; "Perception always
intercedes between reality and ourselves," Barry (1997: 16) says.

> [The] optical system represents an interface between the brain and the
> environment. Characterized by cells responsive to minutely differen-
> tiated and specialized aspects of the environment, the optical system
> is a symphony of millions of nerve cells firing in particular patterns,
> responding to each of the component parts of the final image such as
> direction, degree of slant, shape, and color, through the activation of
> specialized areas within the visual cortex. No neutral response ever
> achieves its complex meaning alone, however. Within the visual sys-
> tem, cells work separately and in concert with one another to achieve
> and to inhibit certain responses, and there is continual feedback among
> the parts. Perception is a dynamical system that utilizes the input from
> the body's sensory systems, synthesizes this with memory and under-
> standing, and creates from both an integrated sense self and mind.
> (Barry, 1997: 34–35)

In the history of vision, there is a movement from regarding vision as what
is a largely uncomplicated registering of the outside world, to theories of
vision as a most complex cognitive-perceptual construction of a social reality. Seen in this view, one may claim that the external world is created
though vision through the imposing of determinate structures that are constituting a firm ground for human action.

Technology-Laden Vision

Even though scholars like Crary (1990, 1995, 1999) emphasize the theoretical and socioeconomic developments preceding the formulation of a
modern theory of vision, there are numerous technical changes that have
both been part of and helped advance the visual culture of modernity (for
an overview, see Klein, 2004; Pauwels, 2006; Schwartz and Przyblyski,
2004). Following French archeologist André Leroi-Gourhan (1993), the
French technology philosopher Bernard Stiegler (1998) speaks of the concept of *epiphylogenesis*, a term denoting the entanglement between the
development of the human as a species and the technological development
demonstrated over time. Rather than being two separate trajectories, where
humans first developed and thereafter invented technology, Leroi-Gourhan
and Stiegler claim that humans were in fact developing into *Homo sapi-
ens* through the dynamic interaction with technology; technology is not

simply the outcome from embodied and cognitive human development (i.e., an effects) or preceding such changes (i.e., a cause), but is exactly what is closely bound up with the human developmental trajectory. Hansen (2006: 299) explicates this position:

> Human beings . . . evolve by passing on their knowledge through culture, and this means that humans are 'essentially' technical and have been so from their very 'origin.' In order to differentiate from strictly zoological evolution, Stiegler thus defines human evolution as irreducibly both bio-logical and cultural; it occurs as a process that he dubs 'epiphylogenesis,' evolution through means other than life. (Hansen, 2006: 299)

The term *epiphylogenesis* thus denotes the double development of tech-nological means and biological changes; life is inherently technological and is what is helped, shaped, and formed by technology. In Stiegler's view, technology ("techno-genesis") is always what is prior to society ("socio-genesis"):

> Becoming technological is originarily a derivation: socio-genesis reca-pitulates techno-genesis. Techno-genesis is structurally prior to socio-genesis—technics is invention, and invention is innovation—and the adjustment between technical evolution system and social traditions always encounters moments of resistance, since technical change, to a greater or lesser extent, disrupts the familiar reference points of which all culture consists. (Stiegler, 2009: 2)

Although Leroi-Gourhan and Stiegler speak of epiphylogenesis over hun-dreds of thousands of years, it is noteworthy that the relationship between technology and vision may be examined in a shorter time perspective. The alleged visual turn in contemporary society is here the outcome from a great variety of new media, developed since the early modern period, beginning perhaps with Galilei's invention of the telescope, an optical device than enabled new forms of visuality. Since the middle of the sixteenth century, a long series of optical devices and machinery have been contrived and brought to the market (Gitelman and Pingree, 2003). Also other, more major technological innovations such as the railroad have brought new opportunities for vision and visuality. Schivelbusch (1986) is pointing at the railroad as a new technology that radically shifted the focus on space and visuality. Another modern innovation was architecture based on glass and steel, enabling new social spaces shaping vision and visuality:

> The railroad reorganized space. In architecture, a similar reorganiza-tion occurred with the introduction of glass and steel as new building materials . . . Both the railroad and the glass buildings were direct ex-pressions of the multiplied productivity brought about by the industrial

revolution. The railroad brought new quantities of goods into circulation; the edifices of glass architecture—railroad stations, market halls,
exhibition palaces, arcades—served as places of transit and storage.
The spatial capacity of glass architecture stands in a similar relation to
the capacity of traditional architecture as the railroad's capacity stands
to that of preindustrial transportation. (Schivelbusch, 1986: 45)

The railroad was perhaps the most important modern technical innovation prior to the electrification at the end of the nineteenth century, and
Schivelbusch (1986) is here speaking of the emergence of a "panoramic
vision" as one of the novel experiences brought by the railway; "[t]he railroad first and foremost, is the main cause for [the] panoramization of the
world," Schivelbusch (1986: 62) says. When being inside the train, the passenger could enjoy a scenery never seen before; landscapes passing before
the passenger who could for the first time experience a new form of "scopic
vision." The emergence of new technologies and the new visual media (i.e.,
the *phenakistiscope,* the *zoetrope,* the *stereoscope,* etc., in the 1830s; Gitelman and Pingee, 2003) brought a new visual culture specific for modernity.
When cinema was invented by the brothers Lumière a few decades later,
there was a substantial demand and appetite for visual entertainment. The
panoramic vision offered by the railways was part of a general reformulation of vision and visuality. Today, vision and visuality are widely studied
by a range of university disciplines, and for the critics, the emergence of
computer technologies and the Internet represents yet another shift in focus
similar to that brought by the railways some 150 years ago. For instance,
the film theorist Jonathan Beller (2006: 3) claims that "the industrialization of vision has shifted gears": "With the rise of internet grows the recognition of the value-productive dimensions of sensual labor in the visual
register. Perception is increasingly bound to production." In addition to the
computer-generated images (e.g., computer games) and Internet, new forms
of virtual reality (VR) technologies are experimented upon, showing that
the limits of human perception may be extended into sophisticated technological machineries capable of simulating social reality. There is thus a certain continuity between the emergence of the railway in the first decades of
the nineteenth century and the most advanced form of VR technologies in
the new millennium: Both technologies are contributing to a rearticulation
of what human vision is and what role visuality plays in the contemporary
society. For the enthusiasts (e.g., Steuer, 1992), new technologies are tools
in the hands of humans, potentially capable of offering new and fruitful
human experiences and shaping social life in a meaningful manner; for the
critics, new technologies are always potentially threatening the individual's
integrity and are always of necessity Janus-faced in terms of both enabling
freedom and oppression. For instance, new surveillance technologies are
regularly defended by their spokesmen as being a warrant for freedom and
security while the critics claim that freedom and security do not come for

free, and more specifically at the cost of personal integrity. That is, the glass is either half full or half empty regarding what perspective is taken. However, the key point in this context is that human vision is rarely if ever immaculate and unmediated. Instead, virtually all visual means are distorting, manipulating, or otherwise influencing the vision of the perceiving subject. In addition, human capacities for vision and visuality are always technology-laden and are co-evolutionarily developed in tandem with technological development. As suggested by the French social theorist Paul Virilio in a number of publications (e.g., Virilio, 1989), vision is to an increasing extent mediated vision, and being aware of that condition and the effects of technology are major political and scientific challenges in contemporary times.

Philosophical Aspects of Perception

An important distinction needs to be made between, on the one hand, philosophical perspectives on vision and visuality (examining the epistemologies of the eye), and, on the other, sociological perspectives on vision (theorizing and studying practices of seeing). In this setting, both perspectives will be examined briefly and neither of the discussions is exhaustive. As has been pointed out earlier, vision and visuality have been perennial issues in philosophy since ancient times. In the twentieth century, the perhaps most widely known proponent of a phenomenology of perception and vision is the French philosopher Maurice Merleau-Ponty. For Merleau-Ponty, human perception is a major philosophical issue since perception is, as suggested by the British empiricists John Locke and David Hume in the seventeenth century, the principal means for knowing the external world. Merleau-Ponty here speaks of the "primacy of perception":

> [By] the 'primacy of perception,' we mean that experience of perception is our presence at the moment when things, truths, values are constituted for us; that perception is a nascent logos; that it teaches us, outside of all dogmatism, the true conditions of objectivity itself; that it summons us to the tasks of knowledge and action. It is not a question of reducing human knowledge to sensation, but of assisting at the birth of this knowledge, to make it as sensible as the sensible, to recover the consciousness of rationality. This experience of rationality is lost when we take it for granted as self-evident, but is, on the contrary, rediscovered when it is made to appear against the background of non-human nature. (Merleau-Ponty, 1964: 25)

Perception is then the surface between the individual and the external world. This surface is, however, always fluid and fluxing; technological means are mediating between the human body and the external world that we learn to know through perception. Eyeglasses, prostheses, various technological apparatus are all examples of how human perception is mediated. Merleau-Ponty is thus advancing a phenomenology of the body; the human experience is fundamentally embodied, lived through the body, a matter of embodiment:

> It is my body which gives significance not only to the natural object, but also to cultural objects like words. If a word is shown to a subject for too short a period a time for him to be able to read it, the word 'warm,' for example, induces a kind of experience of warmth which surrounds him with something in the nature of a meaningful halo. (Merleau-Ponty, 1962: 235)

For Merleau-Ponty, Grosz (1994: 86) remarks, "mind . . . is always embodied, always based on corporeal and sensory relations." Merleau-Ponty's phenomenological philosophy has been influential in a range of disciplines and Jacques Lacan is one of the most important followers of his thinking. Lacan was intrigued by Merleau-Ponty's insistence on seeing vision as being embodied at the same time as Merleau-Ponty spoke of the difference between the visible and the invisible rather than the material and the sensible. Says Lacan ([1973] 1998: 71): "*La Phénomenologie* [Merleau-Ponty's most widely known work, *The Phenomenology of Perception*, first published in 1962] brings us back, then, to the regulation of form, which is governed not only by the subject's eye, but by his expectations, his movement, his grip, his muscular and visceral emotions in short, his constitutive presence, directed in what is called his total intentionality." In Norman Bryson's (1988) careful examination of Lacan's theory of vision, vision is of necessity "socialized," embedded in preexisting social relations:

> For human beings collectively to orchestrate their visual experience together it is required that each submit his or her retinal experience to the socially agreed description(s) of an intelligible world. Vision is socialized, and thereafter deviation from this social construction of visual reality can be measured and named, variously, as hallucination, misrecognition, or 'visual disturbance.' Between the subject and the world is inserted the entire sum of discourses which make up visuality, that cultural construct, and make visuality different from vision, the notion of unmediated visual experience. Between retina and world is inserted a screen of signs, a screen consisting of all multiple discourses on vision built into the social arena. (Bryson, 1988: 91–92)

For Lacan, this condition implies that the perceiving subject is never isolated from the social context in which the act of perception or vision is accomplished; "the viewing subject does not stand at the center of a perceptual horizon, and cannot command the chains of signifiers passing across the visual domain," Bryson (1988: 94) says. Instead, Bryson (1988: 94) continues, vision "[u]nfolds to the side of, in tangent to, the field of the other. And to that form of seeing Lacan gives a name: seeing on the field of the other, seeing under the Gaze." For Silverman (1994), contrary to Bryson's (1988) more "sociological" understanding of the term, Lacan's gaze is derived from the early childhood experiences in what Lacan calls *the mirror stage*:

> What Lacan designates the "gaze" also manifests itself initially within a space external to the subject, first through the mother's look as it facilitates the "join" of infant and mirror image, and later through all of the many other actual looks with which it is confused. It is only at a second remove that the subject might be said to assume responsibility for "operating" the gaze by "seeing" itself being seen even when no pair of eyes are trained upon it—by taking not so much the gaze as its effects within the self. However, consciousness as it is redefined by Lacan hinges not only upon the internalization but upon the elision of the gaze; this "seeing" of oneself being seen is experienced by the subject-of-consciousness—by the subject, that is, who arrogates to itself a certain self-presence or substantiality—as a seeing of itself seeing itself. (Silverman, 1994: 274)

The look is thus always subsumed under the gaze, and only under certain conditions, the viewer is becoming aware of the influence of the gaze. Bryson (1988) credits Lacan for discovering what traditionally has been taken as being private, inward, and secluded in fact is "created socially." Vision is what is always already shaped and formed by the image of the other, that is, vision qua gaze. "Man's desire is the desire of the Other," Lacan ([1973] 1998: 235) says. Such desire is what of necessity is penetrating the subject's vision. For instance, in film theory, the feminist thinker Laura Mulvey (1989) has strongly emphasized that the image of women and men in cinema is subject to the Lacanian gaze. In Mulvey's view, cinema is from the outset structured in accordance with a set of binary opposites such as male/active and passive/female. The male gaze is always present in cinema and consequently female subjects are always subsumed under repressive doctrines regarding what is constitutive of femininity and womanhood proper. Mulvey (1989) thus claims, drawing on Lacan, that the spectacle of cinema is shaped by a mode of visuality or an ocular regime that is imbued with paternalist ideologies and beliefs. The cinematic gaze is thus a masculine gaze. Also, the French film theorist Christian Metz (1982) draws on Lacan in his analysis of the medium. For Metz (1982), the cinematic vision, embedded in "perceptual signifiers," is structured in two directions, from the projector to the screen, and from the screen to the viewer:

> There are two cones in the auditorium: one ending on the screen and starting both in the projection box and in the spectator's vision insofar

as it is projective, and one starting from the screen and deposited in the spectator's perception insofar as it is introjective (on the retina, a second screen) When I say that 'I see' the film, I mean thereby a unique mixture of the two contrary currents: the film is what I receive, and it is also what I release, since it does not pre-exist my entering the auditorium and I only need close my eyes to suppress it. Releasing it, I am the projector, receiving it, I am the screen; in both these figures together, I am the camera, which points and yet which records. (Metz, 1982: 51)

The cinematic vision is thus always both "projective" and "introjective"; the gaze is here dependent on the two "cones" coexisting simultaneously. The cinematic gaze is produced through these two directions. Such belief in visual perception as being both a form of reception and a projection was further explored in the clinical psychological methods developed by the psychologist Hermann Rorschach: "Rorschach himself stressed that there is only a difference in degree between ordinary perception, the filing of impressions in our mind, and interpretations due to 'projection.' When we are aware of the process of filing we say we 'interpret,' where we are not to say 'we see,' " Gombrich (1960: 105) remarks (see also Galison, 2004). "Seeing" and "interpreting" (i.e., "seeing as") are in many cases conflating into one single procedure (Coulter and Parsons, 1991).

What Merleau-Ponty and Lacan suggest is that the visual field is not only a means for knowing the world, a form of relay between the knowing subject and the external world. Instead, preconceived ideas, beliefs, and ideologies derived from the external world are always already present in the act of seeing: The perceiving subject is always participating in the gaze of the other. Although Merleau-Ponty aimed at contributing to the field of philosophical phenomenology and Lacan reformulated the Freudian psychoanalytical framework, their ideas are of relevance for what may be called a sociological theory of vision. For instance, the central idea that vision is a collective, social experience is of great importance for any sociological theory of vision.

Sociological Theories of Vision

Sociological theories of vision is here used as an umbrella term including contributions from a range of disciplines including sociology, anthropology, film theory, art theory, cultural studies, media theory, and so forth. These disciplines all share the assumption that human vision is never appearing in isolation but is instead what is bound up with collectively shared beliefs and assumptions about the social world. In addition, sociological theories are not as much concerned with epistemological issues as with practices of seeing. The German-American sociologist Alfred Schutz (1962), drawing on, like Merleau-Ponty, the German philosopher Edmund Husserl's phenomenology, advocates the idea that human beings in order to cognitively handle the complexity of the social world encountered enact *typifica-tions*, stereotyped images of fellow humans in society. These typifications are then used to establish an integrated image of a society in equilibrium, an image that Schutz called the "social world as taken for granted." This social world is then assumed to remain relatively stable over time. What Schutz suggests is that in order to cope with the immense complexity and variety of social reality, typifications are used to reduce variety and struc-ture the social world into neat categories that are co-aligned and brought into harmony. If Schutz's model is followed, a range of social concerns regarding racism, xenophobia, homophily, and so forth may be explained; once a negative stereotype is established, it takes considerable time and intellectual effort to change that attitude. If white people tend to think that black people are more likely to be engaging in criminal activities (one of the most common race stereotypes in, e.g., the U.S., see hooks, 2000), or if older people think that younger persons are careless, then such negative typifications may serve to guide that person's actions notwithstanding their accuracy. The problem is that while typifications may not of necessity be wholly mistaken (some blacks—just like whites—could be criminals, but most are not; some teenagers may be careless, but most are not, etc.), they tend to operate *en bloc* and therefore lack precision. If an elderly person is enraged by some teenagers' behaviours, he or she tends to think of an entire generation or at least large parts of it in such negative terms. For Schutz (1962), typifications are a sociological fact in the Durkheimian sense of the term; they are neither good nor bad but the means through which human beings cognitively structure social reality. Drawing on Lacan's concept of the gaze, one may argue that typifications are effects of the gaze: In a rac-ist society, different ethnic groups maintain that there are significant dif-ferences between the various groups; in a society characterized by little meaningful contacts between age groups and generations, stereotypes are likely to gain a foothold.

Typifications and the idea that the social world is largely taken for granted until proven differently play a role in sociological theories of vision. For instance, the French sociologist Pierre Bourdieu has examined how individuals from different social strata experience and interpret art. Bourdieu (1993: 219) is here citing Nietzsche, referring to what he called "the dogma of the immaculate perception," the idea that the viewer can experience a piece of art without any preconceived ideas or foreknowledge. That is not the case, Bourdieu (1993) says. Instead, the viewer's relation-ship with a piece of art—his or her acts of seeing, one may say—is from the outset a matter of a series of social conditions and previous experience such as social background, education, cultural training, access to economic resources, and so forth. Bourdieu explains:

> There is no perception which does not involve an unconscious code and
> it is essential to dismiss the myth of the fresh eye, considered a virtue

attributed to naïveté and innocence. One of the reasons why the less educated beholders in our societies are so strongly inclined to demand a realistic representation is that, being devoid of specific categories of perception, they cannot apply any other code to works of scholarly culture than that which enables them to apprehend as meaningful objects of their everyday environment. (Bourdieu, 1993: 217)

For the untrained eye, nonfigurative art does not offer any intelligible codes to decipher. Instead, the novice is either deploring the lack of "realistic representations" (i.e., a cottage in the woods, or a landscape with grazing cows) or even dismiss an entire artwork or an artistic tradition as being irrelevant, often in most emotional terms:

Humans can hear, see, and read artworks in a variety of ways—not so much subjectively as intersubjectively—that is, in keeping with shared habits, conventions of perception, and patterns of interpretation. The results of perception and understanding are often articulated emotionally because the articulation in language of the tacit and semi-subconscious thoughts that constitute the ascribing of meaning and value is only possible to a certain degree. (Zembylas, 2004: 112)

Since tacit knowledge, an important element in the experience of art, cannot be fully articulated, the shortcomings of the vocabulary are compensated for by an emotional response. Common sense is a rather blunt tool when examining art, especially more contemporary works of art, saturated with semiotics, codes, and metacodes that the spectator is expected to be capable of interpreting. "Common sense is an unreflected judgment shared by an entire social order, people, nation or even all humankind," Vico (1999: 80) said.[3] Such "unreflected judgment" may be helpful in many cases, but when it comes to art criticism, it is rather useless in terms of not including the specialized discourses of the art world and art criticism. Following Luhmann's (2000) distinction between *first-* and *second-order observations*, common sense is representative of the first-order observations, the untrained vision of the perceiving subject. The detailed understanding of and participation in the community of the art world qualifies for the passing of judgment of a piece of art on the second order, that is, being able to locate a piece of art in a broader cultural, historical, political, and economic context. "Looking at a painting, listening to a piece of music, or simply identifying a work of art (as opposed to another object) from a first-order observer position does not yet imply a capacity for judging the work. The naked eye does not recognize artistic quality," Luhmann (2000: 80) writes. This distinction between first- and second-order observations does not suggest that the untrained and inexperienced visitor in an art museum is representing "an immaculate perception." Quite the contrary: Any vision is already shaped by previous experiences and, to use Bourdieu's (1993) analytical framework, the "cultural capital" of the perceiving subject is of necessity present in his or her ways of seeing. That is, being unfamiliar with the work of, say, Soviet suprematists, a piece of art by Kazimir Malevich may be unintelligible because the person is lacking the cultural competence for decoding the work: "The disorientation and cultural blindness of the less-educated beholders are an objective reminder of the objective truth that art perception is a mediate deciphering operation," Bourdieu (1993: 217) contends; "any deciphering operation requires a more or less complex code which has been more or less completely mastered" (Bourdieu, 1993: 218).

Wittgenstein is providing an illustrative example to Luhmann's distinction between first-order and second-order observations in his *Remarks in the Foundations of Mathematics* (1953). Here Wittgenstein is concerned with claims made by some mathematicians, adhering to the Kantian tradition of critical philosophy, that mathematical axioms are analytical statements true a priori. Wittgenstein (1953) refuses to accept such a position offhand and uses two figures to make his point:

You only need to look at the figure

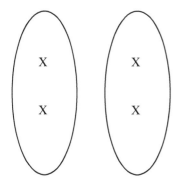

to see that '2 + 2 are 4'—Then I only need to look at the figure

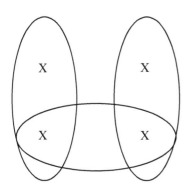

to see that '2 + 2 + 2 are 4'

Figure 2.1 '2 + 2 + 2 are 4' (Wittgenstein, 1953: 52).

What Wittgenstein suggests, to impose Luhmann's categories on his thinking, is that there is in fact a distinction between *first-order* and *second-order observations* in mathematics, and therefore the look of the mathematically untrained eye is deceiving or leads us to the wrong conclusion that 2 + 2 + 2 are 4. If one ignores or brackets what is in fact assumed and taken for granted about mathematical reasoning, one may get the impression that there are no second-order observations but only axioms—Kant's analytic sentences *a priori*—that could be understood by everyone when receiving proper training (representing a long tradition of thinking, starting perhaps with Plato's *Memo* wherein Socrates is helping a young slave boy solving a mathematical problem through a series of inquiries). " 'The axioms of a mathematical axiom-system ought to be self-evident.' How are they self-evident then?" Wittgenstein (1953: 223) asks. The point here is that mathematics is not some kind of uncomplicated "mirror of nature" or self-enclosed regime of interrelated but individually uncomplicated axioms, but is instead an intricate deductive system following its own rules and relying on its own assumptions. The general belief, entertained until modern times (with events such as Gödel's theorem and the emergence of non-Euclidean mathematics; see Kline, 1954, 1972), that mathematics is "pure" and devoid of interests was thereafter gradually abandoned. In addition, what Wittgenstein is suggesting is that vision may be, if not deceiving, at least bound up with a series of assumptions. As has been pointed out by numerous works in the field of epistemology, all observation is "theory-laden," always already relying on a set of assumptions that cannot be dispensed in the research project. Hanson (1958) used the example of Johannes Kepler and Tycho Brahe, two astronomers adhering to complementary theoretical frameworks. While Brahe remained true to the ancient tradition of Ptolemy and Aristotle, Kepler advocated the heliocentric worldview. They were therefore essentially representing two different theoretical traditions of thinking and Hanson asks if they were in fact observing the same things when gazing onto the astral bodies. Hanson (1958: 6–7) says: "Seeing is an experience. A retinal reaction is only a physical state—a photochemical excitation . . . People, not their eyes, see. Cameras, and eye-ball, are blind . . . There is more to seeing than seeing than meets the eyeball." Addressing the commonplace distinction between "seeing" and "seeing that" or "seeing as," Hanson (1958: 22) suggests that "seeing that" is what "threads knowledge into our seeing" and "saves us from re-identifying everything that meets our eye." "Seeing as" is thus what allows physicists to "observe new data as physicists, and not as cameras," Hanson concludes. Physicists (for instance) cannot pay attention to everything observable but must concentrate on what is of particular interest—a scientific procedure that Nicholas of Cusa advanced as *docta ignorantia*, "learned ignorance," in the fifteenth century (Koyré, 1959: 8); the *professional vision* of the physicists—knowledge threaded into seeing—is what guides the professional physicist in his or her everyday work. Since Brahe and Kepler drew on different theoretical frameworks, they were, Hanson (1958: 8) concludes, *not* observing the same thing: "The elements of their experience are identical; but their conceptual organization is vastly different." "Observations of x is shaped by prior knowledge of x," Hanson (1958: 19) contends. Observational data and analytical framework are therefore not fully separate in time and space but are rather co-constitutive into what Rheinberger (1997) calls *experimental systems*.

In a sociological perspective, vision and visuality are inextricably entangled with a variety of social conditions such as the distribution of various resources including cultural training and education. The middle class has traditionally been the carriers of cultural institutions and as a consequence, theorists like Bourdieu (1993) would argue, they have served as the gatekeepers at these institutions. Numerous political attempts have been done to "bring the arts to the people," to workplaces, to the suburbs, to any conceivable place not regularly associated with institutionalized culture production and consumption, but most such attempts are successful for short periods and are eventually terminated (see, e.g., Belfiore, 2002; García, 2004; Gibson, 2002). In other words, culture is not of necessity of interest for everyone, but culture consumption demands a certain competence and cultural capital to digest and render culture meaningful. That is, the access to capital is not only a matter of finding the way to the very location where culture is displayed or provided—a strict matter of *logistics*—but is also what demands significant intangible resources and skills. Vision and visuality are what are deeply seated in the human body and in the entrenched skills and capacities of the perceiving body; seeing is not only believing but more properly having the capacity to make sense out of what is seen and render the sense impressions comprising both first- and second-order observations meaningful.

In summary, philosophical theories of vision are pointing at the ontological and epistemological facets of the act of seeing; vision is here (in the case of Merleau-Ponty and later on Lacan) not only a medium between the human being and external reality but is instead what is from the outset what is infused with norms and values derived externally. Vision is not detached from what is perceived but instead has intricate relationships with the external world. Sociological theories of vision are further underlining this embedded nature of vision. Not only is vision ontologically and epistemologically complex; it is what is fundamentally embedded in social relationships and conditions. In the next section, vision will be examined not only as an individual and social capacity or skill but what is an organizational resource; that is, vision is examined as a form of professional competence employed in organizations.

VISION IN ORGANIZATIONS: PROFESSIONAL VISION

The Concept of Profession

Studies of occupational identities and professions represent a classical field of research in sociology and neighbouring disciplines in the social sciences

(Abbott, 1988; Carr-Saunders and Wilson, 1933; Friedson, 1986; Illich, 1977; Larson, 1977). Professional groups have organized themselves into guilds and other professional communities since at least the Middle Ages (Braudel, 1992; Epstein, 1998; Krause, 1996), and with the emergence of a modern society, professional identities were even more accentuated. In the modern period, professions have been defined and credentialized by the state or organizations—Friedson (1986) here talks about "institutional credentializing"— being given the legitimate right from the state to organize the production of particular kinds of services to the public, including "training or education or prospective members of an occupation" (Friedson, 1986: 64). In addition, the production of professional expertise and legitimacy has been strongly tied to the institution of the modern university, the predominant institution in contemporary society producing, regulating, and controlling the production of systematic and scientific knowledge. However, for emerging professions that has not always been the case. In some cases, prior to the modernization of universities and the establishment of proper scientific procedures, Larson (1977) argues, the university actually in some cases hindered rather than helped the production of systematic scientific and technical knowledge. For instance, in the case of medicine, hindered in its development by incumbent doctrines and beliefs at the universities and various guilds' claims on jurisdiction in the nineteenth century, new medical practices were largely developed at the hospitals amidst the everyday medical practice. Larson (1977: 24) argues that one of the main reason for Paris becoming the world's capital of medical science during the first half of the nineteenth century was its large number of hospitals and that these hospitals were bringing surgeons and physicians together, thereby overcoming the *ancien régime* of guild barriers. When surgeons and physicians collaborated, physicians started to incorporate the localized structural pathology that surgeons had spontaneously applied in the scientific study of specific diseases. The emergence of modern professions and professional authority and credentializing systems is one example of the effects brought by organizational capacities. Larson (1977: 74) emphasizes this organized nature of professions strongly: "[T]he professional project is an organizational project; it organizes the production of producers and the transaction of services for a market; it tends to privilege organizational units in the system of stratification; it works through, and culminates in, distinctive organizations—the professional school and the professional association." Professions are thus defined, somewhat simplified, by their ability to monopolize specific domains of expertise, a definition that Attewell (1990) refers to as being Weberian (after Max Weber) in terms of emphasizing the struggle over power and prestige in a particular field rather than the nature of expertise per se. Herein lies also an important difference between professions (e.g., lawyers and medical doctors, the two most clear-cut and conventional cases, but also more "fuzzy" professions such as engineers or business school graduates) and the occupational groups. For instance, occupational groups do not of necessity make use of less esoteric or specialized knowledge and expertise (think, for instance, of a watchmaker or a carpenter) than professional groups, but they belong to an occupational group less successful in defending and monopolizing the jurisdiction over their domains of expertise. The professional status is in this Weberian view ultimately a matter of power and the ability to establish monopolies or at least significant entry barriers. In the "grey areas" where professional and occupational groups collaborate, there is a strong emphasis on what Gieryn (1983) calls the *boundary work* between the two categories—the long-standing struggle over authority and the right to conduct certain operations among obstetricians and midwives is a well-known and representative case—safeguarding the authority of the privileged professional group. However, the distinction between professional and occupational groups is not a binary one but is to be examined along a continuum ranging from the highly monopolized profession with high entry barriers (e.g., medical doctors) to occupational groups with relatively low or nonexisting entry barriers (e.g., taxi drivers or waitresses) (for a formal categorization of occupational and professional groups, see, for instance, United States Office of Personnel Management's 1998 list of occupational groups). Thus, studies of how professional groups define, develop, and monitor their domain of expertise are also of relevance for occupational groups. Expressed differently, when taking away some of the specific features of the work of professional groups (see Attewell, 1990: 437–438), professional and occupational groups are ultimately defined on basis of their social status.

Studies of professional and occupational groups such as policemen and policewomen (Van Maanen, 1975), managers (Dalton, 1959; Jackall, 1988), fast-food restaurant workers and salesmen (Leidner, 1993), restaurant chefs (Fauchart and von Hippel, 2008; Fine, 1996), restaurant waitresses (Paules, 1991), copy machine repair technicians (Orr, 1996), domestic workers (Cock, 1989; Constable, 1997), meteorologists (Fine, 2007), automotive workers (Graham, 1995), and manufacturing workers (Burawoy, 1979; Roy, 1952) suggest that ideologies, beliefs, and norms guide and structure everyday work and set the boundaries for what qualifies as being legitimate work. However, studies of, for instance, police work (Jermier et al., 1992) show that there is substantial leeway in police officers' work and a diversity in what they regard as being legitimate police work. Under slogans such as "serve and protect" or "crime-fighting" there is substantial space for individual and local translations and enactments of such objectives into actual performances. Such interpretations are socially embedded, i.e., "ideological," in Strauss et al.'s (1964) terms. Lamont and Molnár (2002: 178) discuss the study of Collins (1979), who found a "surprisingly weak correlation between the requirements of educational credentials and the skills/knowledge requirements of jobs":

> Education is often irrelevant to on-the-job productivity, and is sometimes counterproductive. Specifically vocational training seems to be derived primarily from work experience rather than from formal school

training. The actual performance of school themselves, the nature of the grading system and its lack of relationship to occupational success, and the dominant ethos among students suggests that schooling is very inefficient as a means of training for work skills. (Collins, 1979: 21)

On basis of this empirical observation, Collins (1979) argues that education serves to "socialize prospective professionals into status cultures by drawing a line between insiders and outsiders." That is, one does not primarily attend tertiary schooling to learn practical skills but to be trained at thinking and behaving as a member of a particular social group. In fact, Larson (1977: 226) goes so far as to argue that professions are more often defined as being an occupation which tends to be "colleague-oriented" rather than "client oriented." For instance, university professors tend to be more concerned about how colleagues and especially leading researchers regard their scientific contributions than how students perceive and evaluate their teaching. Similarly, Murningham and Conlon (1991) found in their study of 20 professional British string quartets that string quartet where more inward-oriented than oriented towards the audiences when seeking to accomplish musical performance at the peak of their capacity. In order to fully evaluate and appreciate the skills of the professional, you need to be a member of the professional community; professionals always and of necessity appreciate esoteric knowledge. It is part of their training, socialization, and enacted ideology.

As suggested by Strauss et al. (1964), the status of professionals is always reproduced through the adherence to enacted norms and behaviours, including embodied and verbal interaction. On the other hand, professionals not only respond to preexisting institutions and converge towards standardized, scripted behaviour but are, as Scott (2008) underlines, themselves primary "institutional agents," agents contributing to the establishment of new institutions. "More so than any other social category," Scott (2008: 223) writes, "the professions function as institutional agents—as definers, interpreters, and appliers of institutional elements. Professionals are not the only, but are—I believe—the most influential, contemporary crafters of institutions." Seen in this view, there is a complex recursive relationship between individual professionals taking on professional behaviours and symbolism (e.g., dress codes, the use of enacted vocabularies and phrases) and professional communities as active institutional agents establishing new institutional behaviours and conditions.

More recently, professional ideologies emerge from new economic and social conditions. Barley and Kunda's (2006: 55) study of computer programming professionals in the San Francisco Bay Area's Silicon Valley computer industry cluster introduces the term "itinerant professionalism." These itinerant professionals are highly educated and skilled "hired guns," programmers that have chosen to operate on a freelance basis in the industry. For Barley and Kunda (2004, 2006), the concept of professional group is still bound up with clear lines of demarcation between insiders and outsiders:

> Professionalization is typically associated with an occupation's possession of an esoteric body of knowledge, state-mandated licensing, formal training programs, and professional associations that create barriers to entry and a basis for defending their jurisdiction from the expansionist tendencies of other occupations. (Barley and Kunda, 2004: 294)

In summary, professions and professional groups are communities that have been capable of defending their jurisdiction against other social groups. Being a professional is being part of a community that shares a number of experiences, skills, norms, values, and ideologies. As suggested by Charles Goodwin (1995), the professional toolbox also includes specific forms of vision, a set of analytical and visual practices that Goodwin refers to as "professional vision," and Grasseni (2004), referencing Goodwin's work, calls "skilled vision."

Seeing as a Professional

As has been pointed out numerous times, vision and visuality are not strictly a commonsense activity. Already Hermann von Helmholtz found in the middle of the nineteenth century that the capacity to concentrate one's vision and to fix a certain point with one's gaze is largely a matter of training and discipline (i.e., the "increased sensitivity to a limited range of stimuli" [Thomas, 2006: 84]). At the same time, vision, being perhaps the most important sense in everyday life for the majority of human beings, is closely connected to commonsense thinking. Exclamations like "Just look! See for yourself" suggests that even a short glance at something may once and for all verify a specific assumption. In juridical thinking and practice, the use of witnessing relying on their visual impressions and visual tools such as photographs (used since the mid-nineteenth century; Gunning, 1995) have been playing a substantial role. The same goes for scientific practice where various graphs, images, pictures, diagrams, etc., have been developed over the course of history and have been part of the experimental setup in laboratories and research sites. However, in this section, professional vision will be examined as what is effectively removed from such commonsense image of vision and visuality. Being a professional is to be capable of demonstrating a range of skills, competencies, and behaviours that have been enacted and trained within professional communities. The professional must also earn the right to call him- or herself a professional, often through passing through carefully monitored and restricted university education programs or/and by being given certificates or accreditations from organizations given the right to monitor professional organizations. As part of the professional setup, specific modes of vision are often enacted.

To fully qualify as a skilled professional, one must learn to see as a professional. Lawyers are capable of inspecting juridical documents; scientists are trained to examine photographic plates and graphs; medical doctors are capable of undertaking examinations of patients to be capable of articulating diagnoses. Fry (1920) distinguishes *practical vision* guiding us in everyday life, and therefore ceasing "in the moment it has served its biological function," and *curiosity vision* where the vision "[d]wells much more curiously and deliberately upon it" (Fry, 1920: 48–49). In addition, artists are capable of employing what Fry calls *aesthetic vision,* the vision through which we "contemplate works of art" (Fry, 1920: 50) and even more specifically *creative vision,* a form of vision that represents "[t]he furtherest perversion of the gifts of nature of which man is guilty. It demands the most complete detachment from any of the meanings and implications of appearances" (Fry, 1920: 51). Creative vision is a specific kind of gift but it also in opposition to practical vision; it is a form of vision that transcends commonsense thinking and everyday needs and aims for the extraordinary, the "not-yet-to-be-seen." In Fry's (1920) view, vision is what can be trained by the artist and what can be used to accomplished a variety of activities.

Le Regard Médicale/The Medical Gaze

Michel Foucault's *Birth of the Clinic* (1973) is a seminal text bridging professionals, practices of vision, and discursive practices. While Foucault has been largely associated with visuality through his writings on Jeremy Bentham's (1995) invention of the panopticon prison system, connecting vision, surveillance, and penal practices, there is another stream of work from his so-called "archeological period" (Burrell, 1988; Deleuze, 1988a; Eribon, 1991) addressing vision and visuality in other terms. That stream of work is connecting vision not to repressive practices but to epistemological issues and knowledge claims derived from discursive formations such as the clinical medicine developed in what Foucault called "the classical period," the seventeenth and eighteenth centuries. Before examining this connection between seeing and knowing, the panopticon writings will be addressed briefly, if for no other reason because it has been largely influential in the organization theory literature and the reception of Foucault in the social sciences.

For Foucault, Bentham's thinking about a universal structure for disciplinary spaces, the panopticon structure, is a major achievement in the modernity project. Bentham conceived of a generalized model for how a few could overlook the many as a means for rationalizing visual inspection. "[T]he true effect of the Panopticon is to be such that," Foucault (2006: 71) writes, "even when no one is there, the individual is his cell must not only think of himself as visible for a gaze, the real presence or absence of which hardly matters. Power is thereby completely de-individualized." Foucault thus suggests that the panopticon model contributes to a reformulation of power in modern society; power does no longer reside in the body of individuals, in the bodies of kings, prices, cardinals, etc., as during the medieval period (see, e.g., Kantorowicz, 1957), but is transformed into the disciplinary structure of the modern society. As a consequence, to emphasize one single effect of this "de-individualization of power," criminals were no longer punished physically, tortured, or dismembered, a retaliation for the original aggression against the authority's actual body that needs to be repaid literally eye-for-an-eye, but punishment became a matter of confinement and isolation, a separation from the society at large. For Foucault (2000: 58), this is a major contribution to the emergence of the modern society: "I believe that Bentham is more important for our society than Kant and Hegel. All our societies should pay homage to him. It was he who programmed, defined, and described in the most exact manner the forms of power in which we live." Modern society is a society imbued with a variety of forms of surveillance, either in the form of external control or self-discipline and self-surveillance. In perhaps Foucault's most well known work, *Discipline and Punish* (first published in 1975; English edition in 1977), he points out that the Benthamite panopticon model is by no means used strictly in penal institutions but that the principle of the disciplinary space has been translated into other spheres of society, into the school, the factories, the offices: "The prison, the hospital, the school, and the workshop were not forms of supervision of the group itself. It was the structure of supervision which, drawing individuals to it, taking hold of them individually, incorporating them, would constitute them secondarily as a group," Foucault (2000: 77) suggests. The assemblage of power, surveillance, visuality, and discipline in Foucault's genealogical writings based on Bentham's work has been appealing for a number of subdisciplines in the field of organization studies. For instance, labour process theorists and poststructuralist organization researchers (representing two diverging stream of research, see e.g., Wray-Bliss, 2002; Friedman, 2004) have been intrigued by the new forms of surveillance and self-regulation in the new regime of work centered around "empowered" coworkers being responsible for their own output and the administrative work pertaining to their activities (see, e.g., Hassard and Rowlinson, 2002). In the field of accounting research, the Benthamite panopticon model has served as an image of the accounting procedures gradually established (Hopper and Macintosh, 1998).

When addressing vision and visuality in organizations, it is Foucault's (1973) treatise on the emergence of academic medicine that is the perhaps the most interesting work in his *oeuvre*. The themes of surveillance and punishment recurring in Foucault's genealogical writings are more concerned about the gaze that is potentially seeing what is occurring in a confined space; it is a disciplinary gaze intervening into the activities only when needed. *The Birth of the Clinic*, on the contrary, is examining the "medical gaze," *le regard médicale*, that is always already present in the medical practices. It is an omnipresent gaze that is increasingly penetrating all domains of human life, not only in the domain of the sick and the disabled, but also among the healthy, the not-yet-sick subject to "preventive care" and medicalization (Clarke et al., 2003; Rose, 2007). The medical doctor's entire profession is in fact anchored in specific ways of seeing and looking. Foucault emphasizes the very density and scope of the medical gaze:

> Medical rationality plunges into the marvellous density of perception, offering the grain of things as the first face of truth, with their colours, their spots, their hardness, their adherence, the breadth of the experiment seems to be identified with the domain of the careful gaze, and of an empirical vigilance receptive only to the evidence of visible contents. The eye becomes the depositary and source of clarity; it has the power to bring a truth to light that it receives only to the extent that it has brought it to light; as it opens, the eye first opens the truth: a flexion that marks the transition from the world of classical clarity—from the 'enlightenment'—to the nineteenth century. (Foucault, 1973: xiii)

While academic and clinical medicine were largely impotent until the late eighteenth century when Jenner's smallpox vaccination was developed in 1798, and generally, as Collins (1979: 139) emphasizes, "there were no valid medical treatment at all until 1850." Before the mid-nineteenth century, physicians prided themselves on the basis of a training essentially based on ancient works like Galen's medicine. In premodern terms, there was virtually no valid expertise at all in medicine (Collins, 1979). It is then little wonder that no less than four of Molière's comedies addressed medical doctors' work and activities, mocking the medical doctors' incompetence and preposterous claims. The discrepancy between the traditional high status of physicians and their actual capabilities was excellent grist for the mill for the great French comedy writer. Also, Voltaire shared this view, suggesting that "the art of the medical profession consists in amusing the patient for as long as it takes nature to cure him or her" (cited in Blech, 2006: ix).

In Foucault's analysis, the establishment of academic medicine is closely associated with an enclosed and controlled space, that of the clinic: "Following an autonomous movement, the medical gaze circulates within an enclosed space in which it is controlled only by itself; in sovereign fashion, it distributes to daily experience the knowledge that it has borrowed from afar and of which it has made itself both the point of concentration and the center of diffusion" (Foucault, 1973: 30–31). The gradual establishment of the clinic as the central *topos* for the discursive formation on medicine was entangled with the formation of a series of "medical objects, perceptions, and concepts" (Foucault, 1973: 51) that established a specific regime of epistemic knowledge (which Foucault refers to as *savoir*) and a specific regime of practical knowledge, procedures, and skills (referred to as *connaissance*). In the late eighteenth and nineteenth centuries, there was a production of treatises and handbooks in medicine, establishing an operative vocabulary that was shared in the entire field of expertise. In this rearticulation of the purpose, potentiality, and operative procedures of clinical medicine, the procedures of diagnosis (from Greek *dia*, "through, between, across, by, akin of," and *gnosis*, "a seeking to know"—*diagnosis*, "a distinguishing") as a certain practice of seeing was established in the field. Foucault (1973: 55) is here talking about how "seeing and knowing" (*le voir et le savoir*) became intimately connected. However, in order to be known, the *visual inspection* had to be articulated, accounted for verbally: "[I]n clinical medicine, *to be seen* and *to be spoken* immediately communicate in the manifest truth of the disease of which it is precisely the whole *being*. There is disease only in the elements of the visible and therefore statable" (Foucault, 1973: 95). The *seeing* doctor is also the *talking* doctor, the doctor that expresses opinions, thought conjectures, speculations, narratives addressing previous cases, and so forth. In medical practice, visual practices and articulation are bound up with one another to the very point where it is complicated to separate the two. "The clinical gaze has the paradoxical ability to *hear a language* as soon as it *perceives a spectacle*. In the clinic, what is manifested is originally what is spoken," Foucault (1973: 108) writes. In addition, the medical gaze is in its very essence a *pragmatic* gaze, a gaze that refrain from metaphysical speculation; it is a positivist gaze in the original meaning advanced by August Comte, a gaze that avoids speculation about the ultimate causes of the illness but instead seeks to cure it. Says Foucault (1973: 120): "The clinical gaze is not that of an intellectual eye that is able to perceive the unalterable purity of essences beneath phenomena. It is a gaze of the concrete sensibility, a gaze that travels from body to body, and whose trajectory is situated in the space of sensible manifestation. For the clinic, all truth is sensible truth." *Le regard médicale* is a major accomplishment in the "history of ideas" because it frees medicine from the ancient tradition of, for instance, Galen's theory of excess of substances and other doctrines that have failed to prove their scientific or therapeutic value. Instead, medicine is emerging as a field of expertise, a discursive formation, strongly emphasizing the intersection of systematic and disciplined practices of seeing, theoretical perspectives on the human body, and a series of actual practices in the clinic. All these changes are put into practice in the confined domain of the clinic, thereby serving the same role as the laboratory for the scientist, a controlled space isolated yet largely connected to—corresponding to, one may say—the outside society. Foucault's (1973) contribution to the understanding of vision and visuality lies in the emphasis on (1) combining seeing and saying when making knowledge claims, and (2) such procedures of visual inspection and articulation preferably taking place within a controlled space, the central *topos* of the discursive formation. For Deleuze (1988a), it is primarily the first contribution that makes a major difference, that is, the turning of the phenomenological procedures of visual inspection into a question of epistemology:

> This is Foucault's major achievement: the conversion of phenomenology into epistemology. For seeing and speaking means knowing [*savoir*], but we do not see what we speak about, nor do we speak about what we can see; and when we see a pipe we shall always say (in one way or another): 'this is not a pipe', as though intentionality denied itself, and collapsed into itself. Everything is knowledge, and this is the first reason why there is no 'savage experience': there is nothing beneath or prior to knowledge. But knowledge is irreducibly double, since it involves speaking and seeing, language and light, which is the reason why there is no intentionality. (Deleuze, 1988a: 109).

The seeing, *le voir*, the articulation, and the knowledge-claims (either in the form of *savoir* or *connaissance*) are appearing in the same event, in the same procedure of seeing and saying. Standardized procedures and routines for seeing and saying are what is constitutive of modern medicine, Foucault suggests. In comparison to Foucault's genealogical writings on the gaze of surveillance and control, a disciplinary vision increasingly penetrating all spheres of everyday life, the writings on the "epistemologies" of psychiatry and psychology (Foucault, 1967), scientific thinking more generally (Foucault, 1970), and medicine (Foucault, 1973) may appear less thought-provoking and intriguing and more in line with conventional studies of the history of ideas. Still, what Foucault points at is that the very procedure of seeing, vision, is what is central to most sophisticated and esoteric knowledge claims. In virtually all domains of expertise, there are some forms of practice of seeing involved. Seeing is inextricably entangled with knowing in the Westerns episteme.

Studies of scientific practice suggest that the connection made by Foucault between seeing and saying is what is a most intimate and personal experience. For instance, Evelyn Fox Keller (1983) is using the example of how the brilliant physicist Richard Feynman—"the best brain since Einstein" (Shapin, 2008: 221) in the modern scientific folklore—was poorly understood by the authorities in the field of physics to the extent that a fellow physicist named Freeman Dyson decided to help translating Feynman's work into a more adequate form, accessible to the more conventional scientists in the field. Dyson decided that his job was to "understand Dick [Feynman] and explain his ideas in a language that the rest of the world could understand." Dyson here emphasizes Feynman's specific talent for thinking in terms of images and models rather than using equations when proceeding: "The reason Dick's physics was so hard for ordinary physicist to grasp was that he did not use equations . . . Dick just wrote down the solutions out of his head without ever writing down the equations. He had a physical picture of the way things happen and that picture gave him the equations directly with a minimum of calculation. It was no wonder that people who had spent their lives solving equations were baffled by him. Their minds were analytical; his was pictorial" (Freeman Dyson, cited in Keller, 1983: 146–147). Keller's study of the pioneering work of the cytologist Barbara McClintock is in the same manner emphasizing what Freeman Dyson calls "pictorial thinking." One of McClintock's most salient skills was her ability to, in her own terms, develop "a feeling for the organism," an intimate understanding of how the maize plants she studied during her entire career develop and grow. Such almost mystical "feelings," close in nature to the medieval scholastic theologians' emphasis on contemplations on God, is for Keller manifested in McClintock's ability to "see" with the bare eye and with the help of the microscope how the elementary mechanisms of the organism are constituted. Keller (1983) explains this idiosyncratic skill of McClintock:

> For most of us, our concepts of the world build on what we see, as what we see builds on what we think. Where we know more, we see more. But for McClintock, this reciprocity between cognitive and visual seems always to have been more intimate than it is for most. As if without distinguishing the two, she knew by seeing, and say by knowing. Especially illustrative is the story she tells of how she came to see the *Neurospora* chromosomes. Unwilling to accept her failure to see these minute objects under the microscope—to pick them up as individuals with continuity—she retreated to sit, and mediate, beneath the eucalyptus tree. There she 'worked on herself.' When she felt she was ready, she returned to the microscope, and the chromosomes were now to be seen, not only by her, but, thereafter, by others as well. If this were a story of insight arrived at by reflection, it would be more familiar. Its real force is as a story of eyesight, and of continuity between mind and eye that made McClintock's work so distinctive and, at the same time, so difficult to communicate in ordinary language. (Keller, 1983: 148)

Since modern science is what Edmund Husserl (1970: 6) called "fact-minded," only marginally tolerant towards concepts such as "feelings" and primarily interested in transforming data into a form that allows for computability and systematic procedures of comparison (e.g., the procedure of "mathematization"), it is complicated to gain recognition for a body of work that fails to meet these standards for transparency.[4] For instance, McClintock's ideas about transposition, suggesting that the genetic material is in fact much more flexible than what Francis Crick termed the "central dogma" of genetics ("DNA gets *transcribed* into RNA, which gets *translated* into proteins") and introduced in her research programme in the 1940s, was not attaining any more detailed interest until the early 1960s when new research was supporting McClintock's pathbreaking work. Today, commentators like Rose (2007: 47) argue that Crick's central dogma "can no longer be sustained." Keller (1983) here makes the point that "seeing in science" is not unlike "seeing in art": "Based on vision, our most public and our most private sense, it gives rise to a kind of knowledge that requires more than a shared practice to be communicable: It requires a shared subjectivity" (Keller, 1983: 149). In order to see the same things, there is a need for a "shared subjectivity," a mode of thinking that takes a number of things for granted while rendering other problematic. However, the main point in Keller's (1983) two cases—Richard Feynman and Barbara McClintock—is that what we tend to regard as scientific talent does not always proceed along well-known paths but that important insights and ideas may be produced through "pictorial thinking" and thinking where seeing and saying are intimately connected. The capacity to create an intimacy between cognitive and visual human faculties is perhaps one of the distinguishing features of the "scientific genius" (if there is such a dubious thing). Being able to leave the equations behind for a while and step into a mode of thinking that is not restrained by "evidence" is perhaps what enables new thinking. Isabelle Stengers (1997: 21) is, for instance, praising Johannes Kepler and portraying him as one of the true heroes of the emerging sciences for being capable of rendering mathematics a tool in the hands of the practicing researcher and abandoning the philosophical ideas about the circle as being the "mathematical figure of perfection" (see, e.g., Hallyn, 1990). When temporally suspending such doctrines, Kepler was able to on empirical basis to calculate the orbits of the plants and found that the heliocentric system did not operate on the basis of circles but *ellipses*. Scientific procedures and techniques are what keeps the system going and what enables comparisons across time and space, but this increasingly elaborate system is not always of necessity the most fertile ground for new ideas and new thinking. Thus we owe to the creative minds of people like Richard Feynman and Barbara McClintock novel ideas, providing new images of ultimate matter.

The Concept of Professional Vision

While the need for using one's vision is largely taken for granted, the more detailed and intricate aspects of how professional vision is accomplished and what is constitutive of it is subject to empirical research. Contrary to extramural beliefs, professional vision is rarely totally uncomplicated but is always part of the intramural professional debates and controversies; scientists may see different things in the electromagnetic plates; medical doctors may see different things in the same symptoms. In other words, just like professional authority per se is a social accomplishment, based on the mobilization of a range of social resources, professional vision is far from uncomplicated or self-enclosed. Goodwin (1995) studies oceanographers' work, a community of scientists interested in examining the bottom of the sea to understand the geological and zoological conditions of an inspected area. The oceanographers used advanced technologies such as sophisticated cameras to scan the bottom of the sea. The ability to review and interpret the images provided by the camera was an essential part of the oceanographer's scientific activities. Sorting out what is scientifically intriguing from what is only mildly interesting is a praised scientific skill of the oceanographer.

For Goodwin (1995), perception is not what is "located in the psychology of the individual brain and its associated cognitive processes" but is instead what is "[l]odged within, and constituted through, situated endogenous practices" (Goodwin, 1995: 256). Such mode of perception—i.e., professional vision—is "[a] form of social organization in its own right," Goodwin (1995: 256) suggests. In addition, professional vision is in most cases shaped and formed by the various tools and technologies mobilized in the process; professional vision is, in the age of technoscience and the presence of media for storage and representations, *mediated vision*. Therefore, the tools used "[s]hape perception through the way in which they construct representations" (Goodwin, 1995: 256). Finally, for the professional (i.e., the oceanographer), perception and action are "intrinsically linked" (Goodwin, 1995: 256); without the possibilities for perception, there is no action. To use Jonathan Beller's (2006) phrase (albeit used in a Marxist theory context, thereby meaning something entirely different), one may say that for the professional "to look is to labour." Professional vision is the structuring and shaping of human vision under determinate conditions. While Lacan speaks of "the gaze" as the "generalized vision of the other" including the totality of beliefs, desires, and aspirations, the professional vision is the gaze in the more restricted sense of the term, the gaze of the "scientific other," or even more specifically, "the gaze of the scientific discipline." Operating in a discipline engaging in what Thomas S. Kuhn called "normal science," there is a shared set of research problems that are engaging the scientific community. The professional vision of these communities is of necessity penetrated by these research problems. Professional vision is thus the look under the influence of normal science, the legitimate register of things expected to be seen. At times, researchers may even fail to detect new and interesting things—so-called *anomalies* in Kuhn's analytical framework—because their professionalism is strongly shaped by problems at hand.

In another paper, examining the use of professional vision in police work and in juridical procedures during the much discussed Rodney King trial in 1994, where four white officers from the Los Angeles Police Department were charged for beating up the black motorist Rodney King, Goodwin (1994) here suggests that the professional vision and the accompanying rhetoric of the police officers and experts that were called as witnesses during the trial managed to direct attention away from the very act of violence to the police work procedures and routines, thereby managing to make the whole event appear as a situation that was properly handled and where it was in fact the police officers being exposed to a dangerous situation when encountering Rodney King. This amazing trick (for the outsider), to turn the offenders into the victims and make the single person a threat to the four armed police officers, was accomplished through a cunning combination of authorized professional vision and rhetoric. Goodwin (1994) argues that the witnesses, using photos from the crime scene as evidence in defence of the police officers, were capable of accomplishing a series of activities on the basis of their professional vision. First, they were *coding* the occurrences in photos, that is, they were defining and sorting out a series of events in the course of action. Second, the witnesses were *highlighting* specific events as being of central importance for the event, and finally, they were "producing and articulating material representations" (Goodwin, 1994: 606). Goodwin explains that the totality of these operations enabled the witnesses to defend and justify the use of (excessive) violence and portray the entire event as in fact following the prescribed procedures of the LAPD. While the police department had the authority to make use of professionals experts who could legitimately claim the prerogative to articulate a professional account of the situation, Rodney King could not counteract these activities because there is no, Goodwin argues, "professional community of police victims" that could stand up and testify in a similar manner:

> Insofar as the perceptual structures that organize interpretation of the tape are lodged within the profession and not an isolated individual, there is a tremendous asymmetry about who can speak as an expert about the event on the tape and thus structure interpretation of it ... While administrating a beating like this is recognized within the courtroom as part of the work of the police profession, no equivalent social group exists for the suspect. Victims do not constitute a profession. Thus no expert witnesses are available to interpret these events and animate the images on the tape from King's perspective. In the second trial, King was called as a witness, but he could not testify about whether the police officers beating him were using unreasonable force since he lacked 'expertise on the constitution or the use of force.' (Goodwin, 1994: 625)

Examining this sad case from a more theoretical point of view, Goodwin (1994) says that professional vision is a powerful asset or capacity in the hands of professional groups because they can direct attention to issues that are beneficial for the professional group: "Central to the social and cognitive organization of a profession is its ability to shape events in the domain of scrutiny into the phenomenal objects around which the discourse of the profession is organized" (Goodwin, 1994: 626). Second, Goodwin emphasizes rightly that professional vision is "perspectival," i.e., "lodged within specific social entities" and "unevenly allocated" (Goodwin, 1994: 626). That is, professional vision is never capable to speak devoid of interests and political concerns—no matter what is claimed by representatives of professional groups, at times claiming to be able to take a bird's-eye view of things, what Donna Haraway calls a "God trick," claiming that one is capable of taking a "view from nowhere" in Thomas Nagel's (1986) memorable phrase. All vision is situated and context-bound. Moreover, it is "unevenly allocated"; not anyone has the authority to speak on behalf of abstract entities such as "truth," "justice," "democracy," "science," "the routines and policies of the Los Angeles Police Department," and so forth. Professional vision is therefore ultimately based on affiliation with credible institutions. That is, professional vision is rendered legitimate when one is speaking as being the legitimate representative of some institution or organizations. Third, Goodwin (1994: 626) says, professional vision is "[n]ot purely a mental process but instead is accomplished through the competent deployment of a complex of situated practices in a relevant setting." The witnesses called to court had the ability to constitute and make use of an assemblage or ensemble of images and photos, stories and anecdotes, references to police work procedures, policies, and other formally enacted regulations guiding police work, and other relevant resources, to render the acts committed by the four LAPD policemen as meaningful and credible performance. That is, professional vision is always already located within the use of a variety of relevant resources and assets. In order to look professionally, one needs to mobilize a substantial amount of resources to support these activities. In his conclusion, Goodwin (1994) summarizes the argument:

> [P]rocesses of classification are central to human cognition, at times forming the basic subject matter of entire fields such as cognitive anthropology. Through the constitution and use of coding schemes, relevant classification systems are socially organized as professional and bureaucratic knowledge structures, entraining in fine detail the cognitive activity of those who administer them, producing some of the objects of knowledge around which the discourse of a profession is organized, and frequently constituting accountable loci of power for those actions are surveyed and coded. (Goodwin, 1994: 628)

Professional vision is embedded in what Roth and Bowen (1999: 744), examining ecologists' study of lizards in their natural habitat, call "the heterogeneous topology of perception." Roth and Bowen (1999) show that in the study of the reptiles, lizards are undergoing a process where they are inscribed and translated into a scientific protocol enabling a digitalization and mathematization of their bodily features (e.g., length, weight) and their activities (e.g., where they rest, how they move, etc.). It is in the "topology of the the scientific instrument" (i.e., the totality of integrated scientific procedures and instrumentations) that the lizards are "disciplined" and "domesticated"; they are "[m]ade to comply to the disciplinary perceptual machinery . . . and they are made part of the disciplinary perceptual machinery and knowledge structures," Roth and Bowen (1999: 757) claim. The professional vision of the ecologists is bound up with the scientific instrumentation they are mobilizing, and therefore seeing is, in the first place, *believing* in the scientific instrumentation. As John Rajchman (1991: 71) points out in his thoughtful reflection on Michel Foucault's work, "evidence" is in both English and French derived from the Latin *videre*, "to see." Over the course of its history, Rajchman (1991) suggests, the concept of evidence has acquired "the sense of proof, testimony, and clarity of indubitability to the mind." Evidence is the capacity to bring a certain condition into a state of factuality, as what is true under given conditions and under the influence of specific ways of seeing. In the case of the ecologists concerned about the lives and doings of lizards, evidence is what is provided from within the "heterogeneous topology of perception" being used in their research. Roth and Bowen (1999) here emphasize that the professional vision of the ecologists is dependent upon the "observational machinery" being mobilized in their field work:

> Although the research we observed is generally descriptive, the perceptual apparatus involved goes beyond, and transcends, the metaphorical retina, and has a more complex and heterogeneous topology—that is, not a plane or spherical surface. Though the retina is still involved, the recording devices are instruments of different size, quantity, error rates and so on, and the practices associated with them. The field laboratory constituted the observational machinery of the ecologist, and the associated practices constitute the practices of perceiving. But the topology of the perceptual apparatus is neither homogeneous nor homomaterial; it is quite heterogeneous and heteromaterial, and the associated practices have many of the local and *ad hoc* characteristics observed in other studies of scientific laboratories. This topology has a cultural history and constitutes a disciplinary frame (like Dürer's square drawing grid that he interposed between an object and his eye, to see in two dimensions) *for what can be seen and the particular metric that can be employed.* (Roth and Bowen, 1999: 757–758; emphasis added)

Just like Albrecht Dürer's much discussed drawing grid helped structure and divide the object of study into distinct parts—a kind of pixels *avant la lettre*, one may say—the practices of seeing, their professional vision, of the ecologists were taking place within the "disciplinary frame" of the scientific apparatus. Roth and Bowen (1999) thus suggest, in the same vein as Goodwin (1994, 1995), that professional vision is in a multiplicity of ways *disciplined vision*; it is a form of vision under certain conditions and a vision that is aimed at providing evidence in the sense that Rajchman (1991: 73) suggests Foucault positioned the concept, namely in terms of seeing what is not originally seen. Professional vision is the practice of exposing unseen evidences. Given this view of professional vision, there are no instances of *res ipsa loquitur*, "facts speaking for themselves," in contemporary technoscience (Daston and Galison, 2007: 260). The contemporary scientists can never tell a layman to "see for yourself" because all vision is already informed and infused with a range of assumptions that *eo ipso* enables things to be seen. "In science, seeing is more that meets the eye," Rajchman (1991: 75) concludes.

Like any social practice, professional vision can do harm and it can do good depending on the perspective and actual situation. Goodwin's (1994, 1995) contribution lies in seeing vision and visuality not as what are removed from and detached from wider social interests, discussions, and struggles over resources and meaning, but that professional vision is in fact one of the central resources, both individual and collective, that is structuring and organizing social reality. Professional authority is here not only a matter of networking, of writing, or making public and intramural utterances, of mobilizing economic and political resources, but also a matter of the actual practices of looking, of seeing, of calling attention to things that are observed. In other words, vision and visuality are constitutive of professional authority and professional activities and therefore need to be properly theorized, empirically studied, and debated in various social communities and settings. For instance, the juridical practices in the Rodney King trial unravelled by Goodwin (1994) are exemplary in showing that institutional affiliation is of pivotal importance when advocating a certain evidence. As long as there are no "professional community of police victims," it is complicated for individuals ending up in this unfortunate situation to call for credible witnesses. The asymmetry in power is overwhelming and a long-term threat to the juridical system *tout court*.

In the following two chapters, the concept of professional vision will be used and serve as part of the analytical framework when discussing visual practices in first science-based innovation work (in Chapter 3) and in architect work (in Chapter 4). Professional vision is here used as a rather broad term denoting the totality of social and professional practices that draw on the perceiving subject's vision. Such professional vision is seen as an integral component of the firm's resources and assets and is ultimately part of the firm's source of long-term competitive advantage. Again, to engage in professional vision is seeing as a form of labour, a labouring through the senses.

SUMMARY AND CONCLUSION

In this chapter, the concepts of vision and visuality have been examined in some detail. The first thing to notice is that vision and visuality have been subject to considerable philosophical and scientific interest since the first half of the nineteenth century; vision has been radically reconsidered as what is largely a matter of subjective capacities and skills and the human visual organs constituted by the human eye and the brain is by no means functioning exactly the same for all human beings. In addition, an "anthropology of vision" suggests that the European tradition has been particularly concerned with establishing a connection between vision and truth; seeing is ultimately the warrant for determining the truth. Such Eurocentric images of vision are by no means universally shared and in other cultures vision may be restricted and may therefore be secondary to the other senses. When it comes to vision and visuality in organizations, vision is part of a professional setup, a series of skills and competencies that are trained in professional communities and shared by a collective of individuals sharing a number of resources including formal training and expertise, standard operating procedures, working routines, and professional ideologies. Professional vision is thus the very act of vision, a practice of seeing, wherein all the professional skills and experiences are manifested. Professional vision is also closely associated with the capacity of speaking, of accounting for what is seen; seeing and saying are therefore executed in close proximity in professional practice. Constituting oneself as what Foucault calls "a speaking eye" is the prerogative of the professional.

Part II

Practices of Seeing

3 Vision and Visualization in Science-Based Innovation Work

INTRODUCTION

> "Living matter is far from pure indetermination or pure passivity. Neither is it a blind tendency; it is, rather, the vehicle of informed energy."
>
> Simondon (1980: 66)

In this chapter, vision and visuality *qua* professional vision will be examined. Rather than assuming that professional vision is simply located in the scientists' vision, vision is what is distributed over a variety of resources and assets mobilized in the research processes. In order to examine professional vision in scientific work, both a historical, diachronic view and a synchronic view emphasizing technoscientific procedures and resources will be maintained. As is suggested in the chapter, scientific work is not separated from broader social changes and consequently scientific practices but are strongly infused with opportune social values. For instance, as is suggested by some of the students of technoscience, aesthetic norms have always been an indispensable part of any scientific endeavour, and today the use of certain aesthetic features may be observed in virtually any domain of scientific work. Instead of seeing science as what is "ahead of," "beyond," or "outside" society (in Franklin and Roberts's [2006: 13] formulation) and representing "the social" as what is "hopelessly and perpetually lagging behind the sciences," science and society need to be thought of in terms of being largely intertwined; the sciences are part of society and society is both influencing and influenced by the sciences (Greenberg, 1999; Hacking, 2006; Novas and Rose, 2000; Rabinow, 1992; Rose and Novas, 2005). Instead, as Franklin (2001: 337; emphasis in the original), studying genomics research, stresses, "[w]hat we mean by society itself, what we understand the social to be, *is itself one of the things that is changing in the context of new genetics*." Society and the social are terms that are redefined in the light of the new biological possibilities:

> Science is not politics pursued by other means . . . Although internalist history may focus on the intellectual product as the sole object of

investigation and the prime historical mover, scientific work itself, even in the most 'disinterested' fields of inquiry such as the abstract field of mathematics, is unthinkable without the objective conditions giving rise to and supporting it. (Lenoir, 1997: 14)

Franklin and Robert (2006: 13), examining the influence of new reproduction technologies and genetics, suggest that "while it is not helpful to underestimate the radical novelty of many of the new techniques, choices, and dilemmas encountered in the context of new reproductive and genetic technologies, or the difficult issues they present, it is equally unhelpful to overprivilege technological innovation as if they were a force unto itself."[1] Seen in this way, the epistemology of the eye and the practices of seeing in scientific work are inherently social in nature.

In the latter half of the chapter, practices of seeing and ideas and beliefs regarding the value in scientific spectatorship is discussed on basis of an empirical study of a major multinational pharmaceutical company. This study suggests that rather than abandoning practices of seeing in the daily work and relying on machinic vision, the screening of molecules through technological means (what Novas and Rose [2000] call "a molecular gaze" or a "molecular optics," and Myers [2008] calls "molecular vision"), researchers in new drug development activities are strongly emphasizing the professional vision in their work. Advanced technoscientific machinery and apparatuses are then not substituting for direct visual examinations of the molecules investigated.

VISION AND VISUALITY IN SCIENCE-BASED INNOVATION WORK

Early Technologies of Vision

Although modern science and especially the technology-mediated, late modern form that are commonly referred to as technoscience are inextricably entangled with various forms of modern technology, the production of scholarly knowledge has not always been based on minute empirical investigations. For instance, Alexander (2002) is emphasizing the hermeneutical approach in scholarly knowledge production in medieval times:

> Traditionally, true knowledge was based on the interpretation of a canon of ancient texts, which included scripture and the corpus of the ancient philosophers and church fathers. The underlying assumption was that all relevant knowledge was already in existence and was contained within prescribed canon. The search for truth, therefore, consisted of the proper application of the wisdom contained within the bounds of these volumes to the problem at hand. If, as was often the case, the canonical texts were in conflict with each other, the difficulties

would be resolved through the scholastic practice of disputation. Truth, in other words, was arrived at not through new discoveries but through hermeneutics—the detailed interpretation of authoritative texts. (Alexander, 2002: 99)

With the printing revolution, the medieval scholarly production was gradually—very slowly, some researchers argue (Febvre and Martin, 1997)— replaced by new forms of scholarly authority. Eisenstein (1983: 42) argues that after the emergence of printing, to consult different books it was no longer essential to be a wandering scholar and "successive generations of sedentary scholars were less apt to be engrossed by a single text and expend their energies on elaborating on it." As a consequence, "the era of the glossator and commentator came to an end, and a new 'era of intense cross referencing between one book and another began' " (Eisenstein, 1983: 42). Eventually, this gradual change from a hermeneutics of canonical texts was replaced by more empiricist ideas and practices, enabling new forms of knowledge to be formulated. New doctrines, for instance, Copernicus's heliocentric model of the universe, gave birth to new theories and new opportunities: "Unlike the Chinese astronomers," De Landa (1992: 129) remarks, closely following Hanson's (1958) theory about "theory-laden observations, "who had been able to observe the occurrence of sunspots centuries before Galileo simply because their cosmological beliefs did not preclude celestial change, early Western astronomers were unable to 'see' changes in the cosmos. Sunspots, for example, remained 'invisible'—that is, insignificant and anomalous—until Copernicus's idea changed the ways in which European astronomers could look at the heavens." Scientific work became more and more a matter of orchestrating sophisticated assemblages comprising machineries, tools, and other technical devices. The scientific revolution in the seventeenth century brought the telescope, the microscope, the thermometer (albeit not fully accurate until the eighteenth century), and finally in the end of the century the barometer and Robert Boyle's air pump (Butterfield, 1962: 94). These technologies and laboratory equipment opened up new visual practices in the sciences. It is somewhat ironic that Galileo, the great Florentine researcher and the inventor of the telescope, perhaps the most emblematic visual scientific instrument, in fact relied on what Ernst Mach would later call *Gendankenexperiment*, "thought experiment" (Koyré, 1968: 45) to overcome the ancient Aristotelian physics doctrine, suggesting that a body in motion will lose its speed as its "impetus," the energy located inside the body, is gradually consumed. In order to overcome this long-standing doctrine, Galileo did not have recourse to empirical experimentation but to what Koyré (1968: 12) calls "physics *a priori*." In order to defeat the Aristotelian doctrine, Galileo knew he was not only facing scientific and theological argumentation, but also, Koyré (1968) points out, something much worse, namely common sense. Common sense is largely immune to empirical experiments and therefore the "thought experiments" or conjectures served Galileo's purposes better. Therefore, during the early phases of the scientific revolution, science was not primarily empirical but based on philosophical reason and logic. However, British empiricists such as John Locke and David Hume advanced a philosophical doctrine that scientists such as Robert Boyle and others could draw on. The English philosopher Francis Bacon argued in his *Novum Organum* (1620) that "nature should be interpreted through the senses, aided by experiments 'fit and apposite'" (cited in Hackman, 1989: 35). With the emphasis on empiricism and various forms of vision and visuality came a series of new technologies. Shapin and Shaffer (1985) argue that Robert Boyle not only invented the technology he used in his pneumatic research but also instituted a regime of inscription based on what Boyle referred to as "modest witnessing," the use of credible witnesses—recruited from the aristocratic ranks of society and certainly no women or members of the lower social classes—to observe and testify to experiments. Says Shapin (1994: 201): "The rejection of authority and testimony in favour of individual sense-experience is just what stands behind our recognition of seventeenth-century practitioners as 'moderns,' as 'like us,' and, indeed, as producers of the thing we can warrant as science." For Boyle, vision and visuality play a central role in the new emerging scientific regime.

Boyle's empiricism was thus advanced along two routes: the technological path and the institutional path. Taken together, Boyle's program helped stabilize scientific procedures and scientific doctrines. Even though the various and highly subtle doctrines and practices pertaining to inscription procedures (examined in detail in the science and technology studies and actor-network theory literature) played a significant role in instituting science, we are here more concerned about the relationship between visuality and scientific practices. After Boyle's groundbreaking work, advanced technologies were developed in scientific communities all over Europe, serving both as embodiments of underlying doctrines (in Bachelard's [1984] view) and as what helps advancing the doctrines endorsed. In some cases, even the sheer size and advanced technological content helped promote the acceptance of certain theoretical frameworks. Hackman (1989) exemplifies with the Dutch scientist Martinus van Marum's electrostatic generator, which qualifies as what Hackman (1989) calls a "heroic device":

> Scientific instruments were (and still are) used as arbiters between contending theories, and sheer size could give a psychological advantage. A celebrated example from the eighteenth century is the giant electrostatic generator made for the Dutch natural philosopher Martinus van Marum by the English instrument maker John Cuthbertson. It fulfilled all the requirements of a heroic device . . . it was large and constructed to the limits of what was technically possible, This awesome machine with its two glass discs five feet in diameter, produced discharges twenty-four inches long; in modern terms, between 300 000

and 500 000 volts. It was not difficult to understand why Van Marum's fellow scientists could be persuaded by his experimental results. These were the main factors for the early acceptance of Lavoisier's combustion (oxidation) theory in the Netherlands. No apparatus is, however, self-evidently superior. Its value, like that of the experiment, lies in its power of persuasion. Bachelard has likened the instruments to *un théorème réifié*. (Hackman, 1989: 32)

These "heroic devices" served to manifest scientific authority and were also subject to an admiration that draws on what Kasson (1976) and Nye (1994) have called "the technological sublime," the sense of awe mixed with anxiety produced when encountering large-scale technological artefacts such as bridges, skyscrapers, or ocean liners. If nothing else, these scientific technologies represented the beliefs in and expectations on science in the early modern period. In general, the scientific machinery produced emphasized the skilled and professional vision of the scientist; the ability to inspect, examine, read, interpret, or otherwise analyze graphs, figures, traces, or other visual representations provided by the machinery. "[S]cientific knowledge *is* about witnessing. That is what the experimental method is about, the fact of being there," Haraway (2000: 160) argues.

Collective Practices of Seeing

Ludwik Fleck (1934) is one of the most important science philosophers in the modern period underlining the importance of visual practices in scientific procedures. For Fleck (1934), science is not produced by isolated geniuses, the Napoleon Bonapartes of science such as Isaac Newton and Galileo Galilei, but science is, by and large, a communal activity based on what Fleck calls "thought collectives" (*Denkenkollektive*) sharing a certain "style of thought" (*Denkenstile*). For Fleck, there is little scientific thinking that is capable of remaining viable and to continue to circulate unless it is verified and endorsed by the community of researchers. There are no "scientific breakthroughs" emerging from outside the community of researchers because this group is maintaining the jurisdiction over who is capable of making credible accounts; in science, there is no longer room for "amateurs." Here are of course examples of research that eventually have proven to be viable down the road while being ignored by its contemporaries—Mendelian biology, ignored for decades, being perhaps the most well-known case—but in most cases, scientific communities both produce scientific work and verify what contributions are worthy of attention. What is important in the Fleckian view of science is that one must not restrict the concept of "thinking" in the "thought collective" to mere cognitive processes. In empiricist sciences, i.e., in most domains of contemporary technoscience, thinking is always bound up with visual representations, that is, with vision and visuality.

Daston (2008) is emphasizing the intersection between Fleck's episte-mology and visuality and suggests that the socialization into a thought collective is largely a matter of being "experienced":

> For Fleck, learning to see like a scientist was a matter of accumulated experience—not only of an individual but of a well-trained collective. The fault line in epistemology did not run between subjects and objects, the great Kantian divide, but, rather, between inexperience and experi-ence. Unlike the neo-Kantians, who worried about how the subjective mind could know the objective world, Fleck was concerned with how perception forged stable kinds out of confused sensations . . . 'Filters,' or 'theoretical spectacles', or 'worldviews', in neo-Kantian history and philosophy are preconditions for experience, always and necessarily in operation. (Daston, 2008: 100)

What Daston (2008) suggests is that rather than being concerned about the conventional neo-Kantian controversy between subjective and objective knowledge, Fleck is helping us overcome the binary couple of objective/sub-jective in order to recognize a more productive one, namely that between being experienced or inexperienced when it comes to the inspection of visual representations. While the neo-Kantians would say, "When I inspect this photographic plate, I seek to avoid all subjective beliefs and assumptions," the Fleckian researcher would say, "Speaking and looking as a member of this community of researchers, I have learned that these images or blobs are to be examined from this specific perspective." However, being able to speak on behalf of the thought collective is a matter of experience rather than to once and for all iron out all subjective interests. Instead, subjective experiences may be helpful in detecting certain aspects of what is observed. For Daston (2008), rather than being overtly concerned abut the perils of subjectivity, lurking beneath the skin of every man or woman participat-ing in scientific work, scientific work is to be examined as what is already subject to detailed discipline and autosurveillance:

> [S]cientific perception—especially when elevated to the level of system-atic observation, often in carefully designed setups—is disciplined in every sense of the word: instilled by education and practice, checked and cross-checked both by other observers and with other instruments, communicated in forms—text, image, table—designed by and for a scientific collective over decades and sometimes centuries. (Daston, 2008: 102)

As a consequence, the dichotomy subjective/objective is no longer the key issue. Instead, the formation of and lives of thought collectives are proper topics of analysis. More specifically, the question how thought collectives are training its neophytes to subscribe to a specific, at times even idiosyncratic, mode of professional vision is of great theoretical and practical interest. Daston (2008) emphasizes that such a professional vision is not what is immediately given but is instead the outcome from long-term training and a disciplination of the gaze: "The novice sees only blurs and blobs under the microscope; experience and training are required in order to make sense of this visual chaos, in order to be able to see *things*" (Daston, 2008: 99). That is, professional vision is, when following Ludwik Fleck's analytical framework, what is the *outcome* and an *entrenched skill* from scientific work rather than the starting point: "Direct perception is the end and not the beginning of the process of fact genesis," Latour (2008: 94) remarks. Kruse's (2006) study of a life science laboratory in Sweden demonstrates the skills involved when inspecting the visual representations generated by the laboratory machinery and equipment.

> Just how much this ability to look was a product of practice and experience did not become clear to me until I watched a doctoral student try to make sense of the raw data from an analysis she had just completed for the first time . . . Senior colleagues she asked for help gave her advice like 'You have to look at them' . . . The doctoral student became quite frustrated about her failure to understand how others reasoned when interpreting results and about their inability to explain. 'I don't have the experience,' she said, adding that she would have to learn and that interpreting this kind of data probably would be easy once she had grasped it, but right now it was really difficult. An experienced person, on the other hand, could tell with a glance whether a result was good or worthless, including additional factors into her judgment: something may have gone wrong with the sample being analysed, or the machine might be out of calibration or might simply behave 'strangely,' which the experienced person could tell by the same glance. (Kruse, 2006: 111–112)

The challenge for the neophyte, the doctoral student, is both that such "skills of seeing" are in many cases complicated to fully articulate but are acquired through months and years of training and work in the laboratory. Second, the ability to inspect and interpret the images includes not only an understanding of what is possible to see but also an understanding for why they look as they do, i.e., how the instruments were used during the preparation. That is, the visual representations cannot be taken for granted but the skilled scientists need to keep in mind during the analysis how the dots or graphs or whatever form the visual data are presented were produced in the first place:

> The professional vision included applying additional knowledge to the raw data. This additional knowledge not only included what the colours or hues or figures signified, but also how preparations processes and instruments worked and, consequently, how the raw data came to look

like it did. When discussing raw data, the staff often referred to the preparation process, pointing to dots or peaks on graphs and relating them to something that was part of or had happened during the preparation. (Kruse, 2006: 117)

For classical empiricists, the ability to see or otherwise perceive the external world is what is ultimately a warrant for scientific rigour. For the Fleckian, vision is one scientific skill or procedure among others that is collectively constituted and entrenched in actual scientific work, i.e., through training and experience. The ability to engage in professional vision as a legitimate member of a scientific collective is the effect of working in that community over time; looking, discussing, and concluding are all components in such procedures of formulating conjectures, justifications, or falsifications. Michael Lynch (1988), elsewhere subscribing to an ethnomethodological framework (Lynch, 1993), provides a fine illustration to this procedure; here, theories, specimens, visual representations, and other resources are enrolled en route:

> Research teams use laboratory practice to transform invisible or unanalyzable specimens into visually examined, coded, measured, graphically analyzed, and publicly presented data. Such ordering of data is not solely contained 'in perception' but is also a social process—an 'assembly line' resulting in public access to new structures wrested out of obscurity or chaos. Instruments, graphic inscriptions, and interactional processes take the place of 'mind' as the filter, serving to reduce phenomena of study into manageable data. (Lynch, 1988: 156)

In a paper published in 1985, Lynch demonstrates how scientific visuality is accomplished through a number of operations and modifications of the object of study. What Lynch (1985) calls "characteristic features of scientific activity" such as the use of "production of visual display of objects, processes, relationships, and theoretical constructs" is by no means an uncomplicated process but is rather at the very core of the scientific activity: "Visual displays are not only valuable as illustrations in scientific texts; they are irreplaceable as documents which enable objects of study to be initially perceived and analyzed. Such displays systematically transform specimen materials into observable and mathematically analyzable data," Lynch (1985: 37) writes. Lynch speak of this transformation of natural species or tissues into graphical representations as the production of "docile objects," objects that are capable of "behaving" in accordance with a "programme of normalization," i.e., the objects become, with Lynch's phrase, "civilized." Such "programme of normalization" includes a procedure of including three steps: (1) "geometrization," (2) "chronologization," and (3) "mathematization" (Lynch, 1985:

50).[2] The targeted features of the specimen or tissue (a laboratory animal such as a rat or a cell line, both examples of what is called *natura naturata*, "natured nature," constructed in the laboratory in contrast to *natura naturans*, "natural nature) are transformed into a graphical display (e.g., a graph) capturing the temporal sequence of an event (i.e., the metabolism of a drug in the rat's body), and finally the graph, displaying some underlying event, is used for mathematical operations and statistical analysis. "[A] graph . . . is the literary end-point of a series of renderings which transformed cellular arrangements into graphic space," Lynch (1985: 45) notices:

> The graphic display *normalizes* the properties of each animal and each counted terminal. The specimen 'animal' becomes both more than, and less than, a laboratory rat. It becomes *more than* a nervously staring creature living out it its life in a wire cage, since fine structure of its nervous system revealed through dissection of the animal, histological treatment of its issues, and microscopic magnification are not all apparent from the outset. The structures revealed by rendering the animal's remains are virtually abstracted while retaining their attachment to the concrete residues of the animal's body. It becomes *less than* the ordinary animal since the original animal is literary thrown away in favor of the residues retained for inspection. (Lynch, 1985: 57)

While scientists may argue that graphs and other visual representations are capable of objectively capturing an underlying material substratum, studies reported by Roth and Bowen (2003) and Roth (2003) suggest that the ability to read graphs is not a generalized ability among even very experienced scientists. Instead, many graphs produced outside of their own field of expertise are misunderstood or misinterpreted by scientists. Roth and Bowen (2003) and Roth (2003) propose that graphs are always already embedded in an intimate understanding of a specific field of expertise and therefore graphs are not objective accounts of external realities but are rather to be seen as theories and verified empirical data manifested by other (i.e., visual) means; graphs are not "external" accounts of scientific findings but are from the very outset beset by series of assumptions and beliefs. As a consequence, the scientist claiming that the layman should "just look at the graphs" for indisputable evidence does not make sense—such a "looking" must always presuppose that the viewer inspecting the graphs shares a great deal of assumptions with the community constructing the graph in the first place. For Roth (2003), graphs are "conscription devices" being part of the scientists' "rhetorical practices," a component in their totality of resources used when convincing both insiders and outsiders of the value of their contributions. Using the metaphor of the tool in the hands of the experienced artisan where the tool is itself "disappearing" into the artisan's body and there is no longer a clear boundary between hand and tool, the graphs and other visual representations are not "mere representations" but become a constitutive part of the lifeworld of the scientist, an element in their domain of dwelling:

> If signs are understood as tools . . . then our results suggest that graphs with which they [scientists in the study] are familiar are not mere representations. Like tools in the hands of expert practitioners, signs begin to disappear. They are transparent in use and therefore allow the user direct access to a richly textured experience and accumulated knowledge. (Roth and Bowen, 2003: 465)

In summary, graphs and other visual representations are not "external" to the research procedures and setup of the ongoing research endeavours, but are instead direct consequences of the theories and methods enacted and acted upon. Graphs and visual representations are part of "semiotic practices" (Roth, 2003) that cannot be fully disentangled from what Timmermans (2008: 170) calls "disciplinary objectivity" of the community of researchers, that is, "the of insight that comes only with learned experience among peers."

The visual space of the laboratory scientists is produced through a series of operations and transformations; there is no immaculate scientific gaze but all observations are always already deeply embedded in a series of assumptions, beliefs, theorems, theories, and so forth, reified into laboratory equipment and procedures (Roth and Bowen, 1999; Kruse, 2006). In addition, the ability to "see" the species or tissues or whatever scientific object that is studied, organic material has to be civilized, rendered visible for the structured scientific gaze. Lynch 1985: 60) therefore concludes that data are neither "wholly 'out there' in the animal's anatomy, nor wholly constructed out of thin air." In order to accomplish a shared scientific gaze, the procedures preceding and succeeding the very act of visual inspection have to be agreed upon. This makes the scientific gaze simultaneously both more solid and more fragile; more solid in terms of being anchored in a range of procedures and operations; more fragile in terms of being inextricably entangled with a series of agreements that can easily become subject to negotiation as a new scientific result is reported or, on the contrary, there is no such finding reported and a modification of the experimental system is called for.

Vision is, we learn from Fleck, not a matter of a subjective gaze but is always already interpenetrated by the other, the generalized other of the thought collective. To engage in professional vision is to see as a member of a certain community. Digressions from such a view may be a violation of the collectively enacted norms. That is, vision is a form of Lacanian gaze, a vision under the influence of the other. However, this gaze is never wholly self-enclosed but is instead always under the threat of disintegrating or falling apart. That is why specific thought collectives must maintain their authority and jurisdiction over certain "ways of seeing."

VISION AND AESTHETICS

The Concept of Aesthetic and Its Use in the Early Modern Period

One specific aspect of vision and visuality is what may be named the aesthetic factor in science. Aesthetics is commonly defined as "the philosophy of art and beauty" (Shusterman, 2006: 237), first developed by the German philosopher Alexander Baumgarten and thereafter further advanced by his most famous disciple, Immanuel Kant. However, the concept of aesthetics is as old as Aristotle's *Poetics* (Holquist, 2003: 368) but it was not until the end of the eighteenth century that the term was used in a more systematic manner. In Baumgarten's thinking, aesthetics did not in the first place denote "the beautiful" but was introduced as a general conceptualization of a "science of sensory-perception" (Shusterman, 2006: 239). Baumgarten's aesthetic did not only address works of arts and natural beauty but more generally daily practices. Baumgarten's thinking is thus a generalized theory about vision and visuality (Shusterman, 2006: 239). For commentators like Shusterman (2006), the discipline of aesthetic remains "deeply ambiguous, complex and essentially contested," partly because the notions of art and beauty are in themselves ambiguous, and partly because the notion of aesthetics has, Shusterman (2006: 237) says, an "[e]specially complicated, heterogeneous, conflicted and disordered genealogy."

Aesthetics is a rather abstract category, failing to provide wholly self-enclosed concepts and theories and operating on what Vattimo (1992) calls "weak thinking" (Italian, *pensiero debole*), a form of thinking that does not operate on the basis of propositions, demonstrations, and theorems but seeks to capture what is inherently vague and ambiguous. In language games (Wittgenstein) or performative use of language (Austin), terms and concepts may be used in a variety of manners and serve different functions. The concept of aesthetic is largely that of capturing what is residual, what remains after other "proper terms" have been used to denote social reality. The value of terms such as aesthetics lies precisely in their ability to capture what is "in-between," in what Heidegger called the *Zwischenraum*, the "domain in-between." The ability to think in the *Zwischenraum* is the capacity of what Friedrich von Hayek (1978) called "the puzzler," the thinker capable of operating in domains where there are not yet proper terms in place and where new terms have to be invented *en route*. Friedrich von Hayek (1978) used Alfred North Whitehead as an example of a thinker in this tradition, a thinker serving as (to use Foucault's description of

Maurice Blanchot) "a swimmer between two words," capable of thinking what is not yet thought.

Notwithstanding the theoretical and philosophical intricacies, what is of interest in this setting is that rather than conceiving of aesthetics as a term restricted to art, natural beauty, design, and related topics, aesthetics is also a concept that is applicable when examining scientific work. While scientific ideologies tend to emphasize truth, reason, and usability (i.e., the performativity of scientific programs), there is a stream of research underlining the aesthetic qualities of all scientific procedures. Hallyn's (1990) treatise on Copernicus and Kepler shows that the dominant aesthetic ideals of the renaissance period were adhered to by the two great astronomers when creating their scientific models of the heliocentric universe. During the renaissance, symmetry and the "perfected circle" were praised aesthetic norms (Hallyn, 1990: 159). Not only did Copernicus conceive of the universe in accordance with such aesthetic norms; also the churches and the town planning were based on this "script":

> Wittkower [a historian] notes that most churches with a central altar were constructed between 1490 and 1530 . . . after Brunelleschi set an example as early as 1434, with his plan for Santa Maria degli Angeli in Florence. Thus the application to architecture preceded that application to cosmology. From the church architecture, the exaltation of the center spread to town planning, the planning of utopian towns in particular. (Hallyn, 1990: 17)

With Kepler, aesthetics was no longer present in the *form* of the creation but in the "code" underlying to the visual world, i.e., matter. Kepler's Platonist emphasis on mathematics and the distinction between appearance (the perceivable world) and the real (the mathematical representations) helped him abandon the "surface aesthetics" of Copernicus and to—more correctly, we think today—conceive of the universe as a being elliptic in shape and in its mechanical operations. *Ubi material, ibi geometria*—"Where matter is, there is geometry," Johannes Kepler declared (cited in Hallyn, 1990: 170). Hallyn outlines Kepler's program:

> God signifies and communicated to man through nature. Consequently, the practice of astronomy becomes a means of following the contemplative path that leads man to God . . . Understanding the world is ultimately to find the Meaning and the Author in signs. The calculations with which the astronomer discovers his laws or supports his hypotheses contribute to making man more God-like: For the resemblance between man and God is as much a task as a fact. We construct the resemblance by constructing internally the laws that govern Creation. (Hallyn, 1990: 173)[3]

Following Croce's (1995: 28) distinction between "the aesthetics of content" (German, *Gehaltaesthetik*) and "the aesthetics of form" (German, *Formaesthetik*), one may argue that Copernicus subscribed to the latter view of aesthetics while Kepler gave privilege to the content, the intrinsic operations and mechanisms. The consequences from Kepler's Platonist reworking of the universe had significant impact on the history of the sciences, not only in terms of the actual contribution to astronomy, the scientific discipline propelling the entire scientific revolution, but also in terms of method, and more specifically in terms of using mathematics as a tool and a regime of representation which scientists could use when communicating abstract ideas.

Contemporary Science and Aesthetics

In the early modern period, in the late medieval period, and during the renaissance, there was still no major philosophical and practical rift between the arts and the sciences. Art was not a science but a technique, a *techne* (Greek, τεχνη), a speciality of the specific professional group (Le Goff, 1993: 62). Consequently, aesthetics was not a term reserved for certain human activities but was of relevance in all sorts of domains. In the course of history, during the scientific revolution and into the late modern period, science has been increasingly specialized and subject to regulations and procedures for monitoring and evaluation, and the aesthetic components of the work have gradually been subsumed under other features, including rationality and reason. However, when examining various scientific disciplines, there is evidence of aesthetic concerns even in the seemingly most technoscientific disciplines. Jordanova (1989), drawing on a gender theory perspective in her analysis of medicine, emphasizes the aesthetic components in the discipline:

> The aesthetic dimensions of science and medicine are beginning to be paid the more serious attention they deserve, not to display them as cultural ornaments but to demonstrate that aesthetics is constitutive of knowledge. We can see, for example, that 'realism,' used as an aesthetic rather than a philosophical term, has been important within science and medicine by defining modes of illustration, and also, conversely, that scientific and medical ideas were central to realist artistic and literary practices, especially in the nineteenth century. (Jordanova, 1989: 6)

Jordanova (1989) argues that the realist movement in, for instance, literature (Victor Hugo's *Thérèse Raquin* being one example) wielded significant influence on the emerging literature on surgery. Also Cartwright (1995) emphasizes that in the early development of medical visual technologies, women were used as objects of investigation, thereby making the medical technologies subject to a sexualized vision, a form of male gaze into the interior of the female body. Rather providing idealized and thereby somewhat distorted images of the interior of the human body, this emerging corpus of texts presented the human body in a most realistic manner, not failing to account for all sorts of details previously regarded improper and therefore to remain hidden. This tendency to depict the human body "realistically" terminated in the Visual Human Project, where the executed convict Joseph Jernigan from Waco, Texas, donated his body to a project where his remains were put on display on the Internet to further enhance medical education and training (Waldby, 2000). Today, modern surgery, what Hirschauer (1991) calls the "surgical gaze," is based on the ability to combine and "superimpose" the image of the concrete body and single, idealized, or formalized images of the body; "a permanent cross-fading of experience and representation," Hirschauer (1991: 310) says. However, this "surgical gaze" has its roots in the renaissance and the seminal works published by Andreas Vesalius in the mid-sixteenth century. Thacker (1999: 325) argues that Vesalius breaks with the canonical tradition of Galen and emphasizes the visuality of the human body: In *De Humani Corporis Fabrica,* Vesalius's "[r]igorous engagement with contemporary modes of visual representation places great emphasis on the visual (that is, the observable) as the anatomist's primary mode of investigation" (Thacker, 1999: 325). As soon as the human body is located as a *visual object,* that is, an empiricist object of investigation rather than a theoretical construction, there is a divergence between the "messy and grotesque body of the dissection" and the well-ordered and purposeful body of the anatomy treatise that needs to be mediated. Consonant with Hirschauer's (1991) "cross-fading" of experience (observation) and representation (theory), Thacker (1999) points at the frail construction (i.e., the relationship actual body/represented body) emerging on the basis of the anatomist's work to cut up the body and display its parts:

> Every cut is strategic here, as an art of making the interior visible to both anatomical science and (in the anatomy theatres) to the naked eye of the spectator. *The process of dissection is thus a constant negotiation between a potentially disarticulated corpse and the scientific rigor of the anatomy text.* The body that develops during the phase—'the dissected body'—is constantly being incorporated into the anatomical frame, though as a literally opened, unbounded and grotesquely visceral form, it may also threaten the coherence of that same framework. (Thacker, 1999: 326)

In the analytical framework suggested by Karen Barad (2003), employed by Johnson (2008) in her study of an instrument simulating the female urology system used in gynaecology training, the dissected body is a matter of "intra-action," conceived of in terms that enable practices and agency: "[M]atter is instances in its intra-active becomings—not a thing, but a doing, *a congealing of agency . . . matter refers to the materiality/materialization of phenomena*, not to an inherent fixed property of abstract independently existing objects of Newtonian physics" (Barad, 2003: 822; emphasis in the original). The dissected body is thus never an object per se but is always what is constituted as a theoretical and actual object through the very practices and forms of agency involved in the act of dissection. In Thacker's (1999: 327) account, "the body undergoing anatomical dissection is put into liminal space (the visceral, messy body of dissection) specifically so that it may be reincorporated into another discursive-material framework." The visual body, the body put forward in the tradition of Versalius's work, essentially breaking with the Galenic tradition emphasizing universalized principles of harmony applied to the human body, is thus what is composed both of an actual, messy and "grotesque" body, the body on display in the anatomic theatres in the European universities during the period, and the virtual body of the well-ordered and unified theoretical body portrayed in anatomy treatises of the period. In this tradition of thinking in medicine, the visual and the nonvisual are mutually co-constitutive, never reducible to one another.

Vision Machines and Aesthetics

More recently, Joyce (2006) and Burri (2008) have both accounted for the aesthetic concerns in new medical visual technologies such as magnetic resonance imaging (MRI) and radiology, both enabling new forms of visuality and consequently new medical practices. Joyce (2006) outlines a rather straightforward connection between, on the one hand, popular culture of the 1970s and, on the other hand, the new MRI technology:

> In the 1970s, MRI images . . . converged with popular culture aesthetics. Television shows like *The Partridge Family*, the continued presence of Pop Art, and fashions associated with musical genres such as Glam Rock and Disco transformed the world into a vibrant and at times psychadelic hues. The research scientists working on MRI development also chose bright, flashy colours to represent the inner body—a decision that resonated with the aesthetics of popular culture. (Joyce, 2006: 17)

No man is an island, and this too counts for the scientist; the predominant aesthetic regime of the period did, Joyce (2006) suggests, influence the way the information provided by the MRI technology was presented to the analyst. Joyce (2006) even claimed that the entire MRI technology benefited from a pervasive "visual turn" in the period. In addition, radiologists, an emerging professional community within the medical field at the time, could benefit from the new MRI technology and the opportunities for visualization and entrench a position as specialists in examining, interpreting, and narrating the images provided. Joyce (2006: 19) concludes:

"Scientists creatively select, adopt, and appropriate from a range of possibilities to produce new technologies; these decisions, especially in the case of the medical imaging technologies, are intimately connected to the larger cultural context of visualization." Visualization is always a matter of aesthetics and therefore the radiologists' authority and influence in the medical field are ultimately a matter of structuring and controlling artefacts with certain aesthetic properties. Even though medicine is constantly mobilizing and drawing on a range of resources, narratives, and ideologies to safeguard its status and authority, it is, at least partly, also relying on specific forms of aesthetics.

In Burri's (2008) study of radiologists and their struggle to maintain the jurisdiction over their field of expertise, there is again an emphasis on the aesthetic aspects of work. For instance, Burri (2008) visited radiologist conferences and found that there was an observable aesthetic norm in the field, regulating how the visual representations should be organized and thereby rendered meaningful:

> [I]t is clear that the aesthetic quality of images presented at radiological conferences is important. At first glance this seems surprising, as radiologists in their daily work look at thousands of pictures of differing image quality. They are accustomed to images in grey scale and not in colour and do not necessarily depend on perfect or beautiful images to make an adequate diagnosis. Nevertheless, at the radiological congresses I attended, aesthetic features such as the colour and contrast of the digital images were clearly of great importance. (Burri, 2008: 50)

For Burri (2008: 50), aesthetics is a tool in the hands of the radiologists. Since "beautiful images," i.e., images that are easily examined and interpreted, help attract attention, and attention is a means for gaining and maintaining reputation (i.e., status in the field), images play an important role in the community. For the radiologists and other professional or occupational communities working on the basis of visual representations, aesthetics is not "external," "supplementary," or "additional to" the "work proper," the day-to-day operations and procedures, but is rather at the very core of such practices. Images, demonstrating certain aesthetic features, are constitutive of the radiologists' professional status. The studies of Joyce (2006) and Burri (2008) are representative of a general recognition of aesthetics. Piñeiro (2007), studying the aesthetic norms and standards in the community of computer programmers, similarly suggests that aesthetic is always part of any professional or occupational community: "Even in the exact and demanding world of computer programming, there is a place for questions of an aesthetic nature. Regardless of the restrictions forced upon human activity, if there is as much as an ounce of creative work involved or permitted, aesthetic concerns will thrive" (Piñeiro, 2007:

105). The intersections between science and aesthetics are not peripheral as one may think.

MACHINIC VISION AND VISION MACHINES: TECHNOLOGIES OF PERCEPTION AND MEDIATED VISION

The Technogenesis of Vision Machines

Most visual representations demonstrating aesthetic qualities are produced by advanced technoscientific apparatuses (Burri and Dumit, 2008). Therefore, in the following, the intersection between vision and technology will be examined in some detail. It is suggested that most vision, both in technoscience and elsewhere, is *mediated vision*, vision that does not primarily derive from some undistorted eye but from the blending of the human visual apparatus (constituted by retina, the neurological system, etc.) and media for vision and representation. "Microscopes, telescopes, X-ray imagining . . . belong to a long history of perception-enhancing technologies which *embody* scientific observations. They are an essential element in the *technological embodiment of science in its instrumentation,*" the philosopher of technology Don Ihde (1995: 147. Emphasis in the original) notes. The contemporary society is a society fundamentally pervaded by a variety of "vision machines." When we here speak of machines and other technological artefacts, assemblies of technology, the term is used in the sense developed by the French philosopher Gilbert Simondon, as what is not from the outset fixed and ready-made but rather as what is gradually stabilizing and subject to "concretisation" (Dumochel, 1995). For Simondon, a former doctoral student of Maurice Merleau-Ponty at École Normale Supérieur (Beistegui, 2005), the idea of a "purely automatic machine closed in on itself" is misconceived. Instead, all machines and other "technical objects" with superior "technicality" are "open machines," ensembles of technological mechanisms and devices. Consequently, Simondon thinks of technology in terms of *elements, individuals*, and *ensembles* of technologies, all of which are representative of the aggregation of devices into functional units (Simondon, 1980: 9): "Individuals corresponds to machines, devices, and engines; technological elements are best thought of as machine components or simple tools; technological ensembles are vast installations consisting of a variety of machines, devices, and engines, e.g., factories or laboratories," Schmidgen (2004: 9) explains. "The technical object is a unit of becoming," Simondon (1980: 12) suggests, and Stiegler (1998: 67) here uses the term *technogenesis* to denote this process.[4] All technologies are undergoing phases where they are subject to *concretization*, the process where the technical object is given "an intermediate position between the natural and the scientific representation" (Simondon, 1980: 46). Just like organic life is the struggle against disorder (Atlan, 1974), so is the technological object the outcome from the stabilization of elements:

> The machine, as an element in the technical ensemble, becomes the effective unit which augments the quantity of information, increases negentropy, and opposes the degradation of energy. The machine is a [result] of organization and information; it [resembles] life and cooperates with life in its opposition to disorder and to the levelling out of all things that tend to deprive the world of its powers of change. The machine is something which fights against the death of the universe; it slows down, as life does, the denigration of energy, and becomes a stabilizer of the world. (Simondon, 1980: 9)

For Simondon, technical objects are the outcome from processes where different elements (components, mechanisms, functions) are converging towards a unity, constituting the technical object as a coherent organization: "The technical object exists . . . as a specific type that is arrived at the end of a convergent series. This series goes from the abstract mode to the concrete mode; it tends towards a state at which the technical being becomes a system that is entirely coherent with itself and entirely unified," Simondon (1980: 16) says. In Simondon's (1980) view, technical objects are never fully enclosed and immutable from the outset but are rather produced through continuous modifications. As a consequence, technical objects are never separated from their very use. In terms of what we here, after Virilio (1994), call vision machines, there is a form of what André Leroi-Gourhan (1993: 134) calls *orthogenesis*, a dynamic relationship between the technical objects and its use in social and "encultured" settings. Technical objects are capable of being "concretized" through their continuous modification in their use; technologies are never totally stable but are subject to modifications. The concept of orthogenesis—which is an archaeological term, one must keep in mind—suggests that social, economic, and technical progress are mutually constitutive and entangled: "The close interdependence between social institutions and the technical and economic apparatus is borne out by countless facts . . . It is the organization of matter that, in various ways, directly shapes all aspects of human life," Leroi-Gourhan (1993: 147) writes. For Leroi-Gourhan (1993), man is not only the inventor of technology; it is also technology as such that enables mankind to develop. The biological and the technological are two concurrent developmental processes and any attempt at understanding changes and transitions over periods of time—the transition from the Paleolithic to the Mesolithic to the Neolithic periods, for instance—must understand these close interrelations. Thinking of vision in such terms, the technological objects in use (i.e., the telescopes, the microscopes, the photographic plates, and all the scientific paraphernalia) are having a recursive relationship with the looking subject; when vision is failing the technological object is modified, manipulated, or even replaced by a new technological artefact in order to facilitate desired ways of perceiving. In other words, the vision machines employed are open towards social and encultured interests and concerns. Wajcman (2007) summarizes this position:

> [T]he notion that technology is simply the artefact, of rational technical imperatives has been dislodged. Objects and artefacts are no longer seen as separable from society, but as part of the social fabric that holds society together; they are never merely technical or social. Rather, the broad social shaping or constructivist approach treats technology as a sociotechnical product—a seamless web or network combining artefacts people, organizations, cultural meaning and knowledge. (Wajcman, 2007: 293)

In everyday life, human beings perceive at least parts of social reality through screens on computers and other technological devices. The interface, the thin relay between human and the interior of the machine, is becoming our "second nature." Learning to examine and review images on such interfaces is an important skill when becoming visually literate, an increasingly important skill in today's society. Johnston (1999) is referring to the ability of participating in mediated vision as *machinic vision*, a term he uses "[n]ot only [as] an environment of interacting machines and human-machine interfaces but [as] a field of decoded perceptions that, whether or not produced by or issuing from these machines, assume their full intelligibility only in relation to them" (Johnston, 1999: 26). Machinic vision is thus a form of visuality that is always already embedded in the technology, in the functioning of vision machines. In addition, Prasad (2005), studying the use of MRI technology, is using the term *cyborg vision*. In the medical gaze, cyborg vision is the balancing of, on the one hand, the recognition of the technological constitution of vision, and, on the other, the emphasis on the socially and professionally acquired skill of interpreting and examining these images adequately:

> In the cyborg visuality regime, images have become bits of data in cyberspace that can be, and are, manipulated by human beings. This does not men that within this new visual regime, claims towards realism of images are disbanded. If that were so, there would be no reason to have MRI [magnetic resonance imaging] radiological analyses. Cyborg visuality produced by MRI works within different frameworks of realism that does not seek mechanical reproduction of the observed objects(s). MR images produce different reconfigurations of the body, each of which provide a partial perspective of the body and together they constitute the MR radiological gaze. (Prasad, 2005: 310)

Cyborg vision is for Prasad (2005) seeing by means of technology. However, technology does not in any way determine the practices of seeing; it is merely a component in an assemblage of resources being mobilized in the act of professional vision.

Vision Machines in Medicine

One of the earliest examples of mechanic vision is the use of the X-ray technology in German orthopaedic surgery in the last decades of the nineteenth century (Warwick, 2005). The quick spread of the use of X-ray was propelled by a number of social and technical changes in Germany during the period. First, the German state implemented a health insurance program increasing the demands for orthopaedic surgery. Second, the use of the X-ray could support the authority and jurisdiction of orthopaedic surgeons, seeking to become a legitimate niche in the field of surgery. Third and finally, the patients were willing to pay for visual representations showing the injuries or deformities of the patients' bodies. Taken together, the use of the visual techniques such as the X-ray helped establish both new medical practices, supported the status and career opportunities of orthopaedic surgeons, and in general contributed to the visual turn in medicine and society more broadly.

In the U.S., the reception of the X-ray was influenced by juridical concerns, Golan (2004) suggests. While the innovation of the X-ray was more or less immediately recognized by the broader public and was encountered in advertisement, stories, songs, and cartoons—more than "1000 papers and 50 books were published on the subject in 1896 alone" (Golan, 2004: 470)—the community of medical doctors were more skeptical about the use of the X-rays. Above all, medical doctors were concerned they would face charges of malpractice if the X-rays were used, showing in detail the effects of the treatment. However, during the second half of the nineteenth century, lawyers were increasingly using "expert witnesses" (e.g., medical experts) in court and the X-ray was conceived of as a new tool serving as a "silent witness":

> Regular and X-ray photography were part of a new class of machine-made testimonies that rose to dominance during the second half of the 19th century. Ever alert and never involved, machines such as microscopes, telescopes, high-speed cameras, and X-ray tubes threatened to turn human testimony into an inferior mode of communication facts as they purported to communicate richer, better, and truer evidence, which often was inaccessible by other means to human beings. The emblem for this type of mechanical objectivity was visual evidence. 'Let nature speak for itself' became a watchword, and nature's language seemed to be that of photographs and mechanically generated curves. (Golan, 2004: 474)

As Dumit (2004: 112) points out in his analysis of the use of positron emission tomography (PET) in the trial of John Hinckley, the man who shot the American President Ronald Regan in 1981 in an attempt to impress the actress Jodie Foster, what Dumit (2004) calls the *expert images* produced by the PET technology are paradoxical inasmuch as if they are legible, they should not need interpretation, but if they need interpretation they "should not be shown to juries." The use of what Golan (2004) names forms of "mechanical objectivity" was not devoid of controversies and discussions and only after long periods of investigations a number of states permitted the use of X-ray plates. In the recent interest in X-ray plates, the new professional community of radiologists could advance their position and claim spokesmanship of the new technology:

> Mastering the technology, the radiologists emphasized time and again, was not enough. To read the images with any reasonable degree of accuracy—to be distinguished between normal and pathological appearances and between essential and accidental details—one needs to know anatomy, histology, and pathology in detail, and to be familiar with the various ways both normal and abnormal conditions appear on the X-ray plate, Without such knowledge, no meaningful reading of the images was possible. (Golan, 2004: 485)

"The skiagraph [a visualization technology based on X-ray] is never wrong," the slogan of the radiologists ran—"[w]hen errors exists it lies in its interpretations" (Golan, 2004: 485). Contrary to the lawyers' claim, "nature never speaks for itself," the radiologists argued. What was demanded, radiologists insisted, was intricate training and experience in both internal medicine and the functioning of the new technologies. With the technological possibilities of Wilhelm Röntgen's innovation thus came new juridical concerns—a concern similar to that of the use of DNA-typing technologies in juridical procedures today (Daemmrich, 1998)—namely the possibility of "silent witnessing" and visual representations "speaking for themselves" that in turn helped advancing new professional communities such as the radiologists. Dumit (2004) is sceptical regarding the ability of these expert images to operate as objective evidence:

> [E]ven though the brain images are produced by people, the are co-produced by scientific machines, and it is the machines, especially computers, that leave their mark. Scientists . . . increasingly attempt to remove their marks from the image, even though they must still provide the text . . . At the crux of this relationship between the image which (objectively) speaks for itself and the expert who (subjectively) speaks reads its lips is a desire by the court and by everyone else to reduce ambiguity, to make things clear, and clearly acceptable. (Dumit, 2004: 119)

This kind of debates and controversies over the use and significance of visual technologies has continued into the present times as new visual tools have been developed and brought into practice.

The difficulties of professional vision have been addressed in a number of studies of functional magnetic resonance imaging (fMRI) and positron emission tomography (PET) (Alac, 2008; Beaulieu, 2002; Cohn, 2004; Dumit, 2004; Joyce, 2006; Prasad, 2005). As a visual technology, fMRI is based on advanced techniques where the hydrogen protons in brain tissues are induced to emit a signal that is detected by a computer. In the computer, the signals, represented as numerical data, are "[c]onverted into visual representations of the brain" (Alac, 2008: 483) and displayed in many colours on the computer screen. These visual representations are what Dumit (2004: 112) calls *expert images*, "[o]bjects produced with mechanical assistance that require help in interpreting even though they may appear to be legible to laypersons." When looking at the computer screen, radiologists are capable of manipulating the image in a variety of ways, e.g., by rotating the image or scaling up and down. In addition, when inspecting the image, radiologists use gestures and talk to make sense out of what is seen on the screen. "Gesture, talk and the manipulation of the digital screen function together as techniques for managing perception," Alac (2008: 493) writes (see also Nishizaka, 2000). She continues:

> The gestures, together with practitioners' talk, gaze and body orientation turn the physical space occupied by the practitioners into a field of meaning production. In the context of laboratory practice, the multiple 'semiotic fields' . . . such as the field of the digital screen and the one inhabited by material bodies, are superimposed and intertwined, the way in which the images are aligned with the gestures, body orientation, gaze and talk suggests an action-oriented, publicly available, and intersubjective character of seeing. (Alac, 2008: 493)

In addition, the collectively enacted ways of seeing among the radiologists, their professional vision, is based on the ability to move back and forth between the two-dimensional images on the screen and the examined three-dimensional brain of the actual patient subject to fMRI scanning. What the radiologists are examining is in fact a hybrid image that is simultaneously "[m]aterial and digital, concrete and abstract, human and machine, 3D and 2D, action and object, present and future" (Alac, 2008: 502). Alac (2008) is emphasizing that the radiologists are not in fact only strictly looking at the images, but that all procedures of interpretation are strongly relying on talk and gestures to make sense out of the image. That is, radiologists do rarely if ever encounter images that are "self-explanatory" or completely devoid of ambiguities or inconsistencies, but instead there is a variety of aspects that needs to be sorted out, addressed, and determined. Seen in this view, professional vision is, Alac (2008) suggests, emerging as

[a] process situated at the intersection between instruments and technology, practices, settings, and the practitioners' embodied accounts. It describes how the local management of seeing involves previous dealings and cumulative practices of know-how, and how it receives its rhetorical force by reference to the usual procedures of laboratory members. These procedures are nested in larger, historically evolving, socio-technical networks whose specifications are bound to the locally instantiated assemblages of instruments, embodied techniques, and everyday discourses in the laboratory. (Alac, 2008: 503)

Alac (2008: 504) even goes so far to suggest that fMRI images are "visual" and "visible" versions of what was previously not visual; the invisible inside of the human brain is thus turned into a visible medium and is therefore rendered what is open to inspection and becoming subject to the medical gaze. The fMRI technology is therefore what is capable of transgressing the boundary between the visible and the invisible and is also enabling an opening up of new domains of visibility, that of the internal of the human body. However, the concern is that the images shown on the computer screen are in themselves technologically developed, bound up with the operating assumptions inherent to the technology as such (Bachelard, 1984). Barry (1997) emphasizes the difficulties when examining two-dimensional images denoting three-dimensional biological systems:

> What makes reading traditional two-dimensional (2-D) X-ray so difficult for their readers, for example, is their lack of depth, a problem complicated by poor contrast resolution and visual noise. Radiologist training to read them effectively involves a finely tuned discrimination between the normal patterns and textures of the body and the typical patterns and textures of abnormal conditions, because the details— such as small modules of disease like emphysema—are easily lost and may not, or cannot, be seen . . . Human vision is still the most powerful means of sifting out irrelevant information and detecting significant patterns. (Barry, 1997: 34)

The radiologist may then not always strictly "see" a particular abnormality but may develop a certain *sense* or intuitive feeling of something being not quite right or missing in the photographic plate. In order to convey this sense of detecting something interesting, it may be that the radiologists need to use more than verbal accounts of what is observed, and consequently gestures and body language are used in the communication (Alac, 2008). Second, the uses of the images generated and the procedures for interpreting the images and for their further use in the medical practice are fundamentally affected by struggles over authority and jurisdiction within the field of medicine. As a consequence, the fMRI images are not strictly revealing what is "inside the head" but are also a manifestation of scientific regimes and debates and controversies "outside of the patient's head":

> '[S]eeing' of fMRI images is an embodied process achieved through a coordination of 'visual' information with the world of meaningful actions and practical problem-solving. In other words, the visibility is not only relative to what goes on inside the practitioner's head or to what is present on the screen. Seeing is tied to actions that arise out of experiences with the manipulation of objects and everyday practical dealings. (Alac, 2008: 504)

Alac's (2008) study of the use of fMRI images is important because it points at the "overdetermination" of the images produced. First, professional vision is in itself what is precarious in terms of being bound up with assemblages of technology. Second, the images produced are not only strictly inspected and "looked at" but are instead serving their role in medical practice through being examined and discussed through the use of talk, gestures, and other means available when making sense out of the images provided. In other words, professional vision is not a neatly outlined and coherent social practice but is instead what blends and mixes practices of seeing and saying while being bound up with technology and other material and nonmaterial resources constituting a technological assemblage enabling medical vision. The radiologist thus need to admit that it is the machinery, the technoscientific apparatus, that is producing the images to be examined. On the other hand, there is no belief in the *res ipsa loquitur*, the doctrine that "the fact speaks for itself." Instead, it is the radiologists who are the legitimate spokespersons of the visual representations provided. Needless to say, such claims of authority are not entrenched without controversies and struggle. Turning again to the study of Burri (2008), such struggle is part of the everyday work life in hospitals and health care organizations. First, the very access to the machinery is a source of authority and prestige in the field: "Having access to the most advanced scanners makes it possible to undertake research not done elsewhere," says Burri (2008: 45–46). A radiologist testifies to such claims: "These machines are power. The one who has a machine worth two millions at his disposal and may play with it has achieved something in his career" (Radiologist Georg von Alberti, cited in Burri, 2008: 46). Second, once the machinery is put into use, there is a continuous need for engaging in what Gieryn (1983, 1999) calls "boundary work" and Burri (2008) calls "distinction practices," the careful separation between which practices what group is accountable for and what group each individual belongs to. "Distinction practices—rival claims to status and prestige among individuals and groups—are part of the daily routines in hospital research and clinical communities," Burri (2008: 48) notes. Third, when visual representations are produced, there is a discussion on what legitimate claims to authority different groups may make. For instance, radiologists claim that surgeons are not fully capable of "reading" the photographic plates but are rather prone to "see what they want to see" (Burri, 2008: 48). For instance, one radiologist claimed:

> Orthopedists might comprehend something about orthopedics but they do not have a generalized gaze. Other clinicians do not understand the meaning of the images, since there is a lot of hidden information which they overlook. Internists should leave it to radiologists to get that information out of the message. (Radiologist, cited in Burri, 2008: 48)

"A generalized gaze" is thus the distinguishing mark of the skilled radiologist, an unbiased gaze capable of detecting all information that is provided at the same time as an intimate understanding of the technologies used is always already present in the radiologist's gaze. This generalized gaze is an eminent example of what Foucault called *le regard médicale*, the disinterested and "objective" look of the medical professional.

An emphasis similar to that of Alac's (2008) on the connections between visuality, intellectual work, and embodiment is made by Myers (2008) in her study of how protein crystallographers are constructing computer-mediated images of proteins. In the recent shift in focus from genomics to proteomics, where journals such as *Science* and *Nature* publish new protein structures "almost weekly" (Myers, 2008: 163), scientists have turned their attention from "matters of code" to "matters of substance," that is, "[f]rom spelling out linear gene sequences to inquiring after the three-dimensional materiality, structure, and function of the protein molecules that give body to cells" (Myers, 2008: 163). Constructing three-dimensional images of proteins produced by gene sequences is, however, by no means a trivial matter; the protein crystallographer is never provided with information— presented in the form of a so-called electron density map—that is "self-evident": "[t]he crystallographer has few clues as to which parts of the protein fit in which part of the electron density. It is up to the crystallographer to recognize what amino acids fit into particular configuration of electron density," Myers (2008: 183) says. Only through extensive training is the protein crystallographer capable of constructing the image of the protein, and the work is very much a gradual process where a clearer image of the map and the model emerges. In the process of aligning theory, previous experience, and the images being constructed, the crystallographers must learn to develop a "feeling for the molecule" (a term Myers may have picked up from Keller's [1983] biography of Barbara McClintock, talking about McClintock's "feeling for the organism" guiding her pathbreaking work in cytology). Developing such a feeling includes the ability to engage in what Myers calls "the body-work" of crystallographic model building, that is, it is "[t]hrough the labor of constructing, manipulating, and navigating through protein models onscreen, that researchers are literally able to come to grips with—and so make sense of—molecular forms and functions" (Myers, 2008: 166). The experienced protein crystallographer is thus developing significant tacit skills through experience:

> The common lore in the lab is that even if well versed in crystallo-graphic theory, a crystallographer remains a novice until they have fully built their own structure. Working in the tangible medium of interactive computer graphics, modelers-in-training learn how to see, feel, and build protein structures through their embodied interaction with the data. Model-building is thus a kind of training ground for crystallographers to acquire their 'feeling for the molecule', to develop the tacit skills and craft knowledge required to visualize proteins and 'think intelligently about structure.' (Myers, 2008: 181)

The bottom line for the work is therefore to develop a "molecular vision" that is capable of bridging and bonding theoretical models and (emerging) images, to operate in the intersection of "intellectual and physical labor of research" (Myers, 2008: 169), that is, to provide visual representations of what is yet only a theoretical construction of the elementary matter of human biological system. Myers (2008) thus suggests that the visual prac-tices of protein crystallographers are always interpenetrated by the "feeling for the molecule": "Keen molecular vision is, for her [Diane, an experienced crystallographer], an embodied practice of observation and manipulation, where seeing is also a way of feeling what the structure is expressing in its form," Myers (2008: 189) says. The feeling for the molecule is manifested not only in the intellect, in the capacity to draw on sophisticated theoretical frameworks, but also in the very act of seeing/knowing, in the construction of visual forms of what has previously been only articulated in theoretical propositions.

Life on the Screen

Not only are visual practices and the image-making procedures creating struggle and controversies within organizations and firms and between professional communities and disciplines. Advanced technoscientific vision machines are used to make broader social and cultural claims to authority. Cohn (2004) examines the case of how proponents of brain scanning not just claim to have the authority to understand the immensely complicated functioning of the brain, but also claim to be in control of the keys to "life itself." Such claims are ultimately based on a strong epistemological belief in visual representations and their ability to capture and depict organic and biological life.[5] Cohn starts off by arguing that while the human genome project and its various spin-offs (genomics, genetics, pharmacogenomics, etc.) have been enormously influential in term of shaping both the scien-tific disciplines, rendering the "life sciences" the status as the "jewel in the crown"—a position previously held by chemistry in the nineteenth century, and physics in the twentieth century—and the more cultural view of what human life is, it is still failing to offer a credible and intriguing account of how life as such is constituted:

> Life as a gene is consequently a strange life: it is life not alive, a potential or capacity rather than a force or activity, even on the brink of being dissociated completely in labs and test-tubes from living things. Ironically, the reductionist trope of the biological and medical sciences thereby threatens our core conception of life itself. In sum, it is life without much vitality at all and apparently very different from that recounted through the ubiquitous representations of the 'living brain.' (Cohn, 2004: 53)

If the common sense image of life includes some kind of vitalist component, some kind of movement, change, fluidity, instance of continuous modification, then scientific theories need to address such beliefs to be fully credible on broader basis. "By shifting focus from the entire organism to the cell and then to the gene, vitalism was increasingly eschewed, becoming neither possible nor necessary," Cohn (2004: 54) suggests. For most humans, the genetic code is not an image of life that conveys the sense of multitude and variation observed in biological life. Drawing on Agamben's (1998) much-debated distinction between *bios,* denoting human, proper life in its full potentiality, and *zoe,* the "bare life," a lower form of biological and animal life not including the more sophisticated aspects of *bios* (see Esposito, 2008), Cohn (2004: 55) argues that brain scans are used to make claims to capture *bios,* "life itself," in the form of the "mind": "[B]rain scans are not seen to present the 'bare life' of rudimentary elements that DNA conveys, but more evocative of a human existence in its totality, of the essence of that makes us conscious and social, of *bios.*" The various proponents of brain scanning are therefore suggesting that the assemblage of technologies, theories, and methods for analysis they are using are in fact capable of providing inroads to life itself qua mind. For instance, a textbook cited by Cohn (2004) is waxing enthusiasm over the new opportunities: "New imaging techniques make the internal world of mind visible . . . As we enter the twenty-first century functional brain scanning machines are opening up the territory of the mind just as the first ocean-going ships once opened up the globe" (Carter, 1998, cited in Cohn, 2004: 56). Cohn (2004) argues that mind is here used synonymously with life and that prevailing technologies are capable of capturing the elementary forms of life. In doing so, proponents of brain scanning are not only making bold materialist claims but are also participating in an age-long debate over mind-matter dichotomies and relationships without properly addressing it in such terms:

> [W]hat can be witness among researchers at the forefront of the technology is a claim that the mind is being mapped onto and into the brain,

subsumed by a complex materialist paradigm, and so doing away once and for all with any legacy of dualism. The assertion is clear: that ideas of life and the mind will now be contained, enclosed, within the emerging science of the brain. (Cohn, 2004: 59)

As a consequence, such claims—the ability to account for life per se, *bios*, in the form of the activities of the mind—are ultimately based on the belief that visual practices and visual representations are, with Georges Canguilhem's useful term, "in the truth" (*dans le vrai*), surrounded by verified claims and supporting institutions (Rabinow, 1992: 241) and thereby capable of telling "true stories of life." Notwithstanding the broader social, scientific, and cultural implications from the use of brain scanning as a form of what Latour (1988: 85) called a "theatre of the proof," a form of visual demonstration of how the brain is immensely plastic and fluid, changing in its every movement and continuously responding to perceived external events, the most important aspect in this context is the strong reliance on and indeed belief in visual practices, visuality, and visual representations. While the "question concerning life" has been to date a theological, existential, and, at least partially, philosophical question, the proponents of brain scanning are providing an accurate and easily understood demonstration of life—life is mind, and mind is visually represented by brain scanning. Such ready-made answers to existential concerns are legitimate, made available, or even demanded in a society saturated with visual cultures. As a matter of fact, a range of ambiguous and highly complex social and psychological processes—and not just life—are today gaining their legitimacy through their ability to become visually represented. Cohn provides some illustrations: "Many sufferers of schizophrenia, depression, ADHD, chronic fatigue, Gulf War Syndrome are in unison seeking legitimization through the combined capital of an entrenched science and territorial claim of physicality . . . Such knowledge is not merely about confirming a diagnosis, but about how this knowledge is constituting the disease, fixing it as tangible and materially present" (Cohn, 2004: 66). Critics of the visual turn and the substantial influence of "cinematic representations" (e.g., Beller, 2006) would argue that the hegemony of the visual is threatening to exclude all other sources of reason. Vision, the eye, and the act of "having seen for oneself" are in this view becoming not only the *principal* sources of legitimate truth claims but are becoming the *only* sources of legitimate knowledge claims. Firsthand experience and direct inspection are less and less put into question. The hegemony of what Beller (2006) calls the cinematic mode of production is a regime of ocularcentrism taken to its extreme, a form of epistemology almost exclusively relying on visual perception.

In conclusion, there is no "bare eye" or unmediated vision in contemporary technoscience. Technoscience is structured around what Rheinberger (1997) calls "experimental systems" comprising a range of tools and resources including machinery, apparatus, laboratory equipment, but also theoretical schemes and collectively learned and shared practices and procedures. Experimental systems are also set up to address what Fujimura (1996) calls "doable problems," scientific problems that are possible to address within the potentiality of the given experimental system. Such experimental systems are producing visual representations that scientists collectively and individually inspect, examine, and interpret. The professional vision is thus an inextricably entangled component of the experimental system. The scientist's gaze is therefore both the effect of the given experimental system and also what is constitutive of it. Professional vision and the experimental system have a recursive relationship; neither the one without the other. Professional vision is thus always a form of situated vision, a vision bound up with theories, technologies, material resources, and disciplinary practices.

PROFESSIONAL VISION IN SCIENCE-BASED INNOVATION WORK

Bioeconomy, Biocapital, Biomediated Bodies, and Biological Exchange

The pharmaceutical industry is a field of the economy recently undergoing swift changes. Major pharmaceutical companies are struggling to maintain their innovativeness while new biotechnologies and scientific procedures are being developed and thus changing the innovation process. While major pharmaceutical companies used to be rather safe havens for practicing researchers, today the situation has radically changed. Critics argue that pharmaceutical companies are primarily interested in developing so-called "me-too drugs," that is, imitations of commercially successful drugs, rather than engaging in truly innovative work. Angell (2004: 54–55) suggests that over the period 1998–2002, only 12 out of 83 new drugs (14%) in fact were innovative drugs. Angell (2004: 73) regards this as evidence of the lost innovativeness of the pharmaceutical industry, and claims that "big pharma likes to refer to itself as a research-based industry, but it is hardly that. It could at best be described as an idea-licencing, pharmaceutical formulating and manufacturing, clinical testing, patenting, and marketing industry." In fact, the American pharmaceutical industry is spending more money on marketing and administration than on R&D (Angell, 2004: 198). Still, the pharmaceutical industry is a good example of what Pisano (2006) calls a "science-based business," a business that is not just "[a] passive user of science, but also an active participant in the process of advancing science either directly (through in-house research) or indirectly (through sponsored research)" (Pisano, 2006: xii). Pharmaceutical companies not just "apply" scientific know-how but also actively contribute to the production of knowledge in their field of interest, either directly when coworkers are part of research activities in house, or in collaboration with universities, or indirectly through the financing of research programs.

It would be unfair to judge the performance of the pharmaceutical industry solely on the basis of actual output. The production of new drugs needs to be examined in the light of the broader economic, technological, legal, and sociocultural changes over the last decades. The emergence and growth of the biotechnology industry represents a major shift in the world economy. The start for this growth is generally located to the first half of 1970s when Herbert W. Boyer, University of California, San Francisco, and Stanley N. Cohen, Stanford University, managed to develop techniques for so-called "gene splicing," recombinant DNA (rDNA). When Stanford University sought to patent the technique, the university faced both a lack of juridical standards for such a procedure and hostility from the scientific community, regarding the very idea of patenting federally funded research a major departure from the predominant modus operandi and scientific ideologies; research findings should be public and not sheltered by juridical concerns, a majority of scientists believed (Smith Hughes, 2001; Jong, 2006). However, in the early 1980s, the U.S. Supreme court passed legislation in favour of Stanford's application and new opportunities for biotechnology research were opened up. Later, major biotechnology breakthroughs such as the polymerase chain reaction (PCR), a staple technique in biotechnology work, provided further fuel for the emerging industry (Rabinow, 1996a). Today, the biotechnology and pharmaceutical industries are regarded as two closely interrelated branches of the life sciences industry that are arguably playing the same role in the twenty-first century as the manufacturing industry (e.g., the automotive industry) played for the last century (Oliver, 2000).

Research in the domain of anthropology also shows that Western pharmaceutical companies are capable of weaving intricate networks of practices, resources, and coalitions en route (Lakoff, 2006; Petryna, 2006; Rabinow and Dan-Cohen, 2006; Rajan, 2006). Seen in this view, the development of new drugs is a complex aggregate of practices comprising politics, power, biomedical scientific know-how, and capital. The strong emphasis on the biosciences as the principal drivers in today's scientific work must be understood in the context of the changing role of medicine in everyday life in the Western world. While medicine, beginning at the end of the eighteenth century, was used to regulate health, today the jurisdiction of medicine is substantially broader. Rose (2007) is here talking about the "politics of life itself":

> At the risk of simplification, one may say that the vital politics of the eighteenth and nineteenth centuries was a politics of health—of rates of birth and death, of diseases and epidemics, of the policing of water, sewage, foodstuffs, graveyards, and of the vitality of those agglomerated in towns and cities . . . [t]he vital politics of our own century looks quite different. It is neither delimited by the poles of illness and death, nor focused on eliminating pathology to protect the destiny of

the nation. Rather, it is concerned with our growing capacities to control, manage, engineer, reshape, and modulate the very vital capacities of human beings as living creatures. It is, I suggest, a politics of life itself. (Rose, 2007: 3)

One of the most important changes in contemporary capitalism is thus the emergence of "a new economic space"—"the bioeconomy"—and "a new form of capital"—"biocapital" (Rose, 2007: 6. See also Cooper, 2008). Some researchers, scholars, and commentators have embraced the idea of the bioeconomy, while others take a more sceptical stance. Enriques and Goldberg (2000) talk about a "life-science revolution" in a *Harvard Business Review* paper, and Jeremy Rifkin (1998) is anticipating what he calls *the biotech century*. Moreover, Richard Oliver (2000) speaks of *the coming biotech age*. In contrast to such enthusiastic accounts of the potentials of the new biopharmaceutical industry, critics such as Jürgen Habermas (2003), emphasizing the ethical aspects of the new possibilities of manipulating life on the level of its elementary components and processes, and Hopkins et al. (2007), undermining the very idea of a biotech revolution on the basis of empirical evidence, e.g., patents and financial performance of the biotech industry (see also Pisano, 2006), advance a somewhat more tempered idea of an emerging bioeconomy. While this new economic regime is promising to offer new medicines and therapies for a variety of illnesses—in many cases, critics contend, derived from the "lifestyles" of the Western world including obesity and diabetes—previously unseen, there are also some aspects that are calling for ethical debates and discussions, for instance, in the emerging field of stem cell research, a field of research that has been banned or restricted in some Western countries (e.g., the U.S. by the Bush administration) but embraced as the future of the life sciences in others (Brown and Kraft, 2006; Franklin, 2005; Rubin, 2008; Waldby, 2002). It is then no wonder that the bioeconomy has brought a new category of professionals—the *bioethicists* (Rajan, 2006; Salter and Salter, 2007). For instance, the recent "tissue economy," the trade with and storage of organic tissues and specimen, is one such domain of discussion (Waldby and Mitchell, 2006).[6] Do individuals, for instance, have to agree that tissues from their bodies are stored and become subject to scientific examinations, or would that be a violation of the individual's integrity? Or how should the black market for organ donation be regulated and controlled?

Clough (2008) suggests that the latest advancement in the life sciences and in the field of biotechnology has introduced a new paradigm for how the human body is conceived. From the late nineteenth century, the human body was regarded an autopoietic organism that was capable of regulating itself through a number of intricate mechanisms. In the late twentieth century, the human body is instead seen as a "biomediated body," a body that is not essentially enclosed and self-regulated but rather as an open system capable of being affected by both medical technologies and pharmaceutical substances. Drawing on the pioneering work of Norbert Wiener (1950), Clough (2008: 2) suggests that in Wiener's view, life is to be defined in *informational* terms; information is "the local organization against entropy, a temporary deferral of entropy" and that persisting information structure is life (see also Hayles, 1999: 104)[7]. However, prior to Wiener's work, the German physicist Erwin Schrödinger, one of the greatest scientists of the nineteenth century, suggested in his book *What Is Life?* (1946) that one can identify a "code-script" underlying all forms of life. Such declarations has rendered Schrödinger the status of "the founding father" of modern biology and its various subdisciplines (Kay, 2000: 61). The biomediated body is not enclosed or self-regulated but is rather a *space* where different possibilities and limitations are to be examined in detail; no longer removed from scientific and economic interests and residing in its own self-regulating biological potentiality, the body becomes what is subject to continuous modifications and amendments, in many cases directly related to economic interest:

> [T]he biomediated body is a historically specific mode of organization of material forces, invested by capital into being, as well as elaborated through various discourses of biology and physics, thermodynamics and complexity, metastability and nonlinear relationality, reconfiguring bodies, work and reproduction. (Clough, 2008: 2)

What Clough (2008) calls the biomediated body is also subject to what Thacker (2005) calls *biological exchange*, a term defined as "*the circulation and distribution of biological information, be it in a material instantiation, that is mediated by one or more value systems.* Biological exchange is the ability to render the biological not only as information, but as mobile, distributive, networked information" (Thacker, 2005: 7; emphasis in the original). The biological exchange is based on the capacity to simultaneously render biological materials informational while maintaining their organic form. That is, the biological organism is not reduced to the level of information, but the various forms of interventions (e.g., medical therapies) are examined in informational and, more specifically, *mathematical* terms. Thacker (2005) explains:

> The aim of biological exchange is not to render everything digital and immaterial, despite the industry hype over fields such as bioinformatics and genomics. Rather, the aim of biological exchange is to enable a more labile, *fluid mobility across media*—to the extent that it is literally immaterial whether the DNA is in a database or in a test tube . . . The aim of biological exchange—and by extension the aim of the current intersection between biology and computers in genetics and biotechnology—is to define biology as information while at the same time asserting the materiality of biology. Biological fields such as genetics

and biotech are unique in this respect, for, like the economics categories of production and labor, they always require material interactions at some level. (Thacker, 2005: 9)

This view of information is in conflict with Bloomfield and Vurdubakis's (1997) use of the term, denoting a "basic unity" in a "unifying representational schema" with the managerialist ambition to "transcend heterogeneity" and impose new forms of "translatability":

> Information has come to be the key term in an epistemic master narrative which translates all problems of knowledge into problems of coding . . . It constitutes the basic unity of a unifying representational schema, the means which allows diverse objects of knowledge such as economics, molecular biology, psychology, electronics, computer science, etc., to achieve mutual translatability, and thus holds the promise of a universal language of knowledge in the context of which heterogeneity can be transcended. (Bloomfield and Vurdubakis, 1997: 645)

A decontextualized concept is central to what Bloomfield and Vurdubakis (1997) call a "technocratic utopia," a world where everything can be translated into information and easily lends itself to computation. Porter (1995: 7) is here talking about an "ideal of mechanical objectivity," knowledge based "completely on explicit rules," as something that is not fully attainable because the tacit components of knowledge cannot be easily translated into information.

While Norbert Wiener (1950) thought of the biological organisms in reductionist informational terms ("the body *is* information"), Thacker (2005) suggests that in the regime of biological exchange, the body proper is—to use a Bergsonian and perhaps even Deleuzian view (See Bergson, 1988; Deleuze, 1988b; Massumi, 2002)—split into an *actual* and a *virtual* component coexisting in simultaneity; the actual body is the body proper subject to various manipulations and the virtual body is the informational body, the totality of information that can be extracted through scientific procedures and regimes of mathematization (recall the case of the surgeon's ability to bridge practices and observations of the patient's body with theoretical models). This view is not exactly Wiener's (1950) but the French philosopher Raymond Ruyer emphasized in the 1950s and 1960s that in order to function as information, it needs to be grounded and embodied in a material substratum; information is not a transcendental category, existing in some sphere devoid of time and space, but always exists in a medium.[8] "Information requires a frame to be constituted as information," Lenoir (2004: xxii–xxiii), addressing Ruyer's thinking, argues, "and that frame is provided by the active constitution and assembly of human embodiment . . . Vision, indeed any system involving 'information,' requires an interpreter, and that interpreter is the material human body grounded in the wetware of our sensorimotor systems." No information *an sich*, but only *für mich*, in other (Kantian) words. Wark (2004), on his part, suggests a synthesis of the two perspectives (Wiener's and Ruyer's) and says that information is "at once material and immaterial" because it can "[e]xists independently of a given material form, but cannot exists without any material form. The biomediated body, subject to biological exchanges, is never single-handedly reduced to the level of its informational content. The trick of the contemporary life sciences is, Thacker (2005) suggests, to maintain the material features of the biological organism while enabling the informatization of its features and functions; the body is then both immutable and material and fluid and informational at the same time:

> [T]he main challenge put forth to the pharmaceutical industry is not how to develop sustainable and effective treatments, but rather *how to transform material products continually into the long-term generation of information*. What generates economic value, from this standpoint, is an infrastructure for the production of information, yet without ever completely severing the link to the patient's biological body. (Thacker, 2005: 80–81; emphasis in the original)

What is increasingly being arrived at in the field of the life sciences is that there are no direct or uncomplicated links between informational content, the hereditary structure of the genome, and the phenotype. There is in fact an excess of information in the DNA—so-called junk DNA constituted as much as "95–97% of the genome" (Kay, 2000: 2)[9]—and in the emerging field of proteomics, it has been shown that each sequence of DNA may produce a series of different proteins, thereby making the linear connection in the "central dogma" of genetics (DNA → RNA → proteins) much more complicated (Jones, 2004: 107). The announcement of the identification of specific genes and gene sequences capable of "generating" certain diseases and medical conditions in media is thus tenuous and often demands more detailed studies to further advance the connection between (for instance) gene and disease. However, the predominant idea that biological organisms can be fruitfully translated into informational terms is a central guiding principle for the contemporary life sciences.

Biomedicalization

One of the consequences of the biomediated body is that my body is no longer in the strict sense a gift of nature, a piece of *natura naturans*, an instance of "natural" nature, but becomes what must be continually attended to and in various ways *managed* (in the conventional sense of the term), that is, is subject to what has been called a *medicalization*. Conrad (2007: 4) defines medicalization as "[a] process by which nonmedical problems become defined and treated as medical problems, usually in terms of illness and disorders." He continues: "The key to medicalization is definition. That is, a problem is defined in medical terms, described using medical language, understood through the adoption of a medical framework, or 'treated' with a medical intervention" (Conrad, 2007: 5). The biomediated body is the central entity in the regime that Clarke et al. (2003) speak of as *biomedicalization*:

> Biomedicalization is our term for the increasingly complex, multisite, multidirectional processes of medicalization that today are being both extended and reconstituted through the emergent social forms and practices of a highly and increasingly technoscientific biomedicine. (Clarke et al., 2003: 162)

They continue:

> Biomedicalization is characterized by its greater organizational and institutional reach through the meso-level innovations made possible by computer and information sciences in clinical and scientific settings, including computer-based research and record-keeping. The scope of biomedicalization processes is thus much broader, and includes conceptual and clinical expansions through the commodification of health, the elaborations of risk and surveillance, and innovative clinical applications of drugs, diagnostic tests, and treatment procedures. (Clarke et al., 2003: 165)

Clarke et al. (2003) have chosen to add the prefix *bio* to the term medicalization to underline the connection between a more broad-ranging medicalization in society and the emerging biopharmaceutical and biotechnological paradigm, and the biomediated body in a regime of biomedicalization is subject to constant care and concern. While illness and bodily decay used to be the influence of wear and time on the organism—the *durée* of the organism, its "lived time—it is now increasingly the effect of what may be described as "mismanagement."

Although the term *biomedicalization* is capable of explaining a variety of social practices, it is important to keep in mind that the process of biomedicalization is socially embedded and that there are no inevitable determinative forces rendering virtually all individual illnesses and concerns a matter of the hereditary material. Shostak and Conrad (2008) point at the sequence of genetics-geneticization-medicalization as the process wherein findings in genetics are turned into credible explanations for diseases and other forms of "deviancy" (e.g., homosexuality). Genetics is the scientific study of the human genome and geneticization is "[t]he process by which 'differences between individuals are reduced to their DNA codes, with most disorders, behaviours, and physiological variations defined, at least in part, as genetic in origin' " (Lippman, 1991; 19, cited in Shostak and Conrad,

2008: S288). Once geneticization is established as a credible explanation for a disease, a medicalization can be prescribed. Shostak and Conrad (2008) suggest that genetics and genomics are "critical components" in the abstract system of knowledge that support medicine's jurisdictional claims, and therefore the discovery of new genes and associated traits (e.g., "the depression gene") would be quickly used to advance a medicalization of those traits. Examining the three cases of genetics of depression, homosexuality, and variation in responses to chemical exposures demonstrates that there is no straight line between findings in genetics and genomics and medicalization. In some cases, social responses and interpretations of research findings prevent or further reinforce such medicalization processes (Conrad [2007] here speaks of the "demedicalization" of a condition). For instance, in the case of depression, many forms of depression are today seen as a genetically caused disease and that instituted perspective is the result, Shostak and Conrad (2008: S304–S305) argue, "[o]f cultural definitions, institutional forces, and political and economic interests that arose decades ago." These earlier events "ensure that genes associated with depression are understood to be causes of a disease condition," Shostak and Conrad (2008: S304–S305) suggest. Seeing depression as what is genetically determined was in short an explanation that did not violate any instituted social beliefs and did not threaten any competing scientific research program, and consequently depression could be translated into the sequence genetics-geneticization-medicalization without any major objection from social groups.[10] On the contrary, when the "gay gene" was sought for, a project rendering homosexuality a genetically derived "condition" (even though homosexuality were regarded a disease well into the 1970s in countries like the U.S. and Sweden—as late as 1979 in the latter case—the concept of disease was carefully avoided), this led to strong and negative responses from the gay community which undermined the possibility for translating genetic markers into anything more than a scientific curiosity of limited theoretical and practical value:

> The case of homosexuality vividly demonstrates how social movement activism can reinforce a critical juncture, especially by shifting regimes of credibility . . . That is, in contrast to the case of depression, in which there is a very little redundancy in events preceding and following the critical juncture, in the case of homosexuality, social movement organization, mobilization, and institutionalization are woven throughout the sequence in which genetics research is embedded. (Shostak and Conrad, 2008: S307)

Shostak and Conrad's (2008) three case studies suggest that medicalization/biomedicalization is not an innate or determinate force or process wholly in the hands of scientific elites and major pharmaceutical and biotechnology companies. Instead, what is regarded as a credible explanation for a medical condition and what should be regarded as "normal" and what is "pathological" (with Canguilhem's [1991] phrase) are ultimately decided by social communities. "[G]enetic information does not always lead to geneticization, nor does geneticization invariably lead to medicalization," Shostak and Conrad (2008: S310) conclude. They continue: "[T]here is a lack of consistent fit among genetics, geneticization, and medicalization. Examining this lack of consistent fit reveals that genetic information takes its meaning from its embeddedness in different moment in sequence of events and their social structural consequences." Not all genetic markers identified are endowed with the status of being granted further research activities, eventually leading to practically useful therapies and commercially successful drugs. There are still possibilities for selection and choices among competing alternatives and these alternatives are socially embedded.

Biosocial Anxieties in the Age of Biomedicalization

Notwithstanding the research findings of, for instance, Shostak and Conrad (2008), given the changes in how technoscience and the life sciences can shape and form the human body and render its tissues a source of economic activity, it is little wonder that a certain degree of anxiety in broader circles regarding where these technological and scientific advancement may take us in the future (Franklin, 2007; Franklin and Roberts, 2006). As Braidotti (2008) has emphasized, discussing Jürgen Habermas's book *The Future of Human Nature* (see Rabinow [2008: 20–25] for a summary and analysis), the more conservative reactions have been outright technophobic and call for a "moral universalism": "Seldom has the future of human nature been the subject of such concerns and in-depth discussions by our wise public intellectuals as in our globalized age . . . This technophobic reaction to our bio-technological progress has led to a return to Kantian moral universalism," Braidotti (2008: 10) says. At the same time that Braidotti is sceptical of such moral universalism, she is claiming that contemporary capitalism is on the verge of developing forms of "biopiracy":

> Contemporary capitalism is bio-political, in that it aims at controlling all that lives; it has already turned into a form of bio-piracy in that it aims at exploiting the generative powers of women, animals, plant genes and cells. (Braidotti, 2008: 10)

When it comes to the most sordid practices of what Waldby and Mitchell (2006) call the *tissue economy*, the term *biopiracy* may be well founded, but the entire domain of technoscience and the life sciences is a well-instituted and well-regulated domain of social practice. Tragic and deeply disturbing events such as "organ theft" and other violations of human rights are perhaps not as widely spread as one may fear. On the other hand, as soon as there are the scientific and technical possibilities for transplanting organs, there is always a risk of emerging black markets relying on criminal activities. The demand for certain organs appear to be higher than supply and therefore uncontrolled biopiracy may be a growing problem for the future: "Among the most disturbing historical trends," Sharp (2000: 296) writes, "is the tendency within the medical marketplace to exploit the bodies of the poor and disenfranchised, where paupers frequently emerge as being of greater worth dead than alive." Emerging technological and scientific possibilities may increasingly position the world's poor populations as repositories of organic material for the benefit for the financially endowed (Shah, 2006). This a deeply troubling view that certainly demands its cadres of "bioethicists" and thoughtful policies.

Another consequence from the rise of a bioeconomy in control of biocapital is that new biological entities are produced, embodying in the very literal sense the state-of-the-art know-how in the field of the life sciences. Today, there are, for instance, 2,000 to 3,000 types of genetically modified mice in the world (Braidotti, 2006: 101), all displaying specific bioinformational features that are of interest for different research programs. Although these fabricated technoscientific organisms are still animals in the conventional sense of the term, they are also, with Braidotti's (2006: 101) formulation, "[c]yber-teratological apparatus[es] that scramble the established codes and thus destabilize the subject." Just like the hero in Paul Verhoven's *Robocop* (1987), split in two and being the synthesis of biological and technological materials—"Part man, part machine, all cop," the tagline announced—the laboratory animal is part animal (i.e., biological organism), part a disease-producing machinery—a "monstrous" creation serving in the interests of the technosciences, and allegedly (and heavily contested by, for instance, animal rights activists) mankind at large. Landecker (2007) is similarly emphasizing that the specimens of biological research are *mixed bodies*, operating in the borderland between nature and technology:

> [M]ice, and cells of biological research are altered by humans environmentally or physically to do 'unnatural things,' but they are not literally machines. They occupy a form of 'edge habitat,' where organisms with their own natural histories comes into contact with and are shaped by the technological, industrial environment of human beings. Living technologies such as flies, mice, and cultured cells are part of the attempt to stabilize the innate flux and variation of living things as well as to simplify and standardize the objects of research as much as possible . . . Genetically and physically reshaped living matter plays an infrastructural role in making biology the same over time and space. (Landecker, 2007: 25–26)

Laboratory animals are then not just enabling certain scientific possibilities and potentials, but they are also helping to stabilize science across time and space, thereby making science become transparent and open for comparisons. What kind of laboratory animal used in the laboratory work is carefully accounted for in scientific reports and papers to allow for thoughtful replication of experiments and for a review of research results. Thus, the body of the laboratory animal is, as Braidotti (2002: 244) suggests, "far from a biological essence." Instead it is "[a] crossroad of intensive forces; it is a surface of inscriptions of social codes." The laboratory animals, on the level of the hereditary material being "cyber-teratological apparatuses," are eminent examples of what Gaston Bachelard called *un théorème réifié*. The laboratory animals are living and malleable forms of biocapital that can be used in scientific endeavours. Thus one can only agree with Terranova (2004) when she emphasizes the "bottom-up" procedure when investigating the elementary forms of life:

> Mary Shelley's Frankenstein . . . started from the wrong premises. If you want to reproduce the complexities of life, you do not start with organs, stitch them all together and then shock them into life. You start more humbly and modestly, *at the bottom*, with a multitude of interactions in a liquid and open milieu. (Terranova, 2004: 101)

Even though laboratory animals may not appear as terrifying as Mary Shelley's fiend, they are still teratological creations, machines in the etymological sense of the word, derived from the Greek expression for "trick against nature" (Simondon, 1980: xiv). Neither do the laboratory animals, contrary to Frankenstein's monster, speak back; they are devoid of agency and can only hope to attain credible and influential spokesmen.

In the future, the emerging bioeconomy will arguably be propelled by fruitful collaborations between universities and private ventures. For instance, a major impetus for the biotech and pharmaceutical industry in the late 1980s and 1990s was the international Human Genome Project, giving rise to a full mapping of the human genome. Among other things, the Human Genome Project helped to develop new techniques for drug development such as genomics and pharmacogenomics which are promising to develop "personalized medicines" and lower costs for the soaring new drug development expenditures more generally. For instance, in a report published in 2001 by the prestigious consulting firm Boston Consulting Group, it is suggested that "by applying genomics technology, companies could on average realize savings of nearly $300 million and two years per drug, largely as a result of efficiency gains. That represents a 35 percent cost and 15 percent time savings" (cited in Kahn, 2008: 741). However, as Rajan (2006: 28) underlines, the very concept of genomics (and its various forms) "is not a stable referent": "Genomics itself . . . is multiple things, but first and foremost an articulation of experimental with informational science. To this extent, it involves an articulation of different scientific perspectives on biological systems, of mathematics and computational biology on the one hand with molecular genetics and cell biology on the other." Given that new drug development is increasingly becoming "informatized," that is, human responses to various chemical compounds are "mathematized" and rendered calculable—"liquid" in Lakoff's (2006) terms—and thus possible to compare over large samples and populations, new drug development is very much a search for interesting chemical compounds through the use of advanced scanning techniques. Rajan (2006) points at the rhetoric of the industry:

> The pervasive rhetoric surrounding such rapid information generation is, not surprisingly, almost one of breathlessness, conveying a sense of being overwhelmed with a huge amount of (presumably) valuable data that is virtually impossible to keep up with . . . while nobody quite knows the biological significance of even a fraction of it, any piece of information in this haystack could turn out to be extremely valuable, therapeutically and commercially. (Rajan, 2006: 43)

We can here see how the pharmaceutical industry is changing from being based on laboratory practices, including the close collaboration between synthesis chemists and pharmacologists conducting in vitro and in vivo trials to verify the qualities of the compound, to an "information science," the mechanized and computer-supported evaluation of large samples. These changes in the industry, brought on by new scientific procedures, new techniques, new market opportunities, and new juridical frameworks and codes of ethics, are strongly reshaping the professional ideologies of the pharmaceutical industry. Given these newly emerging conditions, the pharmaceutical industry—serving as the nexus between "pure" science and commercial innovation work—is an excellent milieu for studying visual practices.

NEW DRUG DEVELOPMENT

New drug development, an activity comprising both biotechnical and pharmaceutical companies, is here seen as a complex social practice embedded in professional expertise in the technoscientific field of the biolife sciences. Seen in this way, new drug development is an open system of innovation strongly conforming to both regulatory demands and scientific standard operation procedures and the economic and managerial interests that are ultimately determining the day-to-day practices. Historically, new drug development has been strongly influenced by synthesis chemistry (Rajan, 2006: 16) and more specifically the synthesis of small molecules that could be used as the active component in a new compound. Given the vast "molecular space" being examined, much medicinal chemistry (synthesis chemistry work in pharmaceutical companies) is concerned with what Nightingale (1998) calls "number reduction": "[T]here are: 10^{180} possible drugs, 10^{18} molecules that are likely to be drug like, 10^8 compounds that are available in libraries, 10^3

drugs, not only 10^2 profit making compounds. Drug discovery involves reducing the 'molecular space' that profitable drugs will be found in, to a small enough volume that empirical testing can take place" (Nightingale, 1998: 704). In other words, the sense of being forced to navigate vast masses of information—a "tsunami of data" is generated in the industry, Thacker (2005: 128) suggests[11]—and to be demanded to make choices and selection on the basis of incomplete information is nothing new in the industry. However, these traditional methods are today being challenged by a series of new innovations in the domain of biotechnology, genomics, and pharmacogenomics. Especially pharmacogenomics, defined as the integration of "[t]raditional pharmaceutical sciences such as biochemistry with annotated knowledge of genes, proteins and single nucleotide polymorphisms" (Gassman and Reepmeyer, 2005: 239), is of interest for pharmaceutical companies. These techniques/methods are promising to identify "[a]ssociations between genetic markers for drug response and those genes directly involved in the development of different forms of pathology" (Hedgecoe and Martin, 2003: 337). That is, pharmacogenomics are promising to offer more personalized medicines that will (hopefully) eliminate the undesirable side effects.

Speaking in more formal terms, new drug development is denoting, as Hara (2003: 19) suggests, "the causal relationship between chemical and the biological activities, not to the chemical itself." In the process, so-called new chemical entities (NCEs) are related to the biological organisms—initially in in vitro or in in silico studies, and eventually in laboratory animals and thereafter, if proven successful, in humans (volunteers such as students) and ultimately patients. Speaking with Barry (2005), the NCE (and more specifically, the molecule being the active substance in the compound) is "informed" with content and meaning as the NCE is passing through various laboratory and clinical tests en route, proving its efficacy and lack of (intolerable) side effects. More specifically, this inscribing of bioinformational content into the targeted molecule is dependent on a relatively stable relationship between the molecule and the disease being explored. Lakoff (2008: 744) speaks of this relationship as "disease specificity":

> To circulate in the regulated system of biomedicine, a drug is supposed to operate according to its model of the relation between illness and intervention. According to this model—'disease specificity'—illnesses are stable entities that exists outside of their embodiment in particular individuals and that can be explained in terms of specific causal mechanisms that are located within the sufferer's body. Disease specificity is a tool of administrative management. It makes possible to gather populations for large-scale research, and more generally, to rationalize health practice. (Lakoff, 2008: 744)

In domains of medicine where the disease specificity is a source of concern, for instance, in the field of psychopharmacology, drugs targeting the central nervous system, it is much more complicated to develop useful drugs than in domains with a stable target and high degree of "disease specificity" (in, e.g., cardiovascular medicine such as the regulation of hypertension).

The new drug development process includes a variety of heterogeneous resources including:

1. human actors such as chemists, pharmacologists, toxicologists, different functions in the company, corporate managers, academics, doctors, patients, government officers, politicians, activists and the general public.
2. non-human entities such as drugs, materials, instruments and facilities; and
3. institutional and structural factors such as strategies, organizational linkages, human networks, organizational capabilities, funds, markets, regulations, sciences and clinical trials. (Hara, 2003: 32)

New drug development is a complex social undertaking that is constituted like an open system that is carefully corresponding to changes in the external environment. That is, economic, political, and technological changes in the pharmaceutical companies' milieu are much likely to affect how the procedures are arranged and what NCEs and candidate drugs are selected. For instance, the progress of clinical trials of other pharmaceutical companies are of great importance for individual pharmaceutical companies. Even though new drug development is rooted in technoscientific procedures and regulatory demands, there is room for substantial managerial influence in terms of strategies and tactics to secure the long-term competitiveness of the firm.

Professional Vision in New Drug Development

The pharmaceutical industry has undergone radical changes since the early 1990s as the entire field of genomics and pharmacogenomics has gradually been established not only as a field of basic research but as what is having very practical implications for the field of new drug development. The study of PharmaCo (a pseudonym for a major multinational pharmaceutical company) suggests that these changes have brought a new need for competence and technology but also that the pressure to deliver new innovative drugs has increased rather then been lowered. Many commentators and pharmaceutical industry coworkers suggest that these new technologies and scientific practices have in fact not resulted in the increased output that some of the enthusiastic spokespersons claimed they would produce. Instead, pharmaceutical companies are operating under the pressure to adopt new scientific practices and new regulatory demands and these increased costs and lowered output of innovative drugs have caused significant concern in executive communities in the industry and among financial analysts and commentators. It is then little wonder that the largest pharmaceutical companies (e.g., Pfizer) have grown through acquisitions rather than organically. In that respect, PharmaCo is rather representative of the overarching tendencies in the industry. Being historically very successful and having a massive cash flow derived from a small number of successful drugs, the company experienced its first period of downsizing when some activities were outsourced at the beginning of the new millennium. In addition, the company endured a few disappointing new drug applications as newly developed drugs were not approved by the FDA, the American Food and Drug Administration. During the period of the interviews, the company was therefore gradually adjusting to these new conditions, and for some of the older coworkers, used to working in a milieu characterized by joint scientific interests and evolving around laboratory practices, the influence of more conventional managerial decision making came as a bit of a shock. One of the clinical project leaders testified to the new regime of working:

> As we have been given larger and more complex challenges in the pharmaceutical industry and since we have started to fail our projects, there is a certain decision-making anxiety in the organization. Now, we have learned that every single decision may have significant consequences . . . Decisions, normally taken on a certain level, tend to migrate up the organizational hierarchy because no one is willing to make the decision. There's a fear of failing, quite simple. (Clinical Team Leader, Development)

In the end of the first decade of the new millennium, the company is, however, reporting substantial profits and the cash flow is strong, but the company is still struggling to adapt to the new situation. One of the consequences of the pressure to lower costs and to deliver new and innovative drugs is that there is an even stronger focus on abandoning "curiosity driven" and "blue sky stuff"—research that is primarily deriving from the researchers' own theoretical interests and scientific ambitions—and instead what Fujimura (1996) calls "doable problems" are increasingly focused. That is, the pressure to deliver new candidate drugs and, further down the road, new registered drugs has gradually displaced the more lighthearted experimental culture that previously existed at PharmaCo and in the pharmaceutical industry more generally. One such domain where the distinction between possible research methods were contrasted and debated in the firm was first in terms of use of in vivo, in vitro, and in silico testing and, more specifically, what laboratory animals to use in the in vivo testing. One of the researchers pointed at the benefits of different so-called "animal models":

> A mouse weighs like 20 grams in comparison to a dog that weighs 20 kilos. Thus, the amount of use of the substance is one thing. If you look

at rodents and compare a mouse and a rat, then we are a bit unconventional here; by tradition, most of us work with rats . . . There are much more tools [Swedish, *redskap*] there [in mouse models]: Knock-outs [genes] and transgenes and reagence [Swedish, *reagens*] is much better in the mouse than in a rat. (Researcher, Discovery)

Suggesting that the use of mice would provide a whole new set of opportunities, the researcher is critical of the inability to abandon the rat models; adopting a mouse model would open up for a variety of new analytical procedures but that would demand to leave the expertise in rat models behind. Like in domains of technoscience, laboratory practices are path-dependent. In addition, the entire domain of in vivo testing, a field of expertise that the PharmaCo coworkers take great pride in and generally regard as being a source of historically successful projects, has been subject to discussions. As new analytical models and tools in the field of in silico screening (i.e., computer-mediated screening procedures) and in vitro screening (i.e., "in-the-test-tube" screening, using lower specimens such as cell lines as the largest analytical entity) have been developed and successfully applied, the value of in vivo testing has been called into question. However, for the more senior coworkers, in vivo testing is important for controlling the biological effects on "higher organisms." In general, the leap from lower organic systems to higher organic systems has been a concern for the entire field of genetics and genomics. Even though leading scientists in the field such as the Nobel Prize laureate Jacques Monod once claimed "that what is true for the bacteria is also true for the elephant" (Keller, 1983), there is reason to believe that such a seamless change from the micro-level to the macro-level is not possible without some more advanced mechanisms in the hereditary material. One of the researchers addressed this concern:

We ask for evidence for these observations in humans . . . in lower systems, like in a mouse or a cell line. [managers ask] 'Do you observe the same thing there?' No, of course we do not generally do that. Thus we should continue working on it. That must be a wrong attitude . . . I think we are much more comfortable working low down in simple systems, making observations in a cell line, and then slowly working all the way up to mouse, or pig or a primate. (Researcher, Discovery)

As basic research is operating on "lower biological systems" (e.g., a cell line), the pharmaceutical companies are focusing on the interaction between the active substance and the integrated biological system. Therefore, it is not really possible to "extrapolate" results from lower biological systems to higher systems. This makes new drug development work a rather complicated endeavour. The research claimed that there was a lack of risk taking in the company and that many of the managers encouraged an engagement with the lower biological systems, being a "comfort zone" that did not demand the same scientific ingenuity as when moving up to more sophisticated biological systems. In general, the researcher was concerned that the lack of risk taking and the use of standardized "research packages" including methodologies, analytical procedures and ready-made, off-the-shelf substance libraries inhibited innovative and new thinking: "We screen our libraries, the same libraries as in principle all other large pharmaceutical companies are screening. We also use the same enzyme or protein as other companies. I am not concerned there is too little thinking going on for the time being," the researcher argued.

In Vivo vs. In Vitro Screening: Direct Versus Mediated Vision

One of the central topics of discussion in the company was whether in vivo or in vitro or in silico screening was the most adequate and robust analytical procedures for identifying new candidate drugs that would eventually prove to hold water and be registered drugs and launched in the market. Since the top management of PharmaCo had used substantial amounts of statistics, showing that a specific amount of new candidate drugs was needed to produce the desirable number of new registered drugs, the discovery activities were structured in accordance with this "adequate level of output" principle. Consequently, the laboratory researchers, for instance, the synthesis chemists, were evaluated in terms of number of syntheses conducted rather than the quality of the molecules delivered. This emphasis on "molecule counting" was harshly criticized by the laboratory researchers and was regarded as being at odds with both the predominant scientific ideologies and the company culture. In general, PharmaCo was held to be turning into a form of process industry feeling out molecules whose potentiality were never fully evaluated prior to their entrance into the development phases. A variety of stories was told explaining this fierce emphasis on the output of molecules. One of the researchers said that the concept of "the new biology," including a variety of scientific paradigms and technologies such as pharmacogenomics and systems biology, had been brought into the company rather late in comparison to the competitors:

> PharmaCo were rather late to adopt this 'new biology'. We worked for a long time with the traditional procedures for making drugs. We were laggards . . . sure we did jump the bandwagon but later than the most and when we finally did there was a certain degree of panic in some quarters because of our late entrance. Then things went fast . . . I still don't think that we have abandoned the old in vivo work. (Researcher, Discovery)

Being in the position to "catch up" with competitors, the researcher argued, led to a situation where the historically successful methods for developing new drugs were more or less regarded as being obsolete. In general, there has been a strong tendency that new technologies have been developed on the basis of the latest scientific advancement in the field. Another researcher, specializing in laboratory equipment and technology, addressed this issue: "There is a continuous development in the analysis apparatus. There is, I must say, a rather intense development . . . both in instrumentation and technologies of separation" (Researcher, Discovery). However, there was no swift or momentary change from the (old-fashioned) in vivo screening procedures to the (allegedly more up-to-date) in vitro and in silico screening models. The strong local in vivo tradition at these sites was not abandoned overnight but was generally regarded as being very useful in some of the stages of the development of new candidate drugs. One of the researchers emphasized the need for safeguarding the therapeutic effects of a specific molecule prior to its developmental work at the same time as the costs were recognized:

> You are capable of observing quite a bit in the in vivo work but at the same time the in vivo screening is quite heavy and takes a lot of time. You learn a lot and you see a few things; you can never bring the study into the clinic unless you've done the in vivo part. (Researcher, Discovery)

He continued:

> In vivo screening implies a heavy workload. It is no 'high-throughput screening', really. It takes a darn long time . . . Of course, to be able to work with large amounts of substances to select [the most promising one], you certainly need in silico and in vitro models, no doubt about it. (Researcher, Discovery)

Ultimately, one may argue, following the analytical framework advocated in this book, the debate over the costs and benefits of in vivo versus in vitro and in silico screening is matter of professional vision. The in vivo system is operating on the basis of higher biological models (i.e., the laboratory animal's response to a specific compound), and the in vitro and in silico are operating on lower biological models. The in vivo model is therefore providing better opportunities for observing an integrated response to the compound whereas the in vitro and in silico models are only showing the effects in its bits and pieces. Expressed differently, the researchers accustomed to the in vivo procedures were a bit concerned about the idea of mediated vision, vision that was supported by the use of advanced analytical models such as the so-called high-throughout screening procedures. The use of high throughput screening was a recurrent topic of discussion in the study. For instance, one of the researcher pointed at the emphasis on output as the principal argument in favour of this analytical method:

> One of the problems today is that we have become very process-driven and we rely very heavily on high-throughput screening at the

moment. I think that is counter-intellectual, I don't like high-through-put screening. I feel we have to do it, but the sooner we get rid of it, the better. Because it's throwing stuff against the wall and hope that something sticks and saying 'yes, that's worth picking off the wall'. We didn't do that in the old days. There was no possibility doing it, so you have to exercise your brain in what you are going to make. (Researcher, Discovery)

He continued:

My earnest hope and belief is that HTS [high-throughput screening] is a [vanishing] phenomenon and that HTS will be relegated to a minor activity in ten years time. By that time we will have structures of most of the major proteins and that will be modelling in silico and making libraries to test hypotheses. (Researcher, Discovery)

Another researcher similarly deplored the widespread use of high-throughput screening and thought that it would have been much more useful to carefully examine past achievements rather that adopting new fads offhand:

I have never heard anyone within this company ask the question why we were so successful in the end of the 70s and the early 80s. Why were we so creative, how do we manage to produce that many candidate drugs in such a small organization? What were the success factors and how should we reproduce them? Rather than trying to do what we were good at, we were more concerned about what others did. And the grass is always greener in your neighbour's garden: we saw companies investing in bio-technology and micro-biology and the latest fad high-throughput screening, molecular modelling, drug design and all that. I ended up in a situation where I did things because top management should think I was modern up to date and not just an old reactionary, right. Sooner or later you realize that it does not work. You cannot do things you do no believe in. (Researcher, Discovery)

The high-throughput screening is in general a method that is depriving the researcher of his or her analytical skills, all residing in the professional vision of the skilled synthesis chemist or pharmacologist. It is an analytical method that is operating on the basis of *programmability*, the ability to compute a number of parameters that should be checked in the actual molecule. The principal critique against such "automated vision" is that while the procedure may be good at screening large quantities of molecules, the approach is undervaluing *synthetic* thinking, the ability to make connection between two or more seemingly heterogeneous or incompatible parts. In the high-throughout screening paradigm, the professional vision is already inscribed into the program directing the analytical procedure. This approach testifies to the belief that for the researcher *all skills* may be effectively translated into the apparatus; there are no tacit elements that are not captured by the high-throughput screening technology. As a consequence, the researcher's skills, experiences, and know-how are regarded as being a source of competitive advantage that may be subject to automatization and formalized into procedures and technological devices, all for the sake of being able to screen large amounts of substances and hopefully detect the most promising molecule given desirable qualities. Some of the researchers addressed such reductionist and technology-mediated forms of screening, arguing that there is in fact a value in the "procedures of looking": "This lasts step, [including] the human brain and two eyes looking and seeking to interpret, that is a step that cannot be automated, that is very clear. That is a gigantic gap, really" (Researcher, Discovery). Anther researcher emphasized the close connection between motivation, curiosity, and vision in the day-to-day work:

> It is curiosity that is propelling the researcher's work: To look at the gel and the spots on the paper. We see causal relations that no one else has seen previously. I think that is the whole thing; nothing more intriguing than that. (Researcher, Discovery)

In summary, the uses of technologies, tools, and procedures that were undermining the analytical capacities and the prerogatives of the laboratory researcher were criticized for reducing their work to a series of procedures that could individually lend themselves to automatization and what could be called *programmability*, the translation of knowledge work based on both explicit and tacit elements into fixed procedures. In opposition to such attempts at eliminating costly analytical procedures in laboratory work, the laboratory researchers claimed that the ability to examine the effects of the focal compound on higher-level biological systems would help detecting and selecting more solid new candidate drugs. In the present regime, strongly emphasizing the output of new compounds, led to a situation of work overload for the development organization, serving to further refine and carry out clinical trials on the proposed candidate drugs. What the laboratory researchers in PharmaCo suggest is that the ability to use one's professional vision wisely under determinate conditions is potentially a more effective method for identifying and selecting new candidate drugs. The professional vision, comprising all the know-how and experience accumulated over entire careers, is not what is easily being brought into some technology or some laboratory procedure. It is rather what is constitutive of professional identities on both individual and collective levels.

Visual Representations in the Lead Generation and Lead Optimization Phases in New Drug Development

In the early phases of new drug development, in the so-called lead generation, LG (the identification of the active compound in the forthcoming candidate drug), and lead optimization, LO (the "refinement" of the series of molecules provided from the LG phase), a variety of vision technologies was used. For instance, mass spectrometry, liquid chromatography, and X-ray crystallography are widely used methods in medicinal chemistry. According to the interviewees, some of these methods had developed substantially over the last period of time; mass spectrometry is "better and faster" and "more detailed," according to one of the biotransformation analysts at the Distribution Medicine and Pharmacokinetics (DMPK) department. In the case of liquid chromatography, the pumps pushing the substance through the so-called *column*, filled with small pellets separating the substance into its components, had been technically improved and the column was also more dense than previously. Therefore, the data provided was more detailed—"now, we have an adequate degree of sensitivity in the instruments that it is not a major concern anymore," the biotransformation chemist argued—and above all were faster—the time for making one analysis was reduced from 13 minutes to 6 minutes. One of the biotransformation chemists accounted for the new technologies:

> I work with mass spectrometry and liquid chromatography a lot and we have two things limiting us capacity-wise. We are using something called UPLC [Ultra Performance Liquid Chromatography] . . . that have managed to increase the density of the particles in the column. Chromatography is [based on] small balls and the smaller they are the higher is the efficiency in the separation we are aiming at. They [the equipment company] were the first to manage to reduce the particles structure and pack them more densely. In addition, they have built a system capable of handling these pressures, because the pressures are very high. All this has helped reducing the time for analysis with 100%, from thirteen minutes, which was fast for being done the conventional way in biotransformation, to six minutes. (Biotransformation chemist 2, DMPK)

In addition to the improvements in the hardware, the new technologies were complemented with software that could conduct some of the analyses that were previously done by a DMPK analyst:

> What is an important and heavy thing, is this with data-processes, but here we have new software helping us . . . We do not know what we are looking for; we know that we have a *parent* [English in the original] that is eventually transformed into various things and then we need to be able to sort out these unknown things fast and safely. When we do in

vitro studies, which are quite limited, we can still guess what will happen but it is very time-consuming to identify all these things. We have
very low concentrations and there are a lot of background noise that
intervene, so it is not very evident what is happening. But we have this
software we are using and helping us doing all these things very, very
fast. It compares the test with a 'blank' [a reference point substance],
and everything it may find in the test that is not present in the blank is
sorted out as a possible metabolite [products from the metabolism pro-
cess] and then we need to intervene to determine whether this is the case
or not. If we did not have access to that software, we wouldn't be able
to run that many tests. (Biotransformation chemist 2, DMPK)

As a consequence, the new technology helped reduce the time for the analysis
significantly: "It may take you five to ten minutes what previously took you
30–60 minutes, so that is quite a difference," the biotransformation chemist
argued. In general, the new technologies helped reduce the lead times in the
analysis work but also used more information than previously. One of the
biotransformation chemists estimated that the uses of information in the early
phases of biotransformation had increased with a "factor 50," but also added
that this impressive figure is due to the poor previous uses of information.

Another example of how visuality techniques play a central role in the LG
and LO phases of new drug development is the use of modelling and visual
representations in what is called *computational chemistry*. Computational
chemistry is a computer-based science aimed at exploring the geometry of
the molecule, its kinetics, and its various mechanical features on the basis
of computer-based media. Computational chemists use software to predict
how a certain series of molecules are behaving under specific conditions. For
instance, for a synthesis chemist synthesizing a molecule in the laboratory, it
is complicated to know beforehand what the actual molecule will look like;
it could, as one of the synthesis chemists said, be "like a snowball or a reasonably long worm" or it can "open and close itself." Computational chemistry could examine such geometries and is thus a supporting science enabling
a prediction of how molecules will behave under specific conditions. The
output from computational chemistry departments is virtual libraries where
series of molecules—molecules with minor modifications belonging to the
same "family" of molecules—are examined and specified. In addition, computational chemistry produces visual representations of molecules, proteins,
and so forth, thereby helping synthesis chemists and others involved in the
new drug development activities understand how the interaction between
the molecule and the receptor is occurring. Needless to say, when making
such visual representations, a number of assumptions are done, rendering the procedure less complex than it actually is. For instance, when pre-
dicting how a molecule is docked onto a receptor in a protein, it is often
assumed that only the molecule and not the protein can change its form,
and water molecules otherwise intervening in the process are eliminated.

However, notwithstanding such assumptions, there may be some value in providing visual representations of activities at the molecular level. One of the computational chemists thought the visual representations "make quite a difference":

> That is how we can make a difference. You can dock a molecule and show it for your clients, the computational chemists or the synthesis chemists, or the biologists. It is convincing and looks really cool. If you add 3D and you put on the eyeglasses you see it in three dimensions . . . It is very seductive and is easy to believe in, even though it may be totally wrong. (Computational chemist)

If nothing else, visual representation is inspirational and potentially leads to new ideas on how to proceed when refining the molecule: "It may give a few new insights but a large share is inspiration, that people enjoy it and have ideas—'alright, this is what it looks like, let's test a few things' . . . I don't think it hurts, anyway" (Computational chemist). The advanced computer-based media used in computational chemistry is capable of producing highly evocative images that give both the informed viewer and the layman the impression of seeing things as they do in fact appear on the molecular level: "You can add the surface of a protein and its looks really cool," the computational chemist argued.

In the early phases of the new drug development process, the lead generation and the lead optimization phases, synthesis and computational chemists and DMPK experts use a number of visualization technologies (mass spectrometry, liquid chromatology, X-ray crystallography, analytical software) that are of great help when seeking to understand how molecules and receptors interact. However, although these visual technologies promise a lot, it is at times rather complicated to use the technology effectively. For instance, the use of x-ray crystallography, helping to examine the crystal structure of a specific molecule, is an excellent tool when functioning properly, but in practice it is highly time consuming—it may take a few years to examine a molecule that is complicated to crystallize—and the technology is costly. For instance, when being asked to choose between an X-ray crystallographer and hiring another synthesis chemist, the computation chemist did not hesitate for a second to pick the synthesis chemist if the costs were the same:

> If I could choose between a x-ray crystallographer and a chemist I would easily have chosen the chemist who could synthesize the molecules. That depends; x-ray crystallography, it is brilliant if it works all the time; you synthesize your molecule and you get your roentgen structure right away, and it leads forward to new ideas. (Computational chemist)

As suggested, X-ray crystallography is a very useful tool when functioning properly, verifying working hypotheses and potentially leading to new and innovative ideas, but it is also a method that demands analytical efforts and thinking and that is at times complicated to use effectively. In such cases, it may be more useful to have yet another colleague capable of both synthesizing new molecules and formulating new research questions.

Also on a more aggregated level, visualization may play an increasing role. One of the principal scientists in the discovery organization of PharmaCo claimed that the ability to visualize entire biological pathways would be helpful when making decisions in the daily work:

> Visualizing the pathways and the connections, that has a powerful effect . . . The pathways could give you a good feel for what is important. How it can be visualized, I think, has a big impact, yes . . . If you have a visualization, a 3D of the pathway interactions, it's going to make a bigger impact. (Principal Scientist, Discovery, PharmaCo)

Based on the interview material from PharmaCo, one may conclude that the ability to visualize and build models of complicated biological processes at the cellular and microbiological level is of both great analytical and motivational value. One of the concerns appear to be that there are few very well-developed software packages available for such forms of visualization.[12]

In summary, the vision in technoscience is never unmediated vision; it is a vision mediated by technoscientific apparatuses, in turn being based on a variety of technicity such as digital technologies, optics, mechanical devices, and so forth. What is inspected is images that are produced on the basis of a number of integrated and mutually constitutive technologies being part of the technoscientific apparatus. The practicing researcher must always trust in the technoscientific apparatus, that the plates are capable showing underlying matter. In the work of the scientist, there is much doubt, but what cannot be doubted without undermining the entire project is the capacity of the technological apparatus to provide adequate images of what is subject to inspection (Roth, 2009). The expertise and skill involved in professional vision is primarily concerned about detecting and isolating what is present in the visual representations, in the plates, images, and graphs being produced in the science work. This professional vision is indeed, as suggested by Daston (2008: 102), "disciplined in every sense of the word."

SUMMARY AND CONCLUDING REMARKS

"Experimental truth," Shapin (1994: 124) writes, discussing the constitution of modern scientific methodologies, "was to be sought by selfless selves, seeking not celebrity or private advantage but the civic good. This was a conception of the gentlemanly civic actor thoroughly familiar from early modern ethical writing, and English scientific practitioners proposed to reconstitute the natural philosopher on just that civic model." This ethos for the search for truth was established in the early-modern period, during the period of the institutionalization of scientific procedures. In the case of PharmaCo, one may think of the various new technologies and procedures as the extension of this ethos of the "selfless selves," the "view from nowhere" that has been the analytical ideal in much scientific work. The procedures of high-throughput screening are here what is capable of identifying the most promising molecules in large samples on the basis of a number of analytical parameters. While professional vision may not be suspected of, as during Robert Boyle's times, being skewed, corrupt, and prone to succumb to fantasies (Boyle excluded female observers for this reason) or any other "subjective bias," it is today generally regarded as being *too slow* to effectively cover the terrains of billions of molecules enacted by the pharmaceutical companies. The history of the sciences are demonstrating what Ihde (2002: 54) calls a "visualist trajectory," an emphasis on specific ways of seeing, ranging from the visual inspection of the bare eye to the mediated vision of either visual technologies (i.e., Galileo's telescope) or more advanced procedures such as those employed in new drug development work. Science is about witnessing and analysis. Even though witnessing is not always taking place in direct observation—the field of modern physics would, for instance, be inconceivable in such terms—the very idea of witnessing is strongly emphasized in scientific ideologies. Analysis is today by and large a matter of mathematization and taken together the couple witnessing and analysis is no longer a trivial matter of observing and accounting for what is observed but is instead a highly esoteric and specialized procedure demonstrating many local applications and trajectories. Nevertheless, no matter how mediated and technology-laden scientific work becomes, the visual inspection and the witnessing of credible individuals, affiliated with either prestigious research institutions or distinguished and widely respected research communities or research teams, are indispensable components in scientific work. Therefore, it is still based on, *mutatis mutandis*, procedures of visual inspection and articulated in theoretical and methodological terms.

4 Vision and Visualization in Architect Work

INTRODUCTION

> "When I look at the blueprints and inspect various things, I have this feeling that I can enter into the object [the building]. Just through looking . . . I can almost feel how it smells, and I can see all the entities. I am trained to build the house three, four times before I build it in real life . . . Today, there are computer systems which I am really fond of but at the same time that is a substitute for my know-how, the ability to think in 3D or 4D."
>
> Manager, major Scandinavian construction company

In this fourth chapter, the visual practices of architects will be examined. While contemporary technoscience is intimately bound up with a long series of technologies, tools, and visions machines structuring, shaping, forming, and enabling what Paul Virilio (1989) has called a "logistics of perception," the work of practicing architects is less directly determined by technology. Being a professional discipline operating in the intersection between the arts, social planning, and the engineering sciences, architect's work is perhaps more than anything else characterized by the "mutual adjustment" (Thompson, 1967) between a variety of interests and expectations, at times complementary or even contradictory. The built environment should, for instance, be aesthetically appealing, produced at a reasonably low cost, and adhere to principles of sustainable development. The architect is therefore the hub in a complex centre of relations including a range of stakeholders such as clients, local politicians, end users, the broader public, and, not to forget, the community of architects that by the end of the day is evaluating the performance of the commissioned architect. One must not overlook the fact that architects are a professional group and like most professional groups, peer review and credibility from peers are what counts. This does not make professional groups wholly inward oriented; they are rather operating on basis of a set of institutions, routines, traditions, and other factors determining the situation and the actual practice, but it is ultimately only peers—fellow professionals—that are considered qualified to evaluate whether the actual situation was handled professionally or not.

Given the heterogeneous nature of the architect's assignment, architect work is a social practice that embodies a range of different skills and competencies. While the aesthetic skill is what comes to mind when addressing architect's work, architects need to have an adequate training in the engineering sciences including materials science, civil engineering, and construction engineering, an insight into the laws and regulations of the construction industry, and an understanding of how the political system in various more or less explicit ways is controlling and monitoring the built environment. It is still the case that what really counts in the community is the ability to demonstrate capacities for creativity and originality when designing, say, a house. The true heroes of the field are the few well-known star architects that have won many prestigious competitions and that have built the most spectacular buildings. Norman Foster, Frank O. Gehry, Rem Koolhaas, and a handful of such star architects are the most admired and most referenced architects in the community and in the wider public. In addition, a few runner-up firms and "coming men and women" (mostly men, unfortunately) are short-listed by architects. Architects tend overall to pay close attention to what is happening in the field. The combination of the public nature of the work provided, the prestige in buildings, the great amount of money involved, and the political nature of all construction work is paving the way for a "cult of the successful" that in turn is making architecture a most prestigious field. Architecture schools are generally demanding high grades to attend and there is an endemic overproduction of architects; not every architecture school graduate is capable of getting a job in the industry. However, this chapter does not attempt to present a full ethnography of architect work. Instead, it is focused on the visual practices in the discipline, the day-to-day work to design buildings or built environments that are meeting the demands from the various stakeholders. In engaging in this analysis, architect work will be examined as a specific form of knowledge-intensive work in the professional service sector of the economy. Therefore, before engaging in the actual visual practices in the field, the first section of the chapter addresses architecture work in such terms. Thereafter, a literature review is providing some details of how architect work is organized and managed. Thereafter, the literature on visual practices is reviewed and finally, the empirical study is reported. Finally, some concluding remarks are provided.

ARCHITECT BUREAUS AS KNOWLEDGE-INTENSIVE PROFESSIONAL SERVICE FIRMS

Since the beginning of the 1960s, sociologists have been preoccupied with the question of industrial society, a product of the late eighteenth century in the U.K. and Flanders; and the nineteenth century, for the rest of Europe, was about to be displaced by a new economic regime. This economic regime has been named "the postindustrial society" and, more recently, "the knowledge society" and even more specifically, restricting the analysis to the economic conditions, "the knowledge economy."[1] Commentators are suggesting that the new knowledge economy is characterized by a higher degree of intellectual content; while the classic economic production factors—land, work, and capital—have to date explained a substantial part of the economic activities, in the new economic regime, it is "knowledge" that is the principal production factor. Say Powell and Snellman (2004: 201): "The key components of a knowledge economy include a greater reliance on intellectual capabilities than on physical inputs or natural resources, combined with efforts to integrate improvements in every stage of the production process, from the R&D lab to the factory floor to the interface with the customer." Since knowledge is a somewhat ambiguous term, especially in the English language, for once being less nuanced than, say, French or German (offering the distinction between *savoir* and *connaissance*, and *können* and *wissen*, for instance), there is a need for, to use a positivist vocabulary, "operationalizing" knowledge. For instance, patents registered over periods of time have been a long-standing gold standard for the intellectual activities in a country or industry. An examination of such patterns shows that there are reasons to believe in a growth of knowledge—at least knowledge embodied in registered patents. "Clearly, patent trends suggest a recent marked acceleration in the production of new knowledge," Powell and Snellman (2004: 202) remark. After 1987, there has been a growth from 80,000 to 170,000 patents annually in the first years of the new millennium in the U.S. In addition, between 1976 and 1998, there was an eightfold increase in university patents (Powell and Snellman, 2004: 204). Another indication of the emerging knowledge economy is the growth in specialist jobs, and there is clear evidence that the jobs demanding advanced skills and specialized know-how grew faster than the economy at large: "Non-academic science and engineering (S&E) jobs [i.e., knowledge-intensive jobs] grew at more than four times the rate of the total U.S. labor force between 1980 and 2000. S&E employment increased by 159% between 1980 and 2000, an average annual growth rate of 4,9%, in comparison to 1,1% for the entire labor force" (Powell and Snellman, 2004: 205). Other commentators (e.g., Barley and Kunda, 2004) report similar trends. The Western economies are not becoming "service economies" but are rather characterized by their informational and intellectual content.

As a response to the knowledge economy and the knowledge society, organization theorists and management researchers have examined what has been called "knowledge-intensive firms" (KIFs) as a specific form of organization demonstrating certain leadership practices, routines, and other idiosyncratic organizational procedures. Alvesson (2001: 863) is referring to KIFs as firms where "[m]ost work is said to be of an intellectual nature and where well-educated, qualified employees form the major part of the work force." KIFs are thus populated by a variety of experts and specialists whose competencies needs to be aligned and coordinated. It is a standing theme in the literature addressing KIFs that the employees in this particular form of company do indeed demand certain leadership practices and novel forms of motivation. Alvesson (2004: 122) even suggests that the higher amount of know-how in a firm, the less influence top management can execute: "Apart from certain stages such as the foundation and early expansion of a firm and during crises calling for conflict-ridden changes, leadership is probably a less important aspect of KIFs than of many other organizations" (Alvesson, 2004: 137). Therefore, rather than centering the control of the operations on traditional activities, KIFs tend to be managed on basis of what Kärreman and Alvesson (2004: 151) call "cultural-ideological modes of control," aimed at shaping and influencing the identity and the self-image of the coworker. Elsewhere, Alvesson (2004: 137) is talking about the influence of "normative control," the shaping of "[t]he ideas, expectations, and subjectivities of people." The coworkers in KIFs are consequently not as much controlled and monitored by technocratic or bureaucratic means of control but enjoy a significant degree of freedom from direct inspection and detailed regulations regarding working hours, and so forth. On the other hand, this category of workers is exposed to a range of soft forms of control aimed at shaping the image of the knowledge worker as an entrepreneurial, enterprising self, capable of working without detailed managerial guidance or support. What is of specific interest is the time and effort invested in making neophytes enact subject-positions that embody these work values. The socialization into the company (and the profession) is here of central importance. Such subject positions may include work ethos (e.g., "we consultants work long hours to meet customers' expectations"), business attire and general embodied performances (e.g., "it is disrespectful to the clients not to wear proper business attire"), or other aspects relating to the work (e.g., "it is unethical to work with two clients that are competitors at the same time"). Overall, the subject-position is the totality of enacted self-images, demands for performances, professional ideologies, and work ethos that is guiding the professional knowledge worker in his or her day-to-day work. There is a somewhat paradoxical relationship between, on the one hand, the demands on the knowledge worker to be capable of thinking analytically and demonstrating critical reflection, while at the same time being expected to subsume to the overarching corporate policies and ideologies. The knowledge worker is, in other words, expected to think for her- or himself while at the same time fully identifying with the company and the industry. Such inconsistencies are handled through forms of resistance and cynicism. For some researchers, such resistance and cynicism are an indication of a failure of the social system to fully integrate the individual, making him or her fully identify with enacted objectives and predominant ideologies. For others, resistance and cynicism is, on the contrary, an operating mechanism of the social system that enables a reconciliation of opposing objectives and expectations. For instance, Fleming and Spicer (2007) are referencing the Slovenian philosopher and social theorist Slavoj Žižek, discussing the American TV series *M*A*S*H*, where the daily life in an American field hospital during the Korean War is serving as the background. At the field hospital, a number of highly qualified surgeons are working. These surgeons are doing their best to ridicule and poke fun at the military apparatus and the pomp and ceremonials favoured by the military. Dressing somewhat casually and failing to meet the expectations regarding military self-discipline, the surgeons are continuously expressing their contempt for the war and for all things military. At the same time, they are doing their best to help unfortunate soldiers who are wounded in the war; when it comes to medical treatment and bedside care, there is no cynicism or resistance in sight on their part. The military ceremonials and rituals are for the surgeons what the red cloth is for the bull in the bullfighting ring, a source of annoyance that limits the scope of the perspective. For many commentators, *M*A*S*H* has been seen as being representative of an anti-military stance. Žižek does, on the contrary, conceive of the resistance and cynicism demonstrated by the surgeons as a central and even constitutive mechanism of the military apparatus. Only idiots (such as Jaromir Hašek's brave soldier Švejk) are prone to follow the regulations in detail in a war situation; intelligent individuals do the work that matters but escape from marginally important procedures. Resistance and cynicism are indispensable components of the social system in terms of reproducing it over and over. If highly intelligent and enterprising individuals (i.e., knowledge workers) would not be given certain escape routes and arenas for "productive" resistance, they would not function properly. For Žižek, there is a need for an affirmative view of resistance and cynicism and not excluding it from the social system. In knowledge-intensive firms, it is possible to see similar "acts of resistance" on the margin of the corporate system. Knowledge workers, otherwise following all the norms and procedures, may refuse to wear a tie or may bring a coffee mug with some anti-corporate message printed on it, or engage in some other activities that help them to restore their perceived autonomy vis-à-vis their employer and society more broadly. Especially younger coworkers or coworkers nourishing the belief that they are in some way disfavoured by the organization are prone to engage in acts of resistance or express cynicism. However, the most meaningful way is to conceive of such activities or declarations as activities that have a symbiotic relationship with the normal functioning of the organization.

Another central feature of KIFs and knowledge work is the concept of *ambiguity*. Since expertise and detailed know-how in a field are always, by definition, complicated to verify for the outsider, there are a number of activities orchestrated during knowledge work to safeguard that the knowledge worker is capable of demonstrating his or her expertise. First, knowledge workers are often reporting their previous experience, their credentials in terms of university diplomas, courses taken, and so forth, and their assumptions and beliefs to build confidence, both with external clients and with peers. Second, embodied work in terms of body language and proper business attire is part of the performance of the knowledge worker. Third, the vocabulary of the knowledge worker tends to be filled with technical terms and narratives employed to underline the authority of the knowledge work. Taken together, there is a certain variety of processes that helps constitute the knowledge workers as credible and legitimate spokesmen in a specific field. Starbuck (1992) exemplifies:

> Many experts—with awareness—use jargon that obscures their meaning. As a result, clients have to base their judgment on familiar, generic symbols of expertise. Do the experts speak as persons with much education? Have the experts used impressive statistical computations? Are the experts well dressed? Did the expert use data of good quality? Do the experts' analyses seem logical and credible? Do the experts appear confident? Successful KIFs, therefore, pay attention to their symbolic outputs . . . Clients also hire experts to obtain legitimacy instead of expertise. In such circumstances, the client-expert relationship is a charade: the clients choose the advisers who will give wanted advice. (Starbuck, 1992: 731)

In summary, knowledge work and knowledge workers represent a specific form of workers who in many ways are complicated to lead and manage in accordance with technocratic and bureaucratic principles. For instance, since many knowledge workers are professionals, they do not of necessity accept a leader's decision unless they (1) regard that leader as a person qualified to make such a decision, in many cases implying that the person in question should have a similar background or/and more experience than themselves, (2) the decision is correct given a number of contingencies and conditions. That is, the belief in bureaucratic authority may be poorly developed. As a consequence, leadership work in professional organizations is based more on a coaching approach or through norms and objectives rather than direct commands. Knowledge workers do in general represent a new form of "postauthoritarian personality," a personality not overtly impressed by titles and insignia but more concerned about arguments and intriguing storytelling.

Another body of literature of relevance for architect work is what has been called professional service firms (PSFs) (Briscoe, 2007; Empson, 2001; Hitt et al., 2001; Løvendahl, Revang, and Fosstenløkken, 2001; Morris, 2001; Robertson, Scarbrough, and Jacky, 2003; Suddaby and Greenwood, 2001). PSFs represent a number of companies that are offering advanced, knowledge-based services including more traditional professions such as lawyers, management consultants, and medical doctors, but also newer and emerging professional groups such as event managers, stylists, or literature agents. Architect bureaus are PSFs operating primarily in the construction industry but also in other domains including design or event management. In general, PSFs serve in a rather narrow niche in the market and employ knowledge workers that are capable of navigating within this niche. Architect firms are in many ways a typical example of how PSFs work: they are capable of providing a rather distinct service that still includes a diverse set of activities; the service is to be integrated into a broader set of activities (e.g., the very construction of the building, the political work preceding the actual construction, etc.); the architect has a significant influence in the process but is by no means the only authority having a say; the work is commissioned for a restricted period of time, for instance, by the hour by the client. The PSF is therefore dependent on the close collaboration with the client and, at the same time, it will always be the principal supplier of specialist know-how in its field of expertise. The PSF is an idiosyncratic organization in the late modern knowledge economy, a form of organization capable of operating in the network-like and highly relational organization of the contemporary economy while at the same time maintaining its distinct brand, culture, and competencies.

ARCHITECT WORK

Since architects design the built environment around us, their work has from the outset been overtly public. The proverbial "man on the street" has always thought of himself as being in a position to pass judgment, more or less qualified, on the work of architects. In the more scholarly circles, architecture has been a perennial source of discussion and analysis. Many leading architects, such as Le Corbusier (1946), Venturi, Brown, and Izenour (1977), Koolhaas (1978), and Obrist and Koolhaas (2001), have served not only as practicing architects but also as social commentators and social theorists. For instance, the architects and Harvard professor Rem Koolhaas has been particularly successful in combining his work at the leading bureau OMA (Office for Metropolitan Architecture), designing, for instance, the Prada flagship store in the SoHo district in New York City, and more scholarly activities. In addition, influential intellectuals such as Walter Benjamin (1999), and more recently, feminist theorist Elizabeth Grosz (2001) and philosopher John Rajchman (1998) have written extensively on the relationship between society and architecture. Moreover, a number of architecture professors (e.g., Anthony Vidler, 2000) and architects (e.g., Bernard Cache, 1995) are social theorists in their own right, advancing architecture as a principal feature of the late modernity that needs to be taken seriously. In addition to the more broad-ranging social theory on architecture, there are a number of more empirically oriented studies of architect work, reporting from a more sociological frame of reference what architects do or do not do in their everyday undertakings (Blau, 1984; Blau and McKinley, 1979; Gutman, 1988; Ivory, 2004; Kamara, Augenbroe, and Carillo, 2002; Pinnington and Morris, 2002; Winch and Schneider, 1993). As Cohn et al. (2005: 776) remark, given the central importance of architecture in contemporary society and the ideal typical features of architects as a typical professional group, architects have been "relatively neglected" in organization theory and in the literature on professions.

A standing theme in the literature on architect work is that architects are expected to collaborate closely with a number of stakeholders, thereby making the profession largely a *relational activity* (Cuff, 1991). Another recurring discussion is that architects have lost much of their jurisdiction in the field and today it is the clients, demonstrating the financial muscles needed to operate in the field of real estate, that are making the most important decisions, albeit still in close collaborations with architects. In general, there is a sense of lost and much mourned "golden age" in the literature, a golden age that probably is a mere fiction or imagination. In Cohen et al.'s (2005) study of British architects, there was a general sense of loss and a "sentimental longing" (see Gouldner, 1954) for creative elements in the work among the architects:

> Only six people in our sample [out of 42] described themselves as primarily involved in the creative process, and even they believed that they would have to give it up if they wanted upward progression in their organization. Our participants often discussed the creative aspects of work with a kind of sentimental longing. While acknowledging its importance in terms of architectural history and cultural heritage, on a day-to-day basis there was a recognition that it was often subordinated to more pressing, business concerns. (Cohen et al., 2005: 783)

Cohen et al. (2005) did, however, identify three predominant identities among the architects, that of *artists, business people,* and *public servants.* Many architects had abandoned the "artist identity" and thought of themselves as being business-oriented or as being in the service of the general public, safeguarding aesthetically appealing and functional buildings and public spaces. This role of the architect, as being a functionary in the service of society, is of rather recent origin and is closely connected to modernist doctrines and the belief in buildings and built spaces as what is not based on artistic ambitions and ornaments but on function and "user-friendliness." For instance, Walter Gropius, the first director of the Bauhaus school in Dessau, Germany, operating during the Weimar Republic, emphasized this social role of the architect while downgrading the issue of aesthetics:

> Building is not an aesthetic process . . . Architecture which 'continues a tradition is historicist' . . . a new house is . . . a product of industry and as such is the work of specialists: economists, statisticians, hygienicists, climatologists, experts in . . . norms, heating techniques . . . the

architect? He was an artist and is becoming a specialist in organization
. . . building is only organization: social, technical, economic, mental
organization. (Walter Gropius, *Dessau Bauhaus—Principles of Bauhaus Production*, March 1926, cited in Galison, 1990: 717)

In Vienna, one of the epicenters of modernism, Adolph Loos, one of the
most celebrated pioneers of modernist architecture, explicitly denounced
the aesthetic and ornamental features of the architecture of the *ancien
régime*: "I have discovered and given the world the following notion: the
evolution of civilization is synonymous with the elimination of ornament
from the utilitarian object" (Adolf Loos, cited in Galison, 1990: 726). He
even went so far as to claim that ornament was representative of "the sadism
of the eighteenth century" (Klein, 2004: 10–11). In the modernist tradition
of thinking, the architects are no longer a community of beauty seeking
creators, aesthetically inclined and artistically talented creators of spaces
and buildings, but become officers in the service of the modern society.
Notwithstanding such modernist doctrines, no matter what identity the
architects in the Cohen et al. (2005) study took on, they still maintained
the idea that architect work is about creativity:

> It is significant that the architects in our sample continually described
> creativity as the legitimate core of architecture—its defining and dif-
> ferentiating feature . . . as noted, for the majority, creativity was sub-
> sumed within other discursive frames, legitimated in business, or public
> service terms. However, when this happened creativity did not simply
> disappear from view. On the contrary, architects talked at length about
> how it had been 'engulfed,' 'squeezed out,' and 'eclipsed' by the pres-
> sures of the day. (Cohen et al., 2005: 792)

When becoming business-minded or serving the public, creativity is gradually "squeezed out." Thus creativity gradually evaporates or otherwise
mysteriously disappears as other concerns sneak into everyday work.
What remains is, however, the firm belief in the creative capacities of the
trained architect.

Architects represent a highly specialized branch with a high degree,
in Bourdieu's vocabulary, of cultural capital. Blau and McKinley (1979)
emphasize that successful architect firms are not primarily oriented
towards maximizing profit but in contributing with the most interesting
and creative architecture. Architects are, in other words, not in the trade
to make a lot of money but because they have an aesthetic calling, an ambition to make the world a more beautiful place. The aesthetic norms and
objectives collectively enacted in the profession are a standing theme in the
literature. Although the great modernist architect Le Corbusier insisted on
a more engineering-based view of architecture, claiming that a "house is a
machine for living" (*une machine d'habiliter*) and a chair "a machine for

sitting" (Le Corbusier, 1946; McLeod, 1983), it is still today the aesthetic qualities of the work that attract newcomers and is accruing prestige in the field. While architects are not opposed to building cheaply or providing user-friendly buildings, their principal interests evolve around aesthetically appealing buildings.

When it comes to studies of everyday work, when penetrating the surface of "espoused theories" (Argyris and Schön, 1978) and observing what is actually conducted in the daily life, much of the work of architects is routine work and is not always everyday work centered around important decisions regarding aesthetic features of buildings. Ankrah and Langford (2005: 601) report from their study that architect work is by and large formed by the same managerial principles and leadership practices as any other professional service firm:

> Architectural practices are largely informal organizations in which control and coordination are achieved through empathy between organizational members and through direct personal contact, and this is essentially because most of these practices are small. There is decentralization in decision-making with everyone encouraged to think and contribute to problem-solving, although the managing director (usually the founder or a founding partner) plays a pivotal role in coordination. These organizations employ highly trained and skilled individuals who have a high tolerance of ambiguity. Their sense of their own importance creates in them a need for recognition and a desire to impose their identities on the organization. The firms in this business recognize their employees' importance and, accordingly, acknowledge and reward their individual efforts and performance, although to some, not enough. (Ankrah and Langford, 2005: 601)

The collaborative nature of architect work is demonstrated in quantitative research reported by Symes, Eley, and Seidel (1996: 31–38), based on a survey among 610 British architects, suggesting that skills in design and creativity were important, that communication skills are valued, that architects have "special knowledge," that "flexibility and personal style" are necessary, and that marketing expertise is demanded. On the one hand, architects are expected to have detailed knowledge in the very domain of architecture; on the other, they should be able to communicate and collaborate with various stakeholders. Ofori and Kien's (2004) research on the use of sustainable design suggests that the communication with the outside is a major challenge for architects and that it is complicated to translate the belief in the value of sustainable design into actual products: "The findings of the study showed a discrepancy between what architects claim to be convinced about, and knowledgeable in, and their commitment and practices; architects seem to be unable to translate their environmental awareness and knowledge into appropriate design decisions" (Ofori and

Kien, 2004: 34). Another feature of the architect work is its domination of male coworkers and men in executive position in the industry. Fowler and Wilson (2004: 114) found in their study that sexist assumptions and practices were endemic to the field: "Some [male architects] offered psychological explanations for women's subordinate position in the profession, such as the view that women were weaker in 3D perception . . . Other male architects identified fitting jobs for women in less spectacular areas of design—in domestic architecture or interiors" (see also Adams and Tancred, 2000). They concluded their study by suggesting that there is little evidence of any progress towards a less one-sided domination of men in the field:

> [T]here are few grounds for the belief that women are on the verge of 'making it' in architecture. It is not that women lack the cultural capital to do well in the profession, for nobody has doubts about their ability at architectural school level. Rather, we suggest that where markets are less localized and less forthcoming, the room for tolerance and nurture of those with young children becomes reduced. More specifically, in a savagely competitive climate, contracts place a strong premium on instrumental rationality, not least in the use of power to insist on the time discipline of builders and others. (Fowler and Wilson, 2004: 116)

In another study making the gendered nature of the field a topic of critical analysis, Sang, Dainty, and Ison (2007: 1314) emphasized the immediate individual and social costs derived from the gendered industry structure: "The data presented here suggests that women working within the architectural profession are at greater risk of poor health and well-being as a result of occupational stress. Overall female architects appear to experience lower job satisfaction, poorer physical health, higher work-life conflict and higher turnover intentions." These findings are consonant with other studies of, for instance, female construction workers (Eisenberg, 1998) and female civil engineers (Watts, 2009), pointing at the structural sexism as a major challenge for the future in the construction industry.

Being essentially a male domain, architect work is pervaded by what gender theorists may refer to as male norms and values. For instance, there is a not always explicitly articulated but nevertheless rigour hierarchy in most architect offices, locating the chief architect (in many cases also the owner) in the top of the hierarchy and a number of newcomers and administrators at its bottom. In addition, architect work is in many ways shaped and formed by the tradition of participating in competitions, sorting out the best suggestions for the architecture of prestigious and politically important projects. Third, there is often a strong emphasis on individual contributions and ideas and beliefs regarding individual "creativity," "talent," and other praised individual capabilities that are circulating in the field. Like any other field of political, cultural, or scientific production, there is a fierce struggle over resources and authority and individual architects "making it," i.e., winning some prestigious competition or being published in some leading architecture magazine is accruing respect and credibility.

Since this study is not aimed at reporting an ethnography of architecture work en bloc but is primarily concerned with the visual practices of the profession, the next section discusses visual practices from a more general sociological perspective. After that, a number of studies of visual practices and the use of visual representations in architect work will be reviewed.

THE SOCIOLOGY OF VISION AND VISUALITY IN KNOWLEDGE-INTENSIVE WORK

In this section, the uses of visual representations in situ, in organizations, will be examined from a sociological perspective. Here, it is not as much a matter of examining the features and components of visual representations but to examining how visual representations are serving a role in a network of social relations. Speaking from an actor network theory perspective, one may suggest that a visual representation (e.g., a drawing) is an *actant*, what Michel Serres calls a *quasi-object*, an object that oscillates between being a subject, demonstrating its own agency, and an object, an artefact demanding its spokesmanship to function properly. In this view, the visual representation is not a disinterested token in a field of social relations but is what actively forms and shapes social relations in terms of being capable of transgressing the epistemological divide between being object and subject. In a similar manner, Cooren (2004) is talking about "textual agency," a form of agency derived from the ability to "stand in" for other organizational resources: "Created by human beings, these texts participate in the channeling of behaviors, constitute and stabilize organizational pathways, and broadcast information/orders," Cooren (2004: 388) suggests. The primary value of textual agency lies in its ability to "operate at distance," to support the "tele-action" demanded in many geographically distributed firms. Cooren (2004: 388) writes, "[t]extual agency, especially in its written form, enables delegation through *tele-action*, and *tele-communication*. By remaining, these textual agents fabricate relatively fixed spaces and times; they define objectives; they forbid specific behaviors; and they invite or enforce humans to follow specific organizational pathways." Both actor-network theorists and Cooren (2004) and others advocating a view recognizing the agency of visual representations suggest that rather than seeing these artefacts as inert and mute matter, they are in fact resources mobilized in social communities. They are a component in what Schatzki (2002: xii) has called "the site of the social," a most complex term, denoting "[a] mesh of practices and orders: a contingently and differentially evolving configuration of organized activities and arrangements." In the "site of the social," the concept of "practice" is given a central importance. Practice is here rather loosely defined as "a practice is a set of doings and sayings" (Schatzki, 2002: 73). More specifically, Schatzki (2002: 101) says, "practices establish particular arrangements. These arrangements are defined packages of entities, relations, meanings, and positions, whose integrity derives from the organization of practices." Visual representations are one category of entities that are part of the "arrangement" constituting the practice. In Schatzki's (2002) and Cooren's (2004) view, visual representations are what stabilize and render practices/agencies/arrangements durable over time. Agency is, in a visual culture, what is constituted through visual practices (e.g., professional vision) and visual representations.

Designers and the Function of "Meta-Indexicals"

Henderson (1999) studies design work in an American corporation. Rather than being merely one resource among others, the visual representations played a central role in actively structuring and shaping the workplace: "Visual representations shape the structure of the work and determine who participate in the work and what its final products will be," Henderson (1999: 1) says. Henderson (1999) is calling for attention to the fact that rather than being the output from a cognitive and emotional process, the work with visual representation is what is structuring and forming the entire workplace. Moreover, the design work is not restricted to the use of a specific media, but the boundary between generic media (e.g., pen and paper in the sketching phases) and more advanced computer-based media such as CAD (Computer-Aided Design) software is a highly permeable and fluid one; designers tend to use sketching and pen and paper in the early most creative phases and then turn to the computer, but often the process moves back and forth, leaving no significant patterns in their work. Henderson (1999: 8) writes:

> [T]here is no one best way to use a computer-graphics system; firms and individuals engage in many types of mixed paper and electronic practices as well as differential uses, of electronic options. In many companies, experienced design engineers work by hand, and drafters then redraw the designs onto graphics systems. Many designers switch between hand drawings, hard copies from the computer, and the monitor screen, often preferring to work out initial concepts in hand-drawn sketches and returning to paper copies during analytical phases of their work. (Henderson, 1999: 8)

Henderson is talking about this movement back and forth between media as "mixed-use practice," blending "paper and electronic modes of representation" (Henderson, 1999: 168). The value of the visual representations produced in the "mixed-used practice" is the ability of the visual representations to play a "meta-indexical role," that is, to bridge and mix various forms of knowledge, including tacit knowledge and aesthetic preferences:

They serve as a holding ground where commodified and uncodified knowledge can meet, drawing on each other's strength to bring together various levels of tacit knowledge including but not limited to visual knowledge, kinesthetic knowledge, mathematical knowledge (verbal and nonverbal), local and experimental knowledge, and multivisual competencies. This is why they are amenable to mixed-use practices. Such practices take advantage of the strengths of codified and uncodified knowledge as well as the in-between areas that cannot and should not be so simply dichotomized. It is this chameleon, meta-indexical, elastic quality of visual representation that demands mixed practices in the workplace and facilitates multivisual competency to enhance the creativity of individual and group design work. (Henderson, 1999: 12)

Henderson claims rightly that any visualization process include a standardizing, coding, and ordering of the knowledge used in the practice. The engineering disciplines combine a range of skills and know-how, including verbal, visual, kinaesthetic, and mathematical knowledge (Henderson, 1999: 16). Visual representations are capable of integrating these diverse skills. Consequently, many interviewees claimed that there was an intimate relation between sketching and thinking: "I can't think without my drawing board," one engineer exclaimed (cited by Henderson, 1999: 1). Moreover, rather than serving as a means for integrating various operative knowledge bases, visual representations play the role of being what is serving as an interface between the individual and the social, the interior and the exterior; sketching is both an individual act of creation and a communicative act in one single process: They are what Henderson (1999) calls "group-thinking tools": "Sketches facilitate both individual thinking and interactive communication. Because they allow these processes to occur simultaneously, they become group thinking tools" (Henderson, 1999: 27). Group thinking tools are important because they are capable of providing a shared ground for communication and elaborations. At the same time, Henderson warns that visual representations are capable of capturing only a subset of the totality of tacit knowledge involved in the work.

Being able to work with various visual media for representation is part of the designer's professional skills. When constantly working with visual representations, the designers entrench a certain "visual literacy" which equips them with shared ways of seeing, in short a "professional vision": "Constant exposure to and interaction with a way of seeing develop skills in visual reading analogous to verbal reading and writing literacy. Because language is tied to culture, the way we speak both reflects and reinforces our cultural outlook and values" (Henderson, 1999: 44). There is thus an intimate relationship between visual practices and verbal or written accounts of what is observed; seeing influences language and language ultimately sets the boundaries for what may be seen. "Seeing" and "saying" are therefore developed in tandem as part of the professional components.

In Henderson's account, visual practices are not only useful for "insiders" but they also demonstrate tacit components to the "outsiders" (i.e., the nondesigners). Again, it the ability of the visual representations to serve as "visual meta-indexicals" that matter; visual representations qua "meta-indexicals" should have the ability to:

- Transform other ways of knowing, such as verbal and mathematical modes into a visual format;
- Index, reframe, or simply reach the understanding or tacit knowledge of interacting participants;
- Elicit tacit knowledge from participants so that it can be represented in a format readable for others;
- Represent knowledge through the flexibility of sketching in an uncoded format;
- Tap all sorts of visual modes of representation spanning all of the world's art format and history, including abstract (what I have referred to as *multivisual competencies*);
- Expand a given visual lexicon so that new codes can be incorporated;
- Develop and standardize a new lexicon to maintain consistency of meaning (Latour's immutability); and
- Represent different ways of knowing using many different systems of representation at once, including verbal, mathematical, and numerous visual modes. (Henderson, 1999: 199–200)

Visual meta-indexicals thus serve to bridge and bond heterogeneous communities, to capture tacit knowledge, and to bring into harmony, for instance, various sources of knowledge (mathematics, aesthetic knowledge, materials science, etc.). In her conclusion, Henderson (1999: 204) revisits the issue of knowledge and cognitive processes, and suggests that thinking is not "purely a mental activity but is a physical one as well." She continues: "What goes on in the mind is tied to material existence and material practice." Seen in this view, visual representations are serving as *Ersatz* devices, prostheses or tools for thinking. Thought does then not strictly emerge in the cerebral structure of the human brain of the designers and is transferred onto the white surface of the paper through the hand. Henderson rejects such a strict mind-body dualism and causality; the movement of the hand and "the thinking in the brain" (and elsewhere) are mutually constitutive; mind and body are demonstrating a recursive relationship that needs to be carefully examined:

> The mental vision and the paper representation interactively construct one another. The process is not whole vision and then, plonk, drawing. The action orientation of drawing—scratching down visual concepts that may occur fragments and then putting them together as a whole, perhaps after trying various combinations—are part of the whole process. (Henderson, 1999: 204–205)

Finally, Henderson discusses whether the connection between the cognitive processes of the mind and the actual sketching conducted by the designer's hand will be displaced by the series cognition-computer-media visualization, thereby resulting in some new and hopefully productive relationship between mind and hand in the design work. In addition, not only is pen and paper displaced by new media; the new media will per se influence and shape thinking which may enable new design opportunities and new, previously unseen solutions to design problems.

Henderson's work is of great importance for the understanding of visual practices, the use of visual representations, and professional vision because she is strongly emphasizing the mutually constitutive nature of sketching and thinking; in order to think, one must sketch; in order to sketch, one must think. These two embodied and cognitive procedures and capacities are operating around two lines tightly entangled. For the skilled and seasoned designer, the two parallel lines almost merge and become one. In addition, speaking more from a sociological and less from a psychological or epistemological perspective, Henderson (1999) emphasizes the role of visual representations to serve as meta-indexicals, that is, a form of boundary-objects that heterogeneous communities can collaborate around. Fashioned in a Weickian vocabulary, one may argue that sketches and other resources capable of serving as "meta-indexicals" are helping to make sense out of the skills and tacit know-how that are not immediately visible for all coworkers. The visual representations are thus embodying competencies that are not easily represented otherwise.

The Social Role of Visual Representations

Bechky (2003) reports a study of an American manufacturing company, EquipCo, specializing in building advanced machinery. In this work, the design of the engineers, manifested in the visual representation of the blueprint, served to regulate social relations between occupational groups in the workplace. Rather than being some marginal aspect of the work, the prints served a rather central role in regulating and controlling the workplace relations and in constituting and reproducing the boundaries between professional and occupational groups. The point of departure for Bechky's (2003) study is that professional groups continuously engage in boundary work (Gieryn, 1983), that is, they monitor, control, and regulate the relations and the boundaries between professional or occupational communities. "Jurisdiction is contested through public, legal, and workplace claims, for control over task areas . . . These jurisdictional claims act to shift both relations between professional groups and the boundaries of their core work domains," Bechky (2003: 721) suggests. When engaging in boundary work, ultimately aimed at safeguarding the jurisdiction over a certain domain and/or maintaining the authority in the domain, professional and occupational groups mobilize a variety of resources. In these "jurisdictional struggles" (Bechky, 2003: 723), "epistemic objects" such as "drawings and machines" (Bechky, 2003: 729) play a central role. "Epistemic objects" is a somewhat complicated term, denoting that an object is not just any conceivable object at hand but an entity comprising some kind of know-how or other form of valid claims to expertise or authority. One such epistemic object is engineering drawings:

> Engineering drawings epitomized this idea of an epistemic object; they were perceived as showing designers how their ideas worked on paper and communicating to others, such as assemblers [an occupational group], all the information needed for building . . . The drawings detailed the way to build a machine, from the precise terms calling out each part to notes standardizing the manner in which parts should be assembled. Each drawing underwent many revisions on the way to becoming a final representation of the product, and because of this, during the design and prototyping process, the drawings were viewed as open-ended projections of what the product would be. (Bechky, 2003: 729)

The engineering drawings were thus actants in the true sense of the term as being quasi-objects: on the one hand, they were objects produced by the community of highly skilled and professional engineers, capturing all the skills, experience, know-how, in short, all the professionalism of the community of engineers. On the other hand, the drawings were agents in their own terms, having a clearly fixed content and displaying objectives and desirable outcomes. Even though Bechky (2003) did not speak of actants but of boundary objects, the drawings have a central position in regulating the relations between various groups in the firm: "Artefacts were also used to mediate occupational boundaries during episodes of problem solving. When problems arose in the building process, both drawings and machines were used as boundary objects between occupational communities to help solve them," Bechky (2003: 732) notes. In regulating the social relations, the drawings served to exclude the less prestigious groups such as the machine builders from the design phases. Even though the machine builders may have interesting experiences to contribute, engineers insisted on regarding the drawings as enclosed objects, not open to discussions and negotiations:

> I heard almost daily during my year working at EquipCo: 'Build to the print'. The drawings were considered the only authority in the design process; the organization's discourse reinforced the idea that drawings were the sole legitimate means of communication at EquipCo. This rhetoric served a jurisdictional purpose, in addition to supporting the standardization of building methods. Because engineers controlled the drawings and the design process, promoting the use of the drawings supported their jurisdiction over their work and their place in the occupational hierarchy. (Bechky, 2003: 734)

Bechky (2003) identifies a number of features of the epistemic object serving its role as a boundary object capable of defending the professional interests of a certain professional community. For instance, the epistemic object—in this case a drawing—needs to be "somewhat unclear to other groups" (Bechky, 2003: 735), i.e., demanding some allegedly sophisticated and esoteric expertise to be fully capable of decoding and interpreting it:

> For drawings to be powerful as a tool to maintain occupational jurisdiction, they must be somewhat unclear to other groups, because if every aspect of the work were easily codified and understood, engineers would be unable to maintain their status as experts. Therefore, the discourse emphasizing the exclusive use of drawings as an epistemic device was helpful in diverting attention from the less acceptable implications of their abstractness—the fact that drawings were incomplete and, further, not as useful in problem solving at occupational boundaries as the machines were. (Bechky, 2003: 735)

In short, in cases where the machine builders insisted on opening up the drawings for discussions, the engineers tended to claim that "things were not as easy as they appeared" and that there was a difference between an outsider's commonsense thinking and an insider's detailed understanding of certain choices and decisions.

In the concluding section of the paper, Bechky (2003: 746) addresses the role of artefacts in organizations, suggesting that they are "[a]n important part of organizational life: they surround us, and our work and roles are dependent upon them. As an integral part of work processes, objects helps us to accomplish tasks, but not in a merely technical manner. Artefacts, subject to interpretation, participate in the constitution of the social dynamics of organizations." Contrary to Henderson (1999), conceiving of visa artefacts as a communal resource helping heterogeneous communities come together and collaborate, Bechky (2003) is offering a more political (or politicized) view of the role of visual artefacts. Visual artefacts are not of necessity and naturally beneficial for everyone but primarily for the professional or occupational communities that have enacted for themselves the role of experts and principal spokespersons of these epistemic objects. In order to speak on behalf of a visual artefact, one must have entrenched significant resources and expertise and must be regarded as a legitimate member of the community endowed with such rights and skills. Just as visual representations can bridge and bond, they can also separate and isolate them from one another.

A sociological perspective on visual representations underlines the situational and contingent nature of the use and role of visual artefacts. Visual artefacts and their use must then be examined in its setting, in its "context of application." Expressed differently, visual representations have no innate or intrinsic role or meaning prior to their actual use. They cannot be examined *a priori* but only *in situ*, in their very use.

VISUAL REPRESENTATIONS IN ARCHITECT WORK

Being a visually oriented profession, architectural training emphasizes the capacity to see as an architect and to account for the design choices being made. Such capacities of seeing include both the professional gaze where the designed object is evaluated on basis of professional standards and the ability to see the work as an outsider, to understand how the work is perceived by nonarchitects (Lymer, 2009). To accomplish these two objectives, architectural education programs commonly used so-called "critiques," commonly referred to as "crits," where the students' work is presented and reviewed in public by professors, peers, and external professionals and receives feedback from the audience. Lymer (2009) estimates that architectural school graduates undergo between 10 and 15 individual critiques and participate in between 150 and 200 critique sessions during an education program. The critiques are said to "[a]llow students to gain access to the discourse of architecture, pick up ideas, confirm their position as members of the group, access technical expertise and guidance, test out ideas, and compare the responses to their own approaches with those of others" (Lymer, 2009: 149). Similar to the so-called Socratic method in law school education programs and case solving in the tradition of Harvard Business School in management education programs, the critique is a standardized education program feature in architectural training.

As being a visually oriented profession, one distinguishing mark of the architect's competence is to be able to see and inhabit not-yet-built spaces—virtual, not-yet-actualized spaces—by means of what Lymer (2009: 156) calls "the proximal artefacts of the discipline." That is, being able to anticipate forthcoming concerns or construction problems on basis of sketches and models is part of the skills entrenched through the critique sessions. In these sessions, the architectural students are moving back and forth between the professional architectural vision granting intramural norms and values great importance, and the vision of the nonarchitect not seeing the more intricate and "nonvisible" features of the proposed designed object. Architectural students are thus switching between *seeing* the designed object as such and *seeing through it*; in the one case, the designed object is at the center of the relations and examined in itself, while in the other case it is located in a thick relational texture including the various stakeholders of the construction industry and their various interests. "Being a visually oriented profession," Lymer (2009: 158) writes, "architecture is not without its own reflexive awareness of perceptual practice; attention is paid to visualization both in the design process itself and in the communicative function of the presentation—the 'selling' of the design embodied in the presentation." As a consequence, the architectural students must be trained in simultaneously "seeing as an architect" and distancing themselves from this professional vision, enacting a "reflexive awareness of professional vision itself" (Lymer, 2009: 167) to be able to navigate between both the professional standards of practicing architects and the broader community of nonarchitects. "Managing nonarchitectual vision in relations to architecture's proximal artefacts is thus a central architectural competence," Lymer (2009: 167) suggests. Expressed differently, the critiques provides the architectural students with the opportunity to bridge what is visible and invisible for nonarchitects and to develop rhetorical and discursive competencies making sense out of the design choices made by the architect or group of architects. Lymer concludes:

> [C]ritics construe designed qualities as being simultaneously visible and invisible—visible to the critics but invisible potential other viewers. This practice, then, exposes students' work to a variety of pedagogically configured gazes. The students' socialization into a specialized field of competence, in which objects are designed according to professional rationalities that go beyond what is readily visible of accessible to the nonarchitect, is thereby made accountable for the communicative and translational demands of professional praxis. Rather than being a unidirectional process of *estrangement* from ordinary ways of seeing, then, mastering architectural vision is more aptly described as an appropriation of specialized discursive and perceptual competencies, coupled to a refinement of one's ability to configure a set of different gazes or viewpoints in relation to architecture's proximal artefacts. (Lymer, 2009: 167–168)

After finishing a significant period of education and training, including the participation in many critique sessions, the architectural school graduate is capable of seeing both as a member of the professional community of architects and mastering an accompanying rhetoric embedded in a discursive formation on architecture, but also to see as a nonarchitect, that is, to see through the designed object and to locate it in a broader context of the construction industry and society more generally. The skilled architect is a Janus-faced professional in terms of being able to alternate between two distinctly separated ways of seeing and vocabularies in their course of action. Equipped with such skills, the architectural school graduate may navigate in territories beset by various professional standards and economic and social objectives.

In architects' day-to-day work, the general specifications regarding the features of the building, its function, its end user, and other information of relevance for the architect's work are called the *programme* of the building. The programme includes the "content of the building" (Yaneva, 2005: 891, n. 33), that is, its "internal distribution of spaces according to functional needs, general scope and insertion in reality." The programme is formally provided by the client, but in many cases the architect is involved in formulating the programme. When the architect is starting to work on a programme, he or she is developing a *concept*, the main idea of the building, "taken in its relationships with the client demand, the city, the urban fabric, and the broader social, political and cultural context" (Yaneva, 2005: 891, n. 31). The concept is thereafter further specified and turned into detailed decisions regarding the shape and form of social spaces, materials choices, and so forth. When elaborating on the concept, in the very early phases of the process, architects are likely to mobilize a range of visual tools and visual representations that are helping the architect move from the mere image or idea of the building to something more stable and durable, namely the actual sketches and drawings, and, finally, the blueprints used the constructing the building on site. Ewenstein and Whyte (2007) argue that visual representations are objects that play a central role in "mediating knowledge and knowing" (Ewenstein and Whyte, 2007: 81). This somewhat cryptic formulation suggests that the formal knowledge embodied in programs and documents and the know-how, experience, and expertise mobilized by the architect need to be brought together. The architect's ideas and ambitions are not yet formalized in the early stages and the visual representations serve to "communicate meaning symbolically" (Ewenstein and Whyte, 2007: 82). Just as Henderson (1999) conceived visual representations such as drawings to have meta-indexical capacities, the ability to denote many things and to bridge various bodies of know-how in the design work, Ewenstein and Whyte (2007) think that visual representations are heuristic tools for sharing abstract thinking:

> [T]hey [visual representations] communicate meaning symbolically. This helps to articulate, exchange and understand design ideas. Second, they are manifest in the practice as material entities, often physical artefacts, with which practitioners can interact as they generate knowledge individually or collectively. The communicative and interactive properties of visual representations constitute them as central elements of knowledge work. (Ewenstein and Whyte, 2007: 82)

In practice, this means that in the early, more creative stages of the process where the concept is developed, architects engage in substantial sketching activities to sort out the productive ideas that could be further refined:

> In the architectural design firm visual materials are treated as fluid in the process of defining design problems and exploring appropriate solutions. The work of both individual designer and design teams is characterized by copious sketching. Through sketching, red-lining, and generally marking up representations design problems are identified and defined, and corresponding solutions are tested on paper and

on screen. The objects that allow such knowledge work to proceed are fluid materials in which the status of visual representations is often provisional and in flux. (Whyte et al., 2007: 22)

Also, Lymer (2009) stresses the iterative nature of the sketching work and that the work, prior to the public presentation, is essentially an inward operation to stabilize and translate a design idea into a visual form:

> Architects see renderings, sketches, and plans not only to communicate their ideas to clients but also to concretize and visualize their design to themselves in order to assess its architectural qualities. Design is a thoroughly iterative process, in which suggestions are worked up, modelled, assessed, and remodelled. (Lymer, 2009: 158–159)

The sketches are useful "epistemic objects" (Whyte et al., 2007) in terms of being in a liminal position in between, on the one hand, what is fixed enough to serve as a shared arena for a variety of stakeholders, while, on the other hand, being open-ended and fluid enough to be capable of embodying novel ideas and suggestions. The sketch is neither self-enclosed and fixed nor in a state of flux and fluidity, but is capable of productively bridging the two epistemological positions; it is what Yaneva (2005) calls a "multiverse," a patchwork of combined models, sketches, and images but never reducible to either of these visual representations and always "multiple" (see e.g., Mol, 2002): "The final building is never present on any single state or model, but in what all of them together project. That is why the building is a multiple object; a composition of many elements; a 'multiverse' instead of a 'universe' " (Yaneva, 2005: 871). Or in Whyte et al.'s (2007: 22) formulation: "Visual materials are used in a fluid way for sense-making and to develop a shared understanding of meaning. The various stakeholders have a different understanding and appreciation of a design project."

As the work proceeds, the initial sketches become subject to decision making and certain alternatives are abandoned while others are further explored and refined. Consequently, the sketches become less open for discussion and the final architecture is being decided upon. Whyte et al. (2007: 22) say that the visual materials become "frozen"—they are no longer open for negotiations but become semi-stable epistemic objects that take the form of a "fact" in the technoscientific meaning of the term, that is, as something that is becoming increasingly immutable and fixed. "Frozen visual materials are characterized by greater certainty," Whyte et al. (2007: 22) say. Whyte et al. (2007) suggest that architects are capable of using their various visual representations as a tool for supporting their own interests and position: "Practitioners can mediate power relations among themselves by and other stakeholders by managing what is and is not shown, how it is shown and when. Frozen materials can more easily steer meaning and project narrative and thereby influence the kinds of understandings different actors develop. They can become a tool for the exercise of power" (Whyte et al., 2007: 23). On the other hand, Yaneva (2005) suggests that models are used as a shared ground for further discussion about the design of the building:

> Models often travel outside the architectural office to gain powerful allies among clients, sponsors, and future users, community groups and city planning commissions, they are supposed to express concerns, expertise, opinions and expectations, which are furthermore taken into account in design. Thus models incorporate not only a variety of technical concerns, but also a range of other viewpoints. (Yaneva, 2005: 889, n. 15)

One may thus claim that visual representations can both prevent and support further discussions depending on how the architects choose to frame the model; is it still open for negotiations or it is frozen? For instance, when presenting a rather elaborated CAD image of a forthcoming building, outsiders (i.e., nonarchitects) may easily be mesmerized by the seemingly finished design and buy into the concept. The CAD media are simply providing images that outsiders have more problems to dismiss as "mere sketches." On the other hand, if sketches are produced by pen and paper, arguably the most traditional procedure in architect work, there is not the same sense of being a self-enclosed and finished process. As epistemic objects, the CAD image is perceived as more immutable and fixed than the sketch or drawing. The choice between media is therefore what is potentially influencing the decision-making process. In the day-to-day work in architect bureaus, architects are trying to stretch the boundary for what could possibly be done within the framework of a given programme. When stretching the boundaries, the operative limits of the visual artefacts qua epistemic objects are tested. Sketches and other visual representations are capable of bridging opposing terms such as open/closed, fixed/fluid, and so forth, i.e., to serve as a meta-indexical epistemic object. But all epistemic objects such as visual representations and other boundary objects have their limits of what they are capable of accomplishing. During certain conditions, the gap between opposing terms becomes too large or the variety and scope of perspectives and meaning are too wide to be fully captured by the sketches and collective meaning simply fades away, like water pouring into the sand on a beach. Whyte et al. (2007) uses a musical metaphor to capture the sense of loss of shared meaning:

> In experimental jazz, sounds may be on the edge of cacophony, in danger of disintegrating into sheer noise, from which the poorer ensembles are unable to retrieve a meaningful experience. In the same way, without care, meaning may simply evaporate in design work. An inexperienced or inattentive design team could easily lose track

of what was going on and be left only with sheer information. That is not going to happen is a testament to the designers' collective skill. (Whyte et al., 2007: 23)

What, then, are the mechanisms enabling the meta-indexical qualities of epistemic objects such as sketches, CAD images, photos, full-scale models, and the other visual representations deployed by architects? What shared assumptions, beliefs, and skills are needed for effectively deploying visual representations? Nicolini (2007: 578) suggests that there are a number of conditions that needs to be met for visual representations to function properly. First, visual artefacts become meaningful when they are put to use in "[t]he context of complex and 'messy' practice" (Nicolini, 2007: 578), that is, in domains where a variety of skills, resources, and experiences needs to be brought together and aligned. That is, visual representations serve as productive epistemic objects when they are capable of making sense and producing a shared sense of meaning across heterogeneous communities or when participants, both insiders and outsiders, do have a problem to fully articulate their ideas verbally. "Visual artefacts emerge and express their performative power only when they are used within a specific activity and in conjunction with other elements," Nicolini (2007: 578) says. In a well-ordered and neatly structured world, there is less need for visual representations capturing what may be called "weak constructs," ideas and objectives that are not yet articulated or represented but are on the verge of being so. Second, visual representations are, somewhat paradoxical given their role to bridge heterogeneous or inconsistent elements of knowing, relying on a shared set of assumptions. In the later Wittgenstein's conceptualization of language, shared meaning and understanding presuppose shared experiences. Similarly, the using visual media demands both shared experiences and skills and expertise to function as anticipated. Says Nicolini:

> In order to function, so to speak, visual artefacts require a certain amount of work that often remains hidden, what could be called the 'non-visual work' necessary for making visual artefacts work. Put differently, while it is undeniable that a picture is often worth 'a thousand words,' it is also true that pictures and word work together according to a subtle and often unnoticed division of labour. (Nicolini, 2007: 578)

As, for instance, critics have noticed when addressing the ubiquitous use of photographs in contemporary society (e.g., Susan Sontag, Siegfried Kracauer, Vilém Flusser), there is a commonsense belief that photographs are capable of being "self-explanatory," in no need of being explained but, on the contrary, capable of "explaining" or "representing" texts. This fallacy is strongly objected to by, for instance, Susan Sontag (1973: 23), claiming that "photographs, which themselves cannot explain anything, are inexhaustible invitations to deduction, speculation, and fantasy." In the 1920s, the great Weimar social theorist Siegfried Kracauer expressed his contempt for the modern world filled with images and photos not capable of explaining themselves:

> Never before has a period known so little about itself. In the hands of the ruling society, the invention of illustrated magazines is one of the most powerful means of organizing a strike against understanding. Even the colorful arrangement of the images provides a not insignificant means for successfully implementing such a strike. The *continuity* of these images systematically excludes their contextual framework available to consciousness. The 'image-idea' drives away the idea. The blizzard of photographs betrays an indifference towards what the things mean. (Kracauer, 1995: 58)

Both Sontag (1973) and Kracauer (1995) are suggesting that visual representations (e.g., photographs) are not in any way self-explanatory. Instead, they are delusions inviting endless speculations or "fantasies." Speaking in terms of the use of visual representations in architect work, the use of these epistemic objects relies on the shared ability and understanding of what is the limits of the visual representations. If either of the stakeholders in the process assumes that visual representations are capable of enabling more than is actually the case, the intricate network of elements such as visual representations, language, know-how, and so forth may cease to function properly. In conclusion, visual representations do play a role in milieus where heterogeneous resources are mobilized and put to work and where the various actors have an understanding of the purpose, functions, but also limitations of the visual representations. When these conditions are met, visual representations are playing a central role.

The Use of Visual Representations: An Illustration

The noted American architect Frank O. Gehry, one of the most influential contemporary architects and the man behind buildings such as the Guggenheim museum in Bilbao, the Disney Concert Hall in Los Angeles, and the Experience Music Project in Seattle, is well known for his strong reliance on advanced computer media to design his mind-boggling architecture, in many cases defying the conventional view of what architecture is and what role it should play. Boland, Lyytinen, and Yoo (2007) conducted a study of Gehry's work from an organization theory perspective, emphasizing the consequences of the use of 3-D media in the work. Boland, Lyytinen and Yoo (2007: 633) argue that what they refer to as "complex building projects" is a fertile ground for studying a range of topics discussed the conceptual discourse on organizations, including knowledge-intensive work and network organization: "AEC [Architecture, Engineering, and Construction] projects are distributed (designed and constructed by multiple, autonomous actors), heterogeneous (composed of communities with distinct skills, expertise and interests), and sociotechnical (requiring trust, values and norms), as well as IT capabilities and complex fabrication processes)." In the previous, 2-D regime of visual representation, established for generations in the construction industry, actors in AEC projects know, Boland, Lyytinen, and Yoo (2007) argue, how to "encode" visual representations; that is, they are "visually literate" and comfortable with "translating" the two-dimensional images into actual buildings. In Gehry's project, on the contrary, relying on continuous modelling of the emerging building, the 2-D competencies and experiences are no longer fully applicable. Various AEC project coworkers are therefore more closely integrated into the architecture design phase. Rather than working (relatively) much on his or her own, in the 3-D design paradigm represented by Gehry, a range of actors is collaborating more closely:

> [W]hen 2-D blueprints were replaced with digital 3-D representations at the AEC community boundaries, the traditional contract language and associated principles of loose couplings did not provide actors with sufficient ability to understand and negotiate their new roles, or with sufficient understandings of their risk. (Boland, Lyytinen, & Yoo, 2007: 639)

The traditional loose couplings between various actors in the projects were therefore displaced by more tightly coupled relationships. This makes Gehry's project more costly and takes longer to finish, but at the same time, there is a much better collaborative environment where stakeholders and project coworkers can meet. For instance, the chief operating officer in the project reported that "[i]n his 20 plus years of working in the industry, he had spent fewer than eight hours in architects' offices" (Boland, Lyytinen, & Yoo, 2007: 640), but in the Gehry project he was more or less visiting the architect office every week and played a central role in contributing to the architecture. Boland, Lyytinen, and Yoo (2007) suggests that the 3-D regime relied to a larger extent than traditionally on what Thompson (1967) called coordination through "mutual adjustment," the continuous collaboration between various actors and agents.

It may be that there is a poor validity in a research project studying one of the most extraordinary and well-known contemporary architects, Frank Gehry, but notwithstanding such methodological reservations, what Boland, Lyytinen, and Yoo (2007) show is that the use of visual representations and computer-based media enabling advanced 3-D images are having significant influence on how Gehry's projects are organized. While the construction industry is generally held as an example of a loosely coupled system composed of a number of small and medium-sized actors (Dubois and Gadde, 2002), the use of new media is contributing to a more tightly coupled industry structure. Gehry's architecture is at the frontline of what is technically possible to produce and consequently there is a need for a continuous collaboration between a variety of actors. In summary, the study shows that visual representations play a central role in determining what the built environment is or may be; being able to produce intriguing images of buildings is an important driver for change in the industry.

THE USES OF VISUAL REPRESENTATIONS IN ARCHITECT WORK

Introducing Brown Architects and Blue Architects

Brown Architects, a major Scandinavian architect office, has its main office in Gothenburg, Sweden, but is located in a number of places in Sweden and Denmark. Brown Architects is nationally renowned and is a prestigious office attracting some of the most skilled and creative architects, interior decorators, light designers, designers, and engineers in Scandinavia. The office works in a wide variety of sectors pertaining to the built environment including housing, health care buildings, schools, landscape design and architecture, furniture design, and interior decoration. Brown Architects was founded in 1951 and has grown organically and through mergers and acquisitions and is today one of the largest architect offices in Scandinavia. The firm employs about 500 workers in 10 offices. Ninety-nine workers are partners of the firm. In the beginning of the new millennium, Brown Architects won the prestigious national architecture award the Kasper Sahlin prize for a Stockholm Office.

Blue Architects is located in Gothenburg and operates primarily in the Gothenburg metropolitan region and the western part of Sweden but has some projects running in various parts of Sweden. The firm was grounded in the early 1980s when four Brown Architects coworkers, two architects, and two civil engineers started their own company. Blue has today approximately 70 coworkers, whereof about 60 percent are architects and 40 percent are engineers (administrative personnel taken apart). Nine coworkers own the company. The company is organized into three "studios" including 15–20 coworkers having expertise in areas such as housing, schools and "education" buildings, and industry buildings. Blue has affiliated architect bureaus in one place in southern Europe and in South America. Blue is supposed to serve as a "general" architect bureau, having expertise in many fields, but take pride in having many highly successful school buildings in its portfolio.

The Architect's Gaze: Seeing/Knowing

As suggested in studies of architect work (e.g., Cuff, 1983), architects tend to think of their position in the construction industry as being cumbersome in terms of diminishing domains of jurisdiction and the ambition to cut costs throughout the process, ultimately reducing the perceived aesthetic features of the building. Being fundamentally collaborative in nature, architect work is based on a body of know-how, experience, and expertise that at times is complicated to define in clearly bounded and lexical terms. Several of the interviewees addressed this predicament:

> It is complicated to categorize architectural knowledge: What is it really? Here, we still have a problem to define what architects do, what kind of specific knowledge we can offer. This is an attempt to connect people and tacit knowledge and articulate it in discussions and seminars. (Interviewee #1, Brown)

At the same time as the architects felt the need for justifying their competence and role in society at large, they also had a firm belief that they were providing a unique mixture of aesthetic know-how, construction management and engineering expertise, and an understanding of how the built environment was influencing its users and society more broadly. However, this located the architect in an odd position in a society preoccupied with ongoing specialization and "evidence-based knowledge." One of the architects reflected on the situation:

> The architect profession is a bit special . . . combining both technical and artistic features . . . The classical view is that the more clear-cut engineering position uses knowledge that are verified, while for us, in our profession, there are components of intuitive knowledge or knowledge that are entrenched or trained. I do not know if this is true but it is the classic view . . . Nevertheless, it is an issue in the industry as such because I think we have rather poor mechanisms for organized knowledge sharing. (Interviewee #4, Brown)

One of the architects at Blue thought of her and her colleagues' expertise as the capacity to bring a variety of qualities into harmony on an aggregated level, that is, to think of the building holistically and in terms of mediating various demands:

> Above all, this integrated view of the aesthetic features of the building. The engineers are skilled in handling the technical solutions that not all architects have insight into. The engineers are skilled in dealing with the details, the solutions, how to accomplish things. But the overview, that is I would say the unique expertise of the architect or the architect profession. From the very beginning, we are trained in thinking from the city plan, the area plan, from quarter, to building, to layout to exactly how the lamp should be mounted on the ceiling. Constructing a layout includes volumes, layout alternatives, inflow of sunshine . . . accessibility for handicapped users, and so forth. (Interviewee #2, Blue)

One of the interviewees, a younger but yet experienced architect, even expressed some scepticism regarding the use of the term *knowledge* when speaking about the architect's work: "It is tricky to speak of knowledge per se when talking about architects' work because it is just as much about skills and intuition. The process and the work procedures matter just as much" (Interviewee #2, Brown).

In the day-to-day practices, the architects were using a fairly linear model for their work, beginning with the written programme, specifying the function and purpose of the building, and finishing, weeks or months—perhaps even years—down the road with a compete blueprint sent off to the client. The earliest phases, arguably the most creative and innovative phases, where the concept of the building is defined, started with a combination of data collection, creative thinking, visits to the actual site, and other rather seemingly less structured activities. These activities were undertaken to cover most of the information that could be used when designing the building. One of the more experienced architects reflected on the process:

> The challenge is to identify the principal problems within the program and give as good answers to them as possible. Then you can start the sketching process and the program analysis straight away. In many cases, projects are initiated as a rather fuzzy question or in terms of a continuation of a previous project. (Interviewee #3, Brown)

The architect also emphasized the need for visiting the site to create a more detailed understanding of the possibilities or the limitations in the project: "Once you've visited the site and have been thinking for a while, then you may contrive of entire new solutions . . . There needs to be a period of time where you juggle different alternatives . . . One mustn't follow the first instinct," she said (Interviewee #3, Brown).

After the initial phase, including creative thinking and reflection, the collection of relevant data and the retrieval of various "reference photos" from architecture magazines and journals and from the Internet, used as a source of inspiration, the sketching phase begins.[2] In the sketching phase, a series of possible alternatives are given a shape and a form. In a specific experimental mode of thinking, different alternatives are tested against one another and gradually a smaller number of alternatives are selected. One of the challenges in this phase, one of the architects argued, is to not to enclose the design too early but to maintain as many possibilities open as long as practicably possible:

> One important aspect is to avoid fixing some of the parameters, to be capable of maintaining an openness as long as possible. That is accomplished not by designing objects and entities and give them a form. For some clients, this is quite complicated to handle. (Interviewee #2, Brown)

One of the architects at Blue also emphasized the need for "some leeway" in the project: "[In cases] when there are some leeway, where not everything is specified from the beginning" (Architect #2, Blue). As emphasized, for the clients, this modus operandi is posing a challenge for the practicing architect. The clients and other stakeholders want to see as soon as possible what kind of solutions the architect is suggesting, and the willingness on part of the architect to maintain a "fluid state" in the sketching procedure is not always appreciated.

In general, the sketching phase is the event where the programme is being "translated" into visual representations. The role of the skilled architect is to take into account and materialize as much as possible in the programme:

> The challenge is identify the principal problems within the program and give as good answers to them as possible. Then you can start the sketching process and the program analysis straight away. In many cases, projects are initiated as a rather fuzzy question or in terms of a continuation of a previous project. (Interviewee #3, Brown)

In order to handle all the ambiguities and uncertainties during the process, a *concept* was formulated. One of the architects at Blue explained:

> We're trying to establish a concept that we may follow. That is a method for navigating in a complex milieu where it may easily become a mess of buildings and volumes. And when it comes to movements, there is a need for a clear idea to produce a good building. We don't think it is a helpful way forward to sit on our high horses and play the role of misunderstood aesthetes. On the contrary, we need to be as open as possible in both telling what we want to accomplish and how we may follow this road together [i.e., client and architects] (Interviewee #2, Blue)

The sketching phase is therefore the heart of the very profession, the event where entrenched skills, aesthetic norms and values, and external demands and expectations are co-aligned and brought into an acceptable harmony and negotiated order. Many architects are nourishing the belief that they should be capable of contributing with novel solutions to perceived problems, thereby giving the client something he or she was not expecting. One of the architects testified to such values:

> In the sketching method there is an implicit assumption that it is all about identifying the unique features of every assignment on basis of the conditions that we operate under. To create what no one could really anticipate. (Interviewee #4, Brown)

In terms of actual practice, architects make use of a variety of visual representations in their work. This includes photographs and later on CAD images and full-scale models. In the early, sketching phases, photos serve the double role of both being a source of inspiration for the architect him or herself and to capture a "sense" or an "aesthetic idea" the architect would like to convey to the client or other stakeholders. One of the architects explains:

> Quite often, the picture is important. You do the sketching and try to visualize and then you make use of reference pictures. You bring photos and things like that from previous projects. Even in the presentation of one's own project, you make use of photos to capture a certain attitude or feeling or a possible solution for something. (Interviewee #2, Brown)

These "reference photos" served a role not only when discussing with "outsiders" but also when collaborating with colleagues in the office:

> Q: How do you discuss architecture?
> A: A lot of talk derives from reference photos, reference projects; when sketching something or building a model, more often than merely speaking about it. At times you need to help clarifying—a first sketch could be quite vague. You need to explain it: 'this is what I would like to accomplish,' but to just speak about it is quite complicated. (Interviewee #2, Brown)

A similar procedure was used in Blue Architects. One of the architects explained that what was propelling the early creative phases was the use of "photos, photos, photos." She continued to point at the value of photos when communicating with clients: "Examples of good layouts [are collected] but also inspirational photos that we are using in our dialogues with the client to more easily communicate what we are trying to create. Then you display a photo [to the client]: 'something like this, perhaps?' " (Interviewee #2, Blue). One of her colleagues engaged in a similar procedure in the early phases of the work: "There are a lot of magazines and stuff that I try to sift through" (Interviewee #6, Blue). The other main role of photos was as a source of inspiration on the creative work:

> Q: Do you read a lot of magazines and books and so forth to get inspiration in the architect work?
> A: Well, yes I do. You need that, to get inspiration. Quite often during coffee breaks or after the lunch, I sit for a little while in the library. I have no magazines at home because there are many other things, but here there is a good access to journals that I can read. I suppose most of us do. (Interviewee #2, Blue)

References photos and other images are therefore serving a role as what is anchoring and manifesting fleeting and fluid aesthetic norms and values.

Rather than addressing an idea or an image of a forthcoming building in narrative terms, through the use of language, photos provide a handy shortcut between thought and actual representation. Experienced architects (like any other experts), especially those who have collaborated over time in various projects, are of course capable of using a denotative language that through the use of a few distinct phases may convey a sense of what is sought for. Still in many cases, the photo is a tool enabling faster and more accurate descriptions of objectives and desired outcomes. At the same time as they are helpful, photos are deceiving in terms of leading the architect astray and making him or her reuse or reproduce what is already done elsewhere. Such failures to create what is "new" and "previously unseen" represent a violation of the professional ideology of practicing architects and must therefore be addressed as a potential risk when using reference photos:

> You need to build on your experience, on photos you find in the literature, or on excursions. At the same time, it is damn easy to adopt this kind of information so you need to be careful. The foundation for a good solution is in one way or another already present in the very program. (Interviewee #3, Brown)

Also the architects in Blue addressed such "trends" in the field:

> You do not want to do what everyone else is doing but you aim to produce your own angle or your own character. That is very important. But you also need inspiration. If you believe that we should use a certain type of roof, not flat roofs, then you try to find photos of cool buildings having for instance a pointy roof. But you work with other materials and do not use a photo to copy it. It is important when using a photo in the documentation that you are quite precise in telling what you would like to demonstrate with the photo. I think that is important. At times, you see programs filled with photos [not explained]. This is what we want it to look like, what is useful in the picture." (Interviewee #3, Blue)

Another Blue architect was concerned about "path-dependency" in the trade:

> A: This is used systematically, that you check up references and so on.
> Q: Could you ever have this feeling that you are restrained in terms of being too influenced [by other architects' work]?
> A: That is quite possible. But I have not perceived that as a problem, so actually I don't think of that as a form of restraint. I don't think it is a wrong idea to make use of the older references or the previous work of the office. There is, however, a risk that we are

taking it too far, that we are making the same project over and over. (Interviewee #4, Blue)

Some of the architects emphasized that while there is a prescribed and scripted model being used in the profession and in the actual office, more or less linear in its outline, to work with architecture implies to recognize the loops and turns that the process is undergoing. Since there are many aspects to take into account, the process is therefore not always linear and stepwise. One of the architects addressed this issue:

> You don't produce the architecture by thinking [Swedish, "Man tänker ju inte fram arkitekturen"]; it is not a logical consequence; there is no single correct answer to an articulated problem but it is instead a process of testing and decision-making . . . The more dimensions you add and the more you can visualize the faster you can advance. Therefore, the use of models adds a dimension to the sketch. (Interviewee #3, Brown)

As the work proceeds and the actual design is collectively decided upon, architects are at times using more advanced CAD images or full-scale models as heuristic tools to fully represent the idea of the building. In many cases, the use of the CAD was accompanied by intensive sketching and the architects moved back and forth between pen and paper and the computer. This procedure is largely in line with what Henderson (1999: 168) calls "mixed-use practice," a combination of "paper and electronic modes of representation." Says one architect at Blue:

> I start off with paper and pen to find the basic ideas, the foundation. For me, that is quicker and I think have a little bit more freedom. As soon as I find something I believe I can proceed from, I turn to the CAD. I make the construction on the proportions provided and add the map of the terrain. I print it out and continue sketching by hand because now I have the construction to work within. If I feel I have to move down in scale and in details, I return to the computer and use all the tools. So I work back and forth. I think that is an excellent way of working. (Interviewee #2, Blue)

He further explained the work process when designing a major power plant:

> It is a combination, both ways. The first sketch done by Henry was drawn on a Post-it note, I believe. It wasn't too big. It was a box with three solid sides and one in glass. When we work, we move back and forth between working by the hand and with the computer.
>
> Q: How are you doing that?
> A: We try to alter between different media as much as possible. The computer is incredibly precise when you need that and it's fast to

do changes. But when thinking about the entire concept, to think about the causal relations, then it is easier to work by hand with pen and paper.

Q: So you're saving time, quite simple?

A: Yes it does. We're actually working on a sketch done by hand on a paper, on a Post-it note, on a sketch roll, or a piece of paper. Then we define the distances and measures in the computer and use the sketch to see what it looks like. We use 3D animation. We can examine the building from all angles and use photos to get a sense of how it will look quite fast.

Q: But in these early phases, where you identify these elementary forms or formats, then pen and paper is what feels the most natural to use?

A: Yes, that is the case. (Interviewee #2, Blue)

One of the other architects, a Blue, claimed that she was moving back and forth between different media because that gave both an aesthetic freedom at the same time as the constraints of the project were given by the CAD program:

I actually do both ways, but I mostly start with pen and paper . . . if the program is very specific, stating that 'this room should be 13 square meters and this room should be 2 square meters,' then you might just as well start with the CAD because then you drag the surfaces and there is a figure indicating [the size of the surface]. But most of the time I actually start with pen and paper and sketches quite a bit. But that could vary over time. (Interviewee #5, Blue)

However, some of the older architects were more comfortable using the pen in the early stages:

To speak for myself, when you use a pen you don't experience those limitations: You may let your hand run more freely and you can construct these connections between different rooms and get all these different proportions. That is, I think, more difficult to accomplish in a computer. But that is for sure quite personal; the more you work on it the more you perceive the computer as an extension of the pen, I believe that is the case. It is probably a matter of what you are used to . . . I start with sketches and then I move on to the computer. (Interviewee #6, Blue)

Since the CAD software plays a central role in the architect work, the advancement of the CAD package is widely regarded in positive terms among the architects:

As soon as possible, you try to create a 3D image because that makes it so much easier to communicate with the client. It is excellent. The software we are using now, ArchiCAD . . . it is so much better in many ways. You get all the information in the form of 3D rather than just 2D by just pushing a button. As soon as the measures are provided, you get these images. Then they can be further worked on and refined. It is no longer, as previously, a surprise that the building became that tall or received quite odd proportions after finishing the 2D outline. That is very valuable for us as well, but primarily when communicating with the client. Very early, one can plan for the volumes and the inflow of sunshine [into the building] . . . It is often very complicated for many to understand the blueprints. That is where the 3D images play a key role. And we have animated movies showing how one can move inside the building. You can also rotate the building and turn it upside down. All this helps creating an understanding of the building. (Interviewee #2, Blue)

The value of the scale-model lies in its inclusive nature, its ability to add all dimensions and to convey the aesthetic qualities of the building. In addition, a full-scale model is a useful tool for collaboration: "A model is the best item to collaborate around, quite simple," Interviewee #3 (at Brown), declared. Another architect supported this view: "I think the most important feature of the physical model is that more people can participate in the process at the same time, in one way or another" (Interviewee #2, Brown). Also at Blue, full-scale models were used at times, especially in complex projects, such as "in large projects with complex rooms," one architect said. She continued: "When building housing it is quite rarely used because the volumes are so simple and easily understood. But when you have a problem understanding how large building and complex rooms or complicated rooms are integrated, some experimentation is needed. Difficult volumes; you construct a simple volume model, create a construction around it and experiment with different shapes on the roof." (Architect #1, Blue)

For some assignments, for instance when engaging in interior decoration, CAD images were perceived as less useful than full-scale or even large-scale models. One of the interior decorators subscribed to this view: "You cannot just work with CAD. CAD is certainly not the adequate tool when working with interior decoration. You can integrate things but to produce models is complicated," she argued. In terms of being a visual representation, the full-scale model is in between the 3-D image and the actual building, showing all the relationships between the elements in the forthcoming building in three dimensions. The full-scale model is also part of the traditional toolbox deployed in the architect professions and is therefore important for reproducing the image and identity of the practicing architects. If nothing else, a full-scale model testifies to the accumulated and aggregated competence of the practicing architect, a form of embodiment of a variety of tacit and explicit competencies.

The Role of Field Excursions

A third forms of use of visual representations is the tradition in the architect profession to go on excursions, actual visits of built architecture that for some reason may be considered of relevance for the trade or for the focal firm. In Brown, field trips were organized annually and they were greatly appreciated by the coworkers, speaking warmly about the value of such collective experiences from built environments. One of the architects suggested this was an important part of the work:

> To visit the built architecture is of great importance. Then you may observe how the assignment is handled. If it is a church or a housing project, then you examine how the building fits into the city planning and down to the details and what materials are used. For most of us, that is a method to identify solutions to problems; a form of knowledge about how to handle something. (Interviewee #1, Brown)

The architect suggested that there is a limit to how much information an image or a photo may convey and therefore one needs to visit the architecture *in situ*; when visiting buildings, one "apprehends the scale and the space itself; that cannot be accomplished on basis of a picture," Interviewee #1 (Brown) said. This view was endorsed by the one of the architects at Blue, emphasizing specifically the inspiration derived from the excursions:

> In the first place, it is used to get some inspiration, which is of central importance in our profession, I think. It is very important to get impulses from the outside. You cannot create anything unless you get some input. You observe something you dislike and certainly do not want to use, or something that looks nice and that you can make use of—this or that detail. It is never the case that you return to your desk and re-construct the same building, but you notice things that may work [elsewhere], like 'that irregular layout of the windows looks cool' and then you might think that this may be useful in my project. Materials are always exciting . . . it is of central importance to have access to journals, excursions, traveling. Regarding excursions, it is a key idea that we are conducting them all together. That we have shared, common references. (Interviewee #2, Blue)

The field trips had several purposes including providing a firsthand experience form some architecturally significant site and being a collective experience enabling further collaborations when being back at work. Several of the interviewees emphasized that the firsthand experience added a certain spatial and tactile dimension to the aesthetic and visual experiences captured by photos, images, or models (see Pallasmaa, 1996):

First, it is professionally rewarding to visit a place . . . Architecture *is* built environment. You cannot fully experience architecture unless you visit the site. You need to . . . capture it to be able to explore all parts. That is why it's important to go on these excursions and not only consume images in journals. (Interviewee #3, Brown)

One of the architects at Blue was speaking of the "experience of space":

It is all about the total experience of the space [Swedish, *rummet*]. You experience the full size and the dimension in a completely different manner. I think there is quite a bit of a difference when you have looked at the detailed layout plan and when you can walk around. You notice the relationships in the building, the entrance, how you can move in the building, and such things. (Architect #4)

The field trips provided a coherent and integrated experience, including an exploration of "all parts" of the building or the site, thereby providing new experiences and learnings:

You acquire knowledge on a variety of layers. That's why it is such an effective method. Including everything from the formulation of the assignment [Swedish, *förhållningsätt till uppgift*], how a colleague has interpreted the assignment, explored the opportunities of the site, and how the program and the demands have been interpreted. Of course, the design and the form, choice of materials and so forth. On all layers, you may learn new things by visiting finished projects. (Interviewee #4, Brown)

At Blue, the same experiences of observing in real-life settings were accounted for:

The experience from entering a room; how does it feel when entering the building? Is it a spatially generous building or do I feel intimidated? Am I safe and calm here or is it intimidating? How are colours used, for instance? Is it stiff and naked or does it feel cozy [Swedish, *ombonat*]. These experiences you cannot attain from watching a photo. [You notice] 'this feels spacious while in the blueprint it all looked so narrow. What could be the difference? The colouring or is it the light being let in from that direction.' (Interviewee #2, Blue)

As may be noticed in these quotes, the architects at the two bureaus were inclined to use a rather poetic (as opposed to scientific or engineering-oriented) vocabulary, a way of talking that included a series of emotional phrases and metaphors to denote the experience of the built milieus. In many cases, accounting for the experience of space was complicated and words seemed to fail the observer:

There is never the same feeling when you enter [the building]. The experience is quite different. But it doesn't need to be a positive thing, it could be the other way around.

Q: So what is that feeling, what kind of feeling is there?

A: Well, how can you explain that? Quite often you notice things like, 'well, okay, you may do like this and you may do like that.' You need that sense of experiencing something, to get a sense of a new design, a new expression that you haven't thought of yourself. You're looking for these somewhat odd things so to speak. (Architect #6, Blue)

One of the architects at Blue stressed the differences between the talk between architects and with the engineers:

When talking to other architects I use our professional lingo, I guess. That is 'feelings', 'experiences of space'—I believe we are letting ourselves go a bit [Swedish, *svävar ut lite*] . . . [with the engineers] we are talking much more about the details, the selections of materials, but with the architects, I think, we are using more emotional words; values and how we experience space, light, and colouring. (Interviewee #2, Blue)

Many of the architects emphasized the difference between observing a photograph and actually inhabiting the actual space:

You may look at a photo to see that it looks quite cool. You see the façade but not what is behind it; and you don't see the consequences of the choices. In one way, it is quite superficial to browse magazines because you don't really know what is actually built . . . if you enter a building, then you know what has been done. All the way. (Architect #2, Blue)

One of his colleagues also addressed the need for experiencing what is not provided by photos and images:

Those things do not appear in the magazines when you watch a picture. You cannot come close to see 'how does this work,' or 'how did you solve this thing' or 'how did they construct that.' Otherwise, there is very many things that you may see that you cannot understand when looking at a picture." (Architect #5)

More specifically, the field trips and the excursions were an important complement to the sketching procedures in terms of providing a connection between the photo, image, or blueprint and the actual building. The professional vision, what may be called the architect's gaze, is what includes the ability to bridge the two-dimensional image or blueprint and the experience of being in an actual building. When the experienced architect look at an image, he or she is also capable of creating an actual and embodied sense of how its feels to be part of that building, to enter it, to walk around it, to touch and smell the materials and to perceive the interior and exterior spaces. The architect's gaze is thus a form of "embodied professional vision" in Merleau-Ponty's (1962) sense of the term, a vision that engages bodily sensations and created a sense of being in the three-dimensional actual space. Without opportunities for such collective experiences of built environments, this embodied professional vision is never fully developed. One of the architects emphasized this part of the professional development:

> We work quite a lot with two-dimensional tools . . . The experience of being part of the room is very, very important. To understand what one is sketching, to spend time in environments where you can sense how large a space is . . . Then you need to visit places. That's how the brain works. You cannot just look at a sketch. When you have worked for 25 years, then you create an understanding [Swedish, *förståelse*] but never a sense [Swedish, *känsla*] of the space. It is imperative to spend some time on the sites. (Interviewee #5, Brown)

While there was little criticism regarding the value of and use of the excursions and the field trips, one of the executives at Brown, an architect, reflected on the widespread use of this, as he considered it, architect tradition in the construction industry, and asked himself what new practices to make use of to maintain the architects' expertise and jurisdiction:

> In one way, that is [the excursions] the main way for professional development among architects during all ages. I would like to claim that it was the architects who 'invented' that method for knowledge development. The first architects went to Italy or France to get new impressions and ideas. That has been the case throughout history. Today, it is not only architects doing excursions but the whole industry travel to visit places. We start to think that it has been part of our activities and that we are bypassed by the clients who are out there all the time and are more informed than we are. (Interviewee #4, Brown)

Architects make use of a range of visual practices and visual artefacts in their day-to-day work, including sketches, photographs, CAD images, full-scale models, and visits to built architecture to create a shared sense of understanding of how a building should be designed and constructed. These visual representations are epistemic objects that are central to the architects' claim to expertise and understanding and therefore serve as what helps defining the boundaries between their domains of expertise and that of others. Moreover, following Henderson (1999), visual representations serve the role as being meta-indexicals capable of bridging and bringing into harmony a range of capabilities, experiences, know-how, and other resources of relevance for the architect's practice. These meta-indexicals are, however, as suggested by Whyte et al. (2007), not neutral tools accessible for everyone on an equal basis but are instead what can be used to achieve specific desired goals and to accomplish certain outcomes. As such, the visual representations are always embedded in social relations in the construction process. Just as much as visual representations can integrate heterogeneous actors and create a shared arena for discussions, they can erect barriers and exclude certain groups, lacking the right credentials and experiences, from the decision-making process. Visual representations are therefore important components in the assemblage of resources constitutive of the architect's professional vision, the architect's gaze. While the outsider or the neophyte may inspect a "reference photo" and see nothing but a nicely designed house and some appealing features, the professional vision of the architect detects certain axial principles, aesthetic norms and values, trade-offs between alternatives, and overall a generalized view of the professional skills and know-how embodied in the actual building. In addition, the professional vision may unravel a certain "feeling" or "sentiment" or some other highly abstract quality that the architect would like to re-create in the new site. However, at the same time as the architect's gaze is disciplined, just like all professional vision, in many senses of the term, there is still room for new and creative ways of looking and understanding the built environment, leading to discussions and even controversies in the community of architects. One of the architects at Blue claimed that these differences in opinion, articulated during the excursions and other events where buildings were visited, were an important component in the creative work process: "We do all have different preferences and taste and that is what makes it interesting. 'That's what I like'; 'You really think so, I think it is way too cold and stiff'; 'No, that is elegant', someone replies. There are interesting discussions about what has been experienced together not taking place if we visit sites on our own." (Interviewee #2, Blue). Without the capacity to see differently, to inscribe various forms of meaning and value in architectural solutions, the field would not develop further but would stagnate over time. The architect's gaze is thus what is both simultaneously and paradoxically disciplined and open for individual interpretations, idiosyncratic ways of seeing.

In summary, then, the professional community of architects operates in a milieu where they have to take into account a large number of aspects in their work and the same time as they are expected to adhere to and even advance their professional ideologies regarding the aesthetic and practical norms in the built environment. In conducting their work, visual representations, appearing in many forms and playing many different roles, are thus what anchors the highly abstract expertise and know-how of the architect in a concrete and immediately observable artefact, thereby enabling further elaborations between heterogeneous actors. Visual representations and professional visions are therefore at the very heart of the professions and consequently demand a proper theoretization and detailed empirical studies.

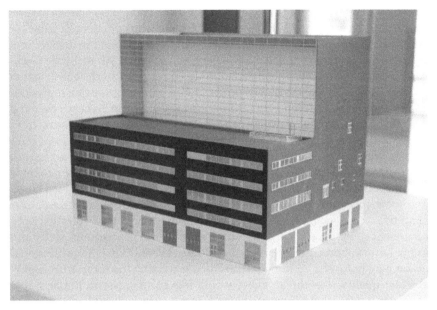

Figure 4.1   Full-scale model, power plant, Blue Architects.

Figure 4.2   Full-scale model, office building, Blue Architects.

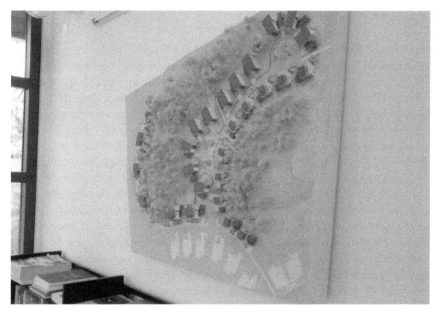

Figure 4.3   Housing project (placed on the wall), Blue Architects.

Figure 4.4   Magazines and journals in the coffee drinking area, Blue Architects.

SUMMARY AND CONCLUSION

Daston and Galison (2007: 368) advocate the fruitful distinction between "theories of vision" (or perhaps even more adequate, "epistemologies of vision") and "practices of seeing" as two distinct analytical approaches. The former discusses the possibilities for accomplishing true or verified knowledge on the basis of visual practices, that is, the epistemological possibilities for vision-based knowledge; the latter program examines how visual practices, "practices of seeing," are developed and used in various domains of expertise in late modern society. While these two programs have bearings on one another, it may be useful to not mix up them entirely since one cannot in most cases, as the saying goes, "both play the game and question the rules." While the "questioning of the rules" clearly belong to the former program, the "understanding of the game" is part of the latter research activities. In this chapter, both epistemologies of vision and practices of seeing have been addressed in the professional community of architects. In conclusion, it may be argued that the professional vision of architects—just as in any other professional community—rests on sediments of assumptions, beliefs, and ideologies regarding the purpose and value of visual representations. Visual representations appear in many forms and play a number of functions and roles. Being neither what is glued nor the glue itself (to use Latour's [1986] metaphor) but always to some extent both, visual representation is central to the architect profession. If nothing else, the empirical study shows that visual representations serve as a meta-indexical resource that denotes both concrete actions and more abstract values and norms. To allude to Latour (1991) one more time, visual representations are what render professional expertise durable. They provide opportunities for professional vision and ultimately help reproduce professional communities and their jurisdiction over targeted domains.

Part III
Concluding Remarks

5 The Primacy of Vision and Its Implication for Organization Theory

INTRODUCTION

"Each book is a pedagogy aimed at forming the reader".

Jacques Derrida (2007: 31)

Jacques Derrida is probably right when saying that all books have some kind of underlying educational ambition, some idea that is expected to be effectively conveyed, or, in some cases even some moral. It is, however, not always customary or *comme-il-faut* to publicly announce such ambitions. If there is a pedagogy of this monograph, it is not one coherent and unified enough to structure and articulate into one single declaration but is rather to be addressed along a number of complementary discussions. The bearing ideas of this monograph have, however, been that the entire aggregate of visual culture and all the "turns" and "shifts" included therein, beginning in the first half of the nineteenth century, and today, almost two hundred years later, continuing to penetrate new domains through the widespread used of new media and the Internet, is a social condition—*un fait social*, a Durkheimian would say—that has been relatively, given its substantial impact on contemporary society, little examined or explored in organization theory. Through drawing on a rather transdisciplinary body of texts, including sociological theory, history, science and technology studies, art history, and so forth, vision and visuality have been portrayed as what is a major social procedure in contemporary social life. The consequences for organizations and organization theory and management studies are substantial. Centered on Charles Goodwin's useful term *professional vision*, organizational activities are seen as what are in many cases, partially or more conclusively, organized around the active visual inspection of the organizational agent. Professional vision is thus a term that is serving as a relay or nexus between a great number of theoretical frameworks, epistemologies, historical studies, and sociological perspectives all sharing the interest for and concern with vision and visuality. The very act of looking, the visual inspection, the gaze (what Lacan and eventually Foucault referred to as *le regard*), is the very act in which decades of research on vision and attention and individually entrenched and acquired skills are collocated and brought together. On the one hand, the professional vision would not be labelled so unless philosophical, scientific, cultural, and ideological changes since the first half of the nineteenth century would have inscribed such epistemological potentialities into the very act of vision. Over the course of almost two hundred years, we Westerners have learned that the very act of looking may, under determinate and highly controlled conditions, enable a detailed understanding of what lies beneath or between (when rejecting ontological metaphors operating on the basis of the Platonist binary couple surface/depth) what is immediately visible. In addition, the professional gaze is also the very act where individually trained and acquired capacities and skills are demonstrated. Being part of what Fleck (1979) calls a "thought collective" is to be able to inspect and review images and photos in accordance with collectively enacted theories and beliefs. The professional vision is therefore never wholly individual and subjective but is always the gaze under the influence of the other, the generalized member of a particular "thought collective." Professional vision is consequently what is bridging and aligning micro and macro, diachronic and synchronic occurrences, the social and the individual. It is an act that embodies the totality of events and theories. It is also an act that lends itself to empirical studies and theoretical elaborations. Seen in this view, an *organizational theory of vision and visuality* is probably derived from a detailed study of professional vision in various domains of interest.

In this final chapter, Some residual issues, not previously addressed, will be attended to. For instance, the importance of new media and how it is shaping the possibilities for vision and visuality in organization and in society more broadly. In the end of this chapter, there will be a more detailed discussion on how theories of vision and visuality and more specifically professional vision is contributing to the theory of organization. The chapter ends with a summary of the arguments advanced in this book.

THE LINE AND THE SURFACE CODE IN VISUAL CULTURE

The philosopher Vilém Flusser (2000, 2002) discusses the difference between visual media and texts. In Flusser's view, human history is characterized by three great media inventions: the use of images, the invention of linear writing, and most recently, in the mid-nineteenth century, the invention of technical images such as the photograph. Flusser says that the earliest images serve to mediate the relationship between humans and the world: "Human beings 'ex-ist,' i.e., the world is not immediately accessible to them and therefore images are needed to make it comprehensible. However, as soon as this happens, images come between the world and human beings. They are supposed to be maps but they turn into screens: Instead of representing the world, they obscure it until human beings' lives finally become a function of the images they create" (Flusser, 2000: 9). Images thus give rise to what Flusser calls "idolatry," the belief in the image's capacity to capture some underlying truth in social reality. Only with the birth of linear writing, first developed in Sumeria and not reaching our present Western form until the Greeks adopted the Phoenician alphabet including symbols for all the vowels, was idolatry replaced by a new form of critical thinking derived from the use of the written word:

> With writing, a new ability was born called conceptual thinking, which consisted of abstracting lines from surfaces, i.e., producing and decoding them . . . Thus with the invention of writing, human beings took one step further back from the world. Texts do not signify the world; they signify the images they tear up. Hence, to decode texts means to discover the images signified by them. The interpretation of texts is to explain images, while that of concepts is to make ideas comprehensible. In this way, texts are a metacode of images. (Flusser, 2000: 11)

In Flusser's perspective, there is a fundamental conflict between the symbolic systems of the image and the text.[1] While images are providing all its information in its entirety in one single moment, texts are revealing its message through the sequential reading of one word after the other; in texts, meaning arrives when the individual words, sentences, and passages are related to one another and constitute an intelligible whole:

> We must follow the written text if we want to get at its message, but in picture we may get at the message first, and then try to decompose it. And this points to the difference between the one-dimensional line and the two-dimensional surface: the one aims at getting somewhere; the other is there already, but may reveal how it got there. This difference is one of temporality, and involves the present, the past, and the future. (Flusser, 2002: 22)

However, it is a mistake to believe that images are more easily understood than texts. As both social theorists like Susan Sontag (1973), addressing the problems associated with decoding photographs in public media and a range of art theorists (e.g., Leppert, 1996), images such as photographs and paintings are by no means self-explanatory, capable of explaining themselves, but are always comprising layers of meaning that need to be carefully examined and interpreted. In fact, media theorists say that the seductive nature of the images lie precisely in their ability to convey a message *en bloc* and through a brief glance. For Flusser (2000, 2002), texts are vehicles for intellectual engagements and analysis and linear writing is therefore a tool for critical thinking, breaking up the images into elements subject to analysis. On the other hand, the idolatry of the image-bound regime is easily transformed into what Flusser calls a "textolatry," "the faithfulness of texts" (Flusser, 2000: 12), the belief that texts are capable of containing ultimate truths. In all fundamentalist thinking, religious as well as philosophical or scientific, textolatry may become an impediment for new thinking. For instance, in the scholastic period of thinking in medieval European society, Aristotelian thinking served as the theoretical framework from which nature and the social world could be examined. When the Aristotelian corpus did not provide any guidance, concerns were simply dismissed as what Thomas S. Kuhn centuries later would call *anomalies*, puzzles neither capable of being explained nor accommodated within the given analytical framework.[2] The scholastic thinkers were succumbing to textolatry and failed to see what is beyond the enacted framework of analysis.

The most recent major even in media is for Flusser (2000, 2002) the invention of "technical images," namely the photograph. For Flusser (2000, 2002), the invention of the photograph is a major event in human history: It is an "[e]vent as equally decisive as the invention of writing. With writing, history in the narrower sense begins a struggle against idolatry. With photography, 'post-history' begins as a struggle against textolatry," Flusser, (2000: 18) writes. The uses of images were abstractions of the first order, representing actual entities or events in the lifeworld of the artists; linear writings are second-order abstractions because they do address the images as objects of analysis, and consequently the use of technical images are "abstractions of the third order": "They abstract from texts which abstract from traditional images which themselves abstracts from the concrete world" (Flusser, 2000: 14). Notwithstanding all the technical issues addressed in Flusser's (2000, 2002) thinking, he is pointing at the significant difference between the *line* and the *surface*, the written language in the form of codes versus immediately perceivable surfaces. The linear code of writing is what promotes analytical and critical thinking and the surface produced by the technical image (e.g., the photograph) is an abstraction of such linear writing. Flusser suggests that while linear writing has for centuries served as the predominant medium for the sharing of thinking and ideas, we are today, when the technical images have been put into movement (e.g., cinema as the movement of photographs to produce an impression of motion—"motion pictures"), returning to a regime of idolatry. "Written lines, although appearing even more frequently than before, are becoming less important than surfaces to the mass of people," Flusser (2002: 22) says. With the birth of the Internet as the predominant mass medium for the distribution of surface code codes, i.e., photos, images, film clips, and so forth, the centuries-old tradition to share information through texts and linear writing is at stake.[3] Although media theorists have shown that basically all new media have been surrounded by a sense of anxiety, for Flusser, the new forms of idolatry needs to be carefully examined and discussed. Drawing on the cybernetic theory of Norbert Wiener and Claude Shannon and Warren Weaver's mathematical theory of information, Flusser argues that there is an inverse relationship between communication and information; the less you inform, the more you communicate; the more you inform, the less is communicated. Technical images are easily communicated; anyone can look at an image and come to some conclusion. But this observation is often deceiving, critics of images claim. Needless to say, the contemporary society is today even more saturated with photos, images, brands, cinematic accounts, and other media relying on surface codes than in, say, the 1920s or in the 1970s. Without falling prey to a critique of contemporary society on the basis of theoretical frameworks and not on the basis of empirical studies, what is of relevance for the understanding of vision and visuality in organizations is that the age of linear writing is perhaps for the first time since its invention challenged by new forms of visual media as the principal form of communication. The frequency of book reading is slowly going down in the Western world and new visual media are constantly introduced. It is then no wonder that in a number of science-fiction movies (e.g., *Blade Runner*, *Children of Men*), the public spaces are filled with visual media that are constantly exposing the citizens and city dwellers to various messages and commercial interests. In these dystopic scenarios, visual media are what remains after all other institutions have collapsed or faded away. Therefore, without taking refuge in a stodgy conservatism, the relative decline of linear writing and reading is a concern not just for theoretical speculation but also for politicians and policymakers. In any case, the surface code of the image or the movie is not what is capable of explaining itself or what is meaningful as such. Instead, it becomes meaningful through proper analysis and understanding, and such understanding does not emerge from the image per se but from the capacity of analytical thinking.

For some media theorists, the relative decline of the written text as the principal medium for communication and the sharing of information is rather cumbersome. For instance, Flusser (2002) claims that there is a close connection between linear writing and reading and rational thought and forms of critical thinking; these activities and practices are what helped "save humankind from 'ideologies,' from hallucinatory imaginations" (Flusser, 2002: 64). In order to think analytically, one must proceed through the linear code. David Jay Bolter (1996) goes even further and claims that the modern subject per se is a product of the practice of linear writing:

> Writing in general and print technology in particular have contributed to a series of related definitions of self in the period from the Renaissance to the 20th century: the self has been regarded as an autonomous ego, the author or the text that constitutes one's mental life. Virtual reality and cyberspace suggest a different definition. The self is no longer constructed as an autonomous, authorial voice; it becomes instead a wandering eye that occupies various perspectives, one after another. This virtual eye knows what it knows not through the capacity for

abstract reasoning, but rather through empathy, through the sharing of the 'point of view' of the object of knowledge. (Bolter, 1996: 106)

If we think there is a kernel of truth in Flusser's (2002) and Bolter's (1996) predictions, the change from text-dominated media to image-dominated media (including many hybrid forms), there is reason for being concerned about the consequences. However, whether the relative loss of writing and reading is posing a threat to the modernist subject and critical thinking remains an empirical question not to be determined *a priori*.

Synthesis: Line as Surface in the Code of Computer Languages

Flusser (2002) suggests that there is an inherent contradiction between linear codes and surface codes and that the history of literacy, scriptural as well as visual, demonstrates a rather intricate dialectics between, on the one hand, the reliance on surface codes (images) and, on the other, linear codes (texts). However, in the case of new media, digital computer-based media that are today constitutive of the everyday lifeworld (Dodge and Kitchin, 2005; Galloway, 2004; Galloway and Thacker, 2007), "Derrida's famous aphorism, 'Il n'y a pas de hors-texte,' has been replaced by its computational equivalent *Il n'y a pas de hors-code*," Hayles (2006: 152) says *apropos* the ubiquitous presence of code. In this new situation, Flusser's analytical framework is only partially applicable. All new media share a number of characteristics accounted for by Manovich (2001: 27–46) such as the use of numerical representations (in the binary code of the processors), the reliance on modularity (i.e., is based on discrete elements such as bits or pixels), the use of extensive automation and variability, and, finally, causing what Manovich calls "transcoding," the interchange between "the cultural layer" and the "computer layer," for instance, in the form of computer interface features being interpenetrating everyday conversations. New media are also based on written code, computer languages on different levels capable of serving as and constituting the interface between the machine and the human user. It is on the very level of the written computer code that the distinction between surface codes and linear codes becomes somewhat confused and blurred. For instance, Mitchell (2005) says that there are no purely visual media; all media presuppose to varying extent the ability of the user to read and to make use of other senses such as hearing and even touching. Assuming that new media are an exclusively visual media is for Mitchell (2005) a fallacy that needs to be critically examined. In contrast, Katherine Hayles (2005) suggests that speech, writing, and code belong to three different "worldviews"—they are fundamentally different and operate on the basis of a number of different human faculties and capacities. In the Western tradition of thinking (that is, in the tradition of Platonist philosophy), speech is deemed the most "authentic" and closest to thinking, whereas writing is more or less regarded as a substitute or a technology abstracting and structuring human thinking. For Derrida (1976), this is a form of what he calls *logocentrism*, a privileging of speech as what is preceding writing, that has significant philosophical and practical implications. While writing is regarded as an abstraction or a technology, a form of *substitute*, code is on the contrary what is even further removed from commonsense thinking and talking. Code is what stands midway between the mathematical and strictly logical operations of the technical assemblage constituting the computer, and the written language used in everyday communication. However, while everyday language is, in the Wittgensteinian tradition of thinking, a form of "language game," an arbitrary use of terms and phrases to accomplish further meaningful interaction, that is, language is connotative and constituted by rather loosely coupled elements that nevertheless hang together, code is strictly denotative. "Code consists of instructions and rules that, when combined, produce programs capable of complex digital functions that operate on computer hardware," Dodge and Kitchin, (2005: 163) state. Code has no meaning beyond its function; *it is what is does*. In the words of computer programmer Ellen Ullman: "We can use English to invent poetry, to try to express things that are hard to express. In programming you really can't . . . a computer program has only one meaning: what it does. It isn't a text for an academic to read. Its entire meaning is its function" (cited in Hayles, 2005: 48). Code regulates the relationship between the machine, the technological apparatus and the external world, the world of the user. This does, however, not suggest a determinist view of code; code is written with varying degrees of expertise and elegance. Just as everyday speech and written texts adhere to certain standards of rhetoric, there are also elements of aesthetics in written code (Piñeiro, 2007).

In a recent exchange of ideas regarding the "ideology of software," Alexander Galloway (2006) has suggested that there are no inherent ideologies in code, at least not ideology in the traditional sense of the term, as a form of set of preconceived ideas that regulate social relations and that effectively ignore social inequalities. Instead, if there is an ideology of the code of software, Galloway insists that it is in terms of being a form of language that is concealed qua linguistic structure. "Language wants to be overlooked," Galloway (2006) suggests:

> Language wants to be overlooked. But it wants to be overlooked precisely so that it can more effectively 'over look,' that is, so it can better function as a syntactic and semantic system designed to specify and articulate while remaining detached from the very processes of specificity and articulation. This is one sense in which language, which itself is not necessarily connected to optical sight, can nevertheless be visual. (Galloway, 2006: 320–321)

For Galloway (2006), there is a "fundamental contradiction" in software in terms of "what you see is not what you get"; code is "[a] medium that is not a medium"—it can never be "viewed as it is" but is instead "compiled, interpreted, parsed and otherwise driven into hiding by still larger globs of code" (Galloway, 2006: 325). If code is a specific form of language, that is a form of "language under cover," a language that is always already serving as something else than it actually is. In addition, the language of code is, Galloway repeats after Ullman (1997) and Dodge and Kitchin (2005), "executable": it operates as what John Austin called an "illocutionary speech act," an expression that when being uttered changes some state of affairs in the world (Galloway, 2006: 325–326), i.e., to speak is to act. The difference is, however, that while any phrase could serve as an illocutionary speech act when agreed upon in a certain community of speakers, the code can only execute its function in a network of technical and linguistic relations that are complicated to change underway. In some cases, it is even impossible to rearticulate the linguistic structure wherein a particular phrase or word can be used. Ullman (1997) claims that in some older computer systems, relying on a computer language that is no longer widely used and consequently less and less trained, used, and understood, a computer system may end up being what Ullman (1997) calls "brain-dead." A brain-dead system is a system still functioning but when too many different programmers have collaborated and worked on different parts of the system to the point where no one is capable of overlooking the entire system, it is brain-dead.

> By the time a computer system becomes old, no one completely understands it. A system made out of old junky technology becomes, paradoxically, precious. It kept running but as if in a velvet box: open it carefully, just look, don't touch. The preciousness of an old system is axiomatic. The longer the system has been running, the greater the numbers of programmers who have worked on it, the less any one person understands it. As years pass and untold numbers of programmers and analysts come and go, the system takes on a life on its own. It runs . . . The system is unmodifiable, full of bugs, no longer understood. We say it's 'brain dead.' Yet it lives, yet it runs. Drain on our time and memory. (Ullman, 1997: 117–118)

Like in the story with the 10 blind Indian men touching different parts of the elephant (see Czarniawska, 1993, for one use of the story) and thereby giving 10 different accounts of what they are in fact touching (such as "a wall" when touching the elephant's side or "a rope" when touching the trunk), the different programmers are seeing individual parts but fail to see the whole system. Such brain-dead computer systems are more common than one would like to think, Ullman (1997) says. Only extensive work is capable of helping the computer system back from its terminal state.

For Galloway (2006), if there is an ideology in software besides being based on language that wants to be ignored *qua* language, it lies in the tendency to "anthropomorphize" itself, that is, to ignore that code is of necessity first machinic and only secondly linguistic in the proper sense of the term:

> [C]ode is machinic first and linguistic second; an intersubjective infra-
> structure is not the same as a material one (even if making such a claim
> unfortunately splits these two symbolic systems into the 'soft' natural
> language versus the 'hard' computer languages). To see code as subjec-
> tively performative or enunciative is to anthropomorphize it, to project
> it onto the rubric of psychology, rather than to understand it through
> its own logic of 'calculation' or 'command.' The material substrate of
> code, which must always exist as an amalgam of electrical signals and
> logical operations exists first and foremost as comments issued by the
> machine. Code essentially has no other reason for being than instruct-
> ing some machine on how to act. (Galloway, 2006: 326)

What is of interest here is that while Flusser (2002) is making an intriguing point regarding the dialectics between linear and surface codes and
shows how different forms of thinking have been derived from the different media, in the present regime, that of digital new media embedded in
computer technology, the linear code is not external to the surface code
(as in the regime of the early Paleolithic paintings) but is rather embodied
in the very media; new media are inextricably bound up with the use of
denotative strings of instructions in the form of linear code. Somewhat
paradoxically, and this is what Galloway (2006) is pointing at when he
claims that code is a "medium that is not a medium" and "what you see is
not what you get," the surface codes produced on the computer interface
are ultimately embedded in strings of instructions; the surface code and the
linear code merge in a meaningful way. In Mitchell's (2005) view, there are
no strictly "visual media" but, both on the level of the interface and on the
level of the machinic operations, linear code and surface code are interacting and recursively constitute one another. One of the consequences is that
the insistence on "the loss of linear writing" may be primarily a matter
of concern in certain communities, failing to maintain a mode of thinking derived from the engagement with linear code, i.e., a form of reading
wherein "one damn thing after another" (Bowker, 2005: 102) needs to be
understood in its totality.

The principal consequence for vision and visuality in organizations is
that it is epistemologically, theoretically, and practically problematic to
separate visual practices in the form of ways of looking (e.g., the gaze,
the glance, staring) from forms of reading. If we assume with Mitchell
(2005) that "there are no visual media" in the same manner as taste always
includes olfactory and tactile capacities, then the use of visual media in
organizations needs to be examined as what is always having some kind
of relationship with other skills beyond their mere visual competence. For
instance, architects not only look at pictures and images; they also touch

and smell built environments and they mobilize a great deal of theoretical know-how when designing and constructing the building. Therefore, when inspecting an image of a building, the embodied expertise and experience are always already present in the architect's vision. The image is then not purely visual but it is always assumed that the skilled architect is inspecting the very image on the basis of such extra-visual skills. Just like with identities, not being separated like beads on a string and mobilized in contexts where they may serve best but are rather always immediately present to various degrees, the five senses are not operating in isolation in everyday life. A phenomenologist philosopher such as Merleau-Ponty (1962) would, for instance, claim that all human existence is of necessity embodied and "enlived" and therefore the five senses are what always accompany human action and human thinking. Cognition and sense impressions are not distinctly separated but largely entangled. The study of visual practices and visuality in organization must recognize this condition.

IMPLICATIONS FOR ORGANIZATION THEORY

The concepts of vision and visuality are important for the understanding how organizations operate and function, and there are several domains of practical work that are affected by how forms of vision and visuality are employed in everyday work. Speaking of theoretical implications, the concepts of vision and visuality may be used to inform the study of organizations in a variety of theoretical frameworks. In the following, knowledge management theory, perspectives on aesthetics and organization, and organization structure will be examined in terms of how organization and practices of seeing are entangled.

Knowledge Management Theory

One of the more dynamic and intellectually intriguing domains of organization studies the last 15 years has been the discussion over the nature of work in knowledge-intensive firms. Using the rather complex term *knowledge management* (Alvesson and Kärreman, 2000), a range of theoretical perspectives pertaining to the development, storing, retrieval, and distribution of intellectual resources have been advanced. Knowledge management is here defined as suggested by Schultze and Stabell (2004: 551): "Typically knowledge management is defined as the generation, representation, storage, transfer, transformation, application, embedding and protecting of organizational knowledge." In this rather diverse corpus of literature, one may at least identify a number of positions and perspectives of relevance for vision and visuality studies in organizations. Amin and Cohendet (2004: 5–6) identify three different perspectives in their review of the literature. First, a *strategic-management approach* employing terms such as "core competencies," "assets," and "rents," to explain how firms are capable of creating sustainable competitive advantage through the use of various intellectual assets (i.e., forms of knowledge). This body of literature is largely relying on quantitative methods and is by and large positivist in its emphasis on aiming to identify models and theories that enable predictions and estimations *ex ante*. The second corpus of literature discussed by Amin and Cohendet (2004) is the *evolutionary theory of organizations* also developed within an economics tradition of thinking, best represented by the seminal work of Nelson and Winter (1982). Nelson and Winter (1982) regard routines and roles as being the "genes of practices," the elementary forms of organizing guiding and structuring practices in firms and other organizations. Seen in this view, organizations are repositories of knowledge in terms of being embedded in a set of standard operating procedures enacted and commonly agreed upon. Finally, Amin and Cohendet (2004) speak about what they refer to as the *social-anthropology-of-learning approach*, an approach that does not primarily emphasize the formal structures and the routines but conceived of knowledge as what is embedded in social relations and what is produced in social interactions. This perspective is often represented in organization theory using qualitative methods and is drawing more on sociological and behavioural theory than economic theory (even though these two fields are never fully mutually excluded). This perspective on knowledge and knowledge management practices rests on what Tsoukas (2005: 5) calls "open-world ontology," an ontology that "[a]ssumes that the world is always in a process of becoming or turning into something different. Flow, flux and change are the fundamental processes of the world. The future is open, unknowable in principle, and it always holds the possibility of surprise." Knowledge is therefore not what is preexisting or preceding actual practices and interactions but is instead what is produced through activities. As a consequence, one must not "take knowledge for granted" (Tsoukas and Mylonopoloulos, 2004: 53), assuming that it has already a particular "form and content." Tsoukas and Mylonopoloulos (2004: S3) continue: "Indeed, one of the common fallacies concerning organizational knowledge is what we may call the apple-tree fallacy: the knowledge individuals make use of in their work is considered to be a collection of freestanding item waiting out these to be plucked from the tree of organizational knowledge." Falling prey to such "fallacies of misplaced concreteness" (Whitehead, 1925), i.e., believing that a complex texture of interrelated and entangled items and events may be separated and examined in isolation, is a form of reductionism *in absurdum*. Instead, knowledge needs to be examined, as suggested by Orlikowski (2002: 252–253), as "[a]n ongoing social accomplishment, constituted and reconstituted in everyday practice." She continues: "As such, knowing cannot be understood as stable or enduring. Because it is enacted in the moment, its existence is virtual, its status provisional." Seen in this view, knowledge is an abstraction, a form imposed upon discontinuous matter, a procrustean bed turning all practices into fixed and packaged entities; what exists is know-how mobilized and used to inform practices in the course of action. Never fully enclosed, nor totally open to modification, know-how is what is emerging in the social relationship between central actors in a field of practice. Knowledge management is in such a perspective, in the open world ontology, what is aiming at turning "[a]n unreflected practice into a reflective one by elucidating the rules guiding the activities of the practice, by helping give a particular shape to collective understandings, and by facilitating the emergence of heuristic knowledge" (Tsoukas and Vladimirou, 2001: 990). Managing knowledge is not about effectively managing "hard bits of information" but, more subtly, "sustaining and strengthening social practices" (Tsoukas and Vladimirou, 2001: 991). In the social-anthropology-of-learning approach, knowledge is no longer what is a fixed stock of routines, patents, or otherwise stable and semi-stable entities of knowledge. Knowledge is, on the contrary, what is produced in actual practice. For the proponents of the social-anthropology-of-learning approach, the followers of economic theory perspectives are succumbing to what Gilbert Ryle (1949) referred to as a *category mistake*—they mistake the output from knowledge work for the knowledge itself. Patents may provide legal protection for work laid down into products and procedures, but they are not in themselves instances of knowledge; it is social practices mobilizing various forms of know-how and expertise that are capable of producing patents as one of its many outputs. In this view, followers of economic theory are mistaking the cause and the effect, thinking of what is the end product as what is the effect. One of the consequences from the social-anthropology-of-learning approach is that there is no knowledge proper per se but only knowledge for us, for social actors interacting in a specific field of expertise. In addition, this renders firms as "distributed knowledge systems" in the strong sense of the term (Tsoukas, 1996: 13); firms are capable of hosting a variety of knowledge resources that are never self-contained or enclosed but are always inherently indeterminate and continually reconfiguring. Such a constructionist view of knowledge is advocated by Gherardi and Nicolini (2001):

> Every attempt to label something as 'knowledge' is made by a specific social community belonging to a network of power relations, and not by a world consisting purely of ideas. Hence, no knowledge is universal or supreme; instead, all knowledge is produced within social, historical, and linguistic relations grounded in specific forms of conflict and the division of labor. (Gherardi and Nicolini, 2001; 44)

If we adhere to a social-anthropology-of-learning approach to knowledge management, studies of vision and visuality need to be considered in similar terms: Since vision is always what is inextricably bound up with language—seeing and saying in Foucault's (1973) term—and more specifically a language that is shared by other members of the thought community (Fleck, 1979) the actor belongs to, professional vision and other forms of visuality in organizations are relational, contextual, situated, and contingent on local conditions. The capacity of seeing, to use one's professional vision, the gaze provided by institutions, traditions, and ideologies, is always taking place within organized communities, communities that share intellectual resources and forms of know-how. In addition, vision and visuality are contributing to knowledge management theory by emphasizing the embodied and perceptual components in all knowledge production; knowledge is by no means an outcome from the strict application of cognitive faculties and capacities but is instead produced through a variety of resources at hand. As students of laboratory practices such as Rheinberger (1997), Pickering (1995), and Knorr Cetina (1995) show, scientific knowledge is produced in what Rheinberger (1997) calls "experimental systems" that are composed of many diverse and complementary parts. The researchers' embodied capacities such as tactile, olfactory, auditory, gustatory, and visual skills are integral to such experimental systems. Researchers must not only think but also look, smell, touch, and hear how the laboratory equipment is functioning. To date, the knowledge management literature has been primarily focused on cognitive and language-laden observations, but knowledge is not only manifesting itself in language but in the very relationship between language and the systematic use of the five senses. The knowledge management literature is thus benefiting from an increased emphasis on embodied faculties, potentially broadening the basis for what counts as proper knowledge.

Aesthetics and Organization

Another field affected by theories of vision and visuality in organizations is the growing field of aesthetics in organizations. Among a variety of "turns" being announced, including the "corporeal turn" (Witz, 2000), the "realist turn" (Reed, 2005), the "visual turn" (Jay, 2002), the "linguistic turn" (Alvesson and Kärreman, 2000; Rorty, 1992), the "practice turn" (Schatzki, Knorr Cetina, and Savigny, 2001), and the "complexity turn" (Urry, 2005), it would be possible to speak about something like an "aesthetic turn" in organization theory. Social theorists such as Postrel (2003) and Böhme (2003) talk about the "aesthetic economy" or a society increasingly concerned about aesthetic features of products. Davenport and Beck (2001), Lanham (2006), and Beller (2006) use the term *attention economy* to capture the same tendency, the reliance on aesthetic features to attract consumers and well as the broader public's attention. Postrel (2003: 4–5) is particularly articulate on this matter: "Aesthetics has become too important to be left to the aesthetes. To succeed, hard-nosed engineers, real estate developers, and MBAs must take aesthetic communication, and aesthetic pleasure, seriously. We, their customers, demand it." She continues with the same emphasis on understanding this new aesthetic orientation in the economy:

> The issue is not *what* style is used but rather *that* style is used, consciously and conscientiously, even in areas where function used to stand alone. Aesthetics is more pervasive than it used to be—not restricted to social, economic, or artistic elites, limited to only a few settings or industries, or designed to communicate only power, influence or wealth. Sensory appeals are everywhere, they are increasingly personalized, and they are intensifying. (Postrel, 2003: 5)

For Postrel (2003), the aesthetic is no longer a domain separated from society at large but instead yet another production factor aimed at increasing the circulation of capital through stimulating desire and demand. The crux is that this production factor is rather fickle and complicated to discuss unless one has developed a fairly elaborated vocabulary addressing the matter. In addition, it is what is embedded in the senses: "Aesthetic is the way we communicate through the senses. It is the art of creating reactions without words, through the look and feel of people, places or things. Hence, aesthetics differs from entertainment that requires cognitive engagement with narrative, word play, or complex intellectual allusion," Postrel (2003: 6) writes. The aesthetic economy is for Postrel representing an economic regime and indeed an epistemology collapsing the age-old distinction between "substance" (an Aristotelian term used rather loosely by Postrel, 2003) and "style."

In organization theory, aesthetics has been debated at least since the 1990s (Guillén, 1997). Monographs and edited volumes published by Strati (1999, 2007), Linstead and Höpfl (2001), Carr and Hancock (2003), Guillet de Monthoux (2004), and Guillet de Monthoux, Gustafsson, and Sjöstrand, (2007) have brought the issue of aesthetics into the field of organization theory. More recent contributions have studied aesthetic concerns among computer programmers (Case and Piñeiro, 2006; Piñeiro, 2007), architects (Ewenstein and Whyte, 2007), financial analysts (Guve, 2007), or health care workers (Macnaughton, 2007; Martin, 2002). Other contributors have examined the concept of aesthetics more broadly as an analytical concept applicable in organization studies (Harter et al,, 2008; Taylor, 2002; Taylor and Hansen, 2005; Warren, 2008), advocating, for instance, concepts such as *aesthetic knowledge*, knowledge that is "[d]riven by the desire for the subjective, personal truth usually for its own sake" (Taylor and Hansen, 2005: 1213) and is "embodied" and goes "beyond words" (Ewenstein and Whyte, 2007: 689, 705). Strati (2007: 62) advocates the term *sensible knowledge* as an umbrella term for what is "[p]erceived through the senses, judged through the senses, and produced and reproduced through the senses." Sensible knowledge is thus embodied and "resides in the visual, the auditory, the olfactory, the gustatory, and touchable [senses] and in the sensitive-aesthetic judgment" (Strati, 2007: 62). Just like Taylor and Hansen (2005) and Ewenstein and Whyte (2007), Strati (2007: 70) suggests that sensible knowledge "evades logical-analytical description and scientific formalization" and is better expressed "evocatively and metaphorically." In addition, just like other commentators of such non-logico-scientific forms of knowing (to inverse Bruner's [1986] term), Strati is emphasizing the embodiment and the creativity of sensible knowledge and underlines its importance in the contemporary regime of accumulation:

> Knowledge rooted in 'practice' and situated organizational learning are distinctive features of the knowledge society characteristic of the contemporary world of industrial and post-industrial production. They emphasize that it is people who create, invent and enact organization, doing so not as individual yet interrelated minds but through their corporality—which enable them to acquire sensible knowledge as well as to engage in intellectual ratiocination—and always in relation to the non-human element that make up the organizational space. (Strati, 2007: 66)

Without falling prey to a form of romanticism regarding the "creativity" and "inventiveness" of aesthetic and sensible knowledge, making such human faculties the "next untapped human resource" supposedly capable of invigorating economic life, it is fair to judge that there is room for a form of knowledge that is stretching beyond the logico-scientific domains of thinking and that recognizes the human senses and the faculties bridging them. That is, aesthetic and sensible knowledge are merely residual elements and analytical perspective but centrally located from a practical perspective, informing human action and thinking in many domains of human endeavours.

If we assume that aesthetic and sensible knowledge will play a role as a production factor in organizations—what positivists call "anecdotal evidence" suggests that such is the case, as for instance the remarkable growth of the computer game industry suggests—visual practices and visuality will serve a key role in organizations. The practices of seeing, the professional vision of the agent, is then at the very center of relations in the new emerging regime of work. For instance, in the case of the computer game industry, Zackariasson, Styhre, and Wilson's (2006) study of a Swedish computer game company suggests that these firms were only interested in hiring what they called "gamers," individuals committed and dedicated to the practice of playing computer games. Similar to restaurant chefs, sceptical towards formal education and emphasizing the value of practical work and learning-by-doing approaches to the work (Fine, 1996), computer game developers are not trained in academic institutions or vocational training schools but are trained primarily through having extensive experience from playing, discussing, debating, and evaluating computer games. In the vocabulary of aesthetic knowledge, they embody a certain professional vision identifying features of the game that reveal whether it is developed by the leading expertise or by less credible communities in the field. Professional vision thus includes aesthetic judgment but also includes other qualities such the economic aspect of the modus operandi, i.e., the ability to undertake a practice in an effective and skilled manner. Professional vision not only examines the outcomes but constitutes the very procedures for producing such output. The theoretical and practical field of vision and visuality in organizations are thus at the very heart of the aesthetic economy or the attention economy outlined and theorized by Böhme (2003), Lanham (2006), and others. Thus, when examining these emerging economic regimes, it is useful to again separate an "epistemologies of the eye" or "theories of vision" on the one hand and "practices of seeing" on the other (Daston and Galison, 2007: 368). In addition, in the aesthetic economy and the attention economy, vision and visuality are not only about the practices of seeing but also about being seen. Entwhistle and Racamora (2006) show in their intriguing analysis of the accumulation and circulation of *fashion capital* at London Fashion Week that in the new regime of economic production, relevant resources such as social and symbolic capital are largely acquired when being visible and seen at the right events and venues. Somewhat paradoxically and largely consonant with what Georges Bataille (1988) speaks of as "the general economy," fashion capital is being generated through simultaneously being consumed and squandered at the "right" events (i.e., events formally or informally sanctioned by leading authorities in the field of fashion such as fashion magazine editors, established designers, etc.); simply by participating at the most interesting shows during the fashion week, the leading figures are both "infusing" (in Selznick's [1949] sense of the term) fashion capital into specific designers while simultaneously getting credit for having the adequate *fingerspitzengefühl* guiding the selection of what is interesting at the very moment. In other words, in Entwhistle and Racamora's (2006) account, there is an intricate and rather esoteric dialectics between both the consumption and generation of fashion capital and "seeing" and "being seen" at the London Fashion Week. The case of London Fashion Week is interesting because it is both underlining the central importance of "practices of seeing" in the industry while at the same time revealing the "epistemologies of the eye" in terms of how an entire regime of signs (see, e.g., Barthes's *The Fashion System* [1983]) is ultimately bound up with instituted modes of seeing and saying.[4] The fashion industry is, in other words, founded on the established routines for determining and sorting out "what's hot and what's not." The professional vision of fashion commentators, fashion critics, and other relevant actors is what is capable of producing pervasive and highly sophisticated social orders pervading all spheres of society, also outside of the rather restricted field of the fashion industry. The fashion industry is perhaps the best illustration to what Jonathan Beller (2006) calls the "cinematic mode of production," the accumulation of value through what Beller calls "visual labour" (see, e.g., Styhre, 2009).

Taken together, vision and visuality in organizations may play a more central role in forthcoming regimes of economic production; professional vision as the integration and embodiment of a series of professional skills and capacities is therefore a highly relevant concept that is applicable in a variety of domains, fields, and industries, all obeying their own instituted beliefs, values, norms, and practices.

Organization Structure

If vision and visuality in the form of professional vision are inscribed as an important feature of organizational activities, it is complicated to assume that organizations are well integrated, coherent, and above all cognitively possible to apprehend in their entirety. Instead, if forms of vision are one of the central capacities underlining the various processes in organizations, one must recognize the transient, temporal, and highly contingent nature of all organization. Although it has been argued that professional vision—that is, *organizational* vision—is rendered stable and fixed through the thought collectives endorsing and sanctioning specific forms of vision, visual perception is ontologically, epistemologically, and methodologically porous, embedded in assemblages of technologies and practices that in themselves are only temporally stabilized. An organization based on professional vision can never become fully removed from the fact that the very act of vision is in itself an open-ended and permeable process. Speaking in terms established in the organization theory, it may be suggested that professional vision is always taking place and is also itself producing environments that are "loosely coupled." Weick (1979: 111) provides the following definition of loosely coupled systems:

> Loose coupling occurs when two separate systems have few variables in common or when the common variables are weak compared to the other variables that influence the system. Two systems that are joined by few common variables or weak common variables are said to be loosely coupled.

Loosely coupled systems are organizations that fails to meet Henri Fayol's insistence on a linear chain of command, from the very top to the bottom of the "organizational pyramid." Instead, the organizations are composed of parts and components that are only corresponding with one another irregularly and poorly. For instance, in academic institutions, often organized around faculties, departments, schools, and so forth, the line organization represented by the rector's office is only marginally capable of influencing the actions and decisions in the various departments or schools; nor are the various parts capable of directly influencing one another. Instead, leaders of such organizations are controlling and managing the activities through what Peter Drucker (1955: 52ff) referred to as "management by objectives." For instance, in academic institutions, one should strive to accomplish "academic excellence" or "attract industry funding" of the research and the professors and coworkers should act in accordance with certain codes of conduct.

In the literature making use of the concept of loose couplings, there is an emphasis on both the loose coupling between the organization and the environment and between organizational parts. For instance, Pfeffer and Salancik (1978: 13) argue that loose couplings is an important "safety device for organizational survival": "The fact that environmental impacts are felt only imperfectly provides the organization with some discretion, as well as the capability to act across time horizons longer than the time it takes for environments to change," Pfeffer and Salacik (1978: 13) explain. On the contrary, institutional theorists such as Meyer and Rowan (1977: 341) argue that organizations are loosely coupled systems in order to maintain what they refer to as "ceremonial conformity," instituted practices and routines that the organization needs to adhere to in order to safeguard long-term survival and short-term legitimacy, while not letting this "conformity" disrupt and intervene in the day-to-day activities: "To maintain ceremonial conformity, organizations that reflect institutional rules tend to buffer their formal structures from the uncertainties of technical activities by becoming loosely coupled, building gaps between their formal structures and the actual work activities" (Meyer and Rowan, 1977: 341). In addition to these uncertainties derived from the firm's environment, one may argue that the reliance on vision and visuality in the form of professional vision is contributing with another form of loose coupling, namely a loose coupling between the actual event of using professional vision, an act that embodies all the uncertainty and situated conditions and contingencies that vision draws on, and the formal authority accruing to the organization. For instance, as shown by Goodwin (1994) in his detailed analysis of the Rodney King trial, the police officers testifying to the fairness of the behaviours of the four police officers were engaging in a highly complex and politically charged act of investing all their prestige and authority in the courtroom to justify the violation of Rodney King. The Los Angeles police would not lose its legitimacy if the testifying police officer would have failed to convince the court that the acts conducted were justified because there was a loose coupling between the professional vision of the testimony and the police department per se. A similar case is the diagnosis of a general practitioner or medical doctor. Almost weekly, there are sad stories reported in the media about GPs failing to formulate a proper account of an individual's health conditions. However, the professional vision of the GP and the authority and legitimacy of the medical profession are again loosely coupled and thereby capable of tolerating such "failed" acts of professional vision. This form of loose coupling is not organizational but *epistemological*; the "ways of seeing" of the profession are regarded as being of a different order than the organizational setting wherein the professional vision is executed.

Another organizational model that is applicable when examining organization structure is what Barbara Czarniawska (1997) calls *actions nets*. Action nets are interactive order comprising actors and practices, evolving over time and tolerating significant changes in routines and actors:

> Action nets are neither people nor groups; they may be large (across several organization fields) or small (a project); the focus of analysis can be a combination or collection of such nets (an organization field). It is from the action net that we deduce which actors are involved, not the other way around. This means, for example, that the net will never continue to exist even when the actors are exchanged for others, or the original actors change their identity (they may become machines), although it always means the change in the character of the net as well; that the changing net may press for a change in the identity of the actors . . . that the actors may be of fixed status (humans and nonhumans)—a fact we would miss if we looked exclusively at human actors and their interactions. (Czarniawska, 1997: 179)

An action net is a dynamic concept, emphasizing the recursive relationship between, on the one hand, actual practices and, on the other hand, instituted routines and procedures:

> The concept of the action net is based on the assumption that organizing (and its special of case: management) requires that several different collective actions be connected according to a pattern that is institutionalized at a given time and a given place. The collective actions concerned need not necessarily be performed within the bounds of a specific 'organization.' On the contrary, an action net may involve a great variety of organizations or organized groups of people of a loose or temporary nature . . . Thus the action net is a general concept referring less to entities concerned with the practice of management and more with useful ways of studying that practice. (Lindberg and Czarniawska, 2006: 293)

Action nets are not to be used synonymously with organization; instead, action nets transgress organizational boundaries and the boundary between human/nonhuman and outline the very activities wherein practices are undertaken and objectives are accomplished. Czarniawska (2004: 780) suggests that action nets as theoretical construct are both capable of embracing "anti-essentialist aspect of all organizing" while recognizing the "solid effects" of organizing, that is, that practices generate material, symbolic, or linguistic effects. Czarniawska (2004) says that the concept of the action net is introduced to minimize what is taken for granted regarding organizational activities prior to empirical analysis. While other theories of organization flatly assume that there are actors, routines, artefacts, etc., involved, the action net perspective regards such "entities" as *products* or *effects* of organizing. Instead, action nets begin with practices which in turn generate a variety of more or less differentiated actors, routines, or standard operation procedures, institutions, professional identities, and ideologies. Czarniawska's (1997, 2004) concept of action net is useful because it seeks to eliminate or at least render problematic a series of assumptions and taken-for-granted beliefs. Rather than starting off with a significant epistemological and theoretical baggage, the action net approach seeks to return to the elementary forms of organizing, the activities that are in themselves capable of producing the entities and institutions that we tend to regard as constitutive elements of organization. What both loosely coupled systems of organization and action nets share is the idea that organizations are never as unified, integrated, coherent, and immutable as is commonly suggested and assumed in commonsense thinking as well as in more scholarly theorizing. Instead, organizations are what Perrow and Guillén (1990) refer to as *refractory tools*. Perrow and Guillén (1990), studying the shortcomings of the American health care system during the AIDS panic in the U.S. in the 1980s, outline their model in a passage worth citing at length:

> Both major perspectives and several other variants, such as network analysis, population ecology, Marxist and ethnological perspectives, take for granted something that should always be problematical. They assume that organizations have solved the basic problems of multiple missions and mandates, conflicting goals, goal distortion, and unauthorized usage of the exploitation of organizational resources. The third perspective, we have been using, makes no such assumption. Instead, it assumes that the goals of the organization are only weakly defined (patient care, yes, but perhaps not all patients), that goals are subject to internal contradictions (a research goal that requires the study of patients may conflict with the goal of patient care), that personal ideologies and beliefs cannot always be set aside (so personnel discriminate against minorities or cannot bring themselves to provide safe-sex education), and even that there is a good deal of chance, accident, an unanticipated interaction that may deflect organizations from goals truly subscribed to by everyone. In this view organizations are very imperfect and even recalcitrant 'tools' in the hands of the authorities who oversees them or the leaders who run them. Organizations will fail much of the time to achieve their official purpose, which is always stated in misleadingly clear, rational terms. (Perrow and Guillén, 1990: 128–129)

Organizational activities are in Perrow and Guillén's view (1990) rather frail constructions, resting on porous grounds and are always under the threat of being disintegrated or falling apart. All organizations are in this view what is on the verge of failing, of breaking down or losing its direction. What keeps them together is not so much strong corporate cultures

(Peter and Waterman, 1982), carefully crafted and well-implemented strategies, or specific managerial tools or techniques such as business process engineering or total quality management practices (Hammer and Champy, 1993; Powell, 1995), but the day-to-day work to maintain the activities that are decided upon and to provide services for end users and other relevant stakeholders. In sharp contrast to the management guru literature view, portraying successful organizations as shiny castles populated by happy, rosy-cheeked, and highly performing members of professionals and occupational communities, in Perrow and Guillén's (1990) view, organizations are always at stake, never to be taken for granted, and rather far removed from the infantile fantasies projected on large, primarily American, multinational companies. As a number of social theorists and organization theorists have suggested (ten Bos, 2001; Parker, 2002; Péteri, 1989), utopia is neither possible nor desirable to achieve. Therefore, the utopian images of successful corporations are concealing the individual, social, and emotional costs involved in creating such a corporation. In many cases, this modern form of fairy tale has proven to in fact be based on systematic manipulation of performance indicators (as in the much-debated case of the American energy company Enron; see, e.g., Carr and Downs, 2004) or other forms of unethical or otherwise deceitful behaviours and practices. Rather than adhering to the management guru view of organizations, the idea that organizations are *refractory tools* is much closer to the everyday functioning of organizations (see also Perrow, 1984, 2007).

When it comes to vision and visuality, Perrow and Guillén's (1990) concept is specifically useful because all vision is, as suggested both in the theoretical analysis of vision and the empirical studies, what is always at stake; vision is an individual capacity, subject to variation between individual experiences and biographies, and always an effect of highly varying skills and capacities for attention. When organizations rely on subjective capacities for vision, the epistemological foundation of the activities is rather frail and the immutable nature of the organization is open for discussion. Vision is part of much knowledge-intensive work ranging from surgery to architect work, from the arts to surveillance practices, from juridical practices to innovation management activities, but the true nature of the professional vision must remain concealed for the outsider. For instance, in the sciences, vision is mathematized (Lynch, 1988) in order to enable a codification of the empirical material and its circulation in scientific communities. Vision has always been subject to much epistemological concern, primarily because it is so closely connected to commonsense thinking ("seeing is believing"), and consequently the vision-laden nature of knowledge work must to some extent be mystified or specialized to protect the domain of expertise from commonsense thinking and questioning (Bechky, 2003). In organizations where vision plays a central role, there is always a risk that routines and practices are falling apart; different experts may perceive an event or an entity differently and all of a sudden the social world as taken for granted is coming to an end and becomes subject to debates and discussions. In vision-based work, the community of seers, the Fleckian thought community, must always seek to coordinate their practices of seeing and saying. Refractory organizations are capable of maintaining their form and activities as long as visual practices are not producing an excess of controversies and debates. When such debates are inhibiting a continuation of the activities, the social organization is threatened and the social interaction may be overturned, ending up in discussions and even painful quarrels. That is the principal contribution to organization theory: (1) That vision and visual practices such as professional vision are ultimately relying on shared epistemological assumptions and beliefs, and (2) that organizations embedded in practices of collective professional vision are of necessity refractory tools. Forms of vision are never effortless or disinterested. Instead, practices of seeing are always demanding the ability to co-align vision, cognition, and experience in a mindful procedure generating some social effect. When failing to accomplish this effect, professional vision is no longer serving its purpose. Such "coming to an end" of professional vision is demonstrated by anthropologist Paul Rabinow (1996b) in his study of the biotechnology company Cetus in Berkeley in the San Francisco Bay Area:

> PR   [*Paul Rabinow*]: What are the limits to curiosity?
>
> TW   [*Tom White, biotechnology researcher*]: Boredom, I've seen curiosity end for some scientists. When it does end it is a totally recognizable element in them. They no longer have the curiosity. They go home five o'clock . . . [w]hen some peculiar result is presented at meetings, they yawn and aren't interested. It is the strangest thing. It's like death in a scientist. They can be productive in a certain sense, but the ability to solve new problems isn't there. (Rabinow, 1996b: 162)

The professional vision of the bored scientists is a form of premature death. Most organizations are capable of accommodating a few individuals no longer being capable of seeing what is interesting in a case, but as this number grows, there is no longer a professional community capable of maintaining its vision on a matter of interest. Such organizations, being on the slippery slope, are indeed refractory tools.

STUDYING PROFESSIONAL VISION: SOME METHODOLOGICAL CONCERNS

The study of professional vision is a complicated methodological question. Since professional vision is inherently split into "the seeing" (observation) and "the saying" (declaration, utterance, inscription) component—individuals make an observation and account for it in an adequate and widely shared vocabulary—there are few possibilities for escaping the influence of language altogether. Learning to understand the dynamics between seeing and saying in specific communities such as scientists, architects, designers, fashion journalists, etc., demands a certain closeness and even intimacy with these communities. Oscillating between seeing and saying is an almost effortless activity for the skilled and experienced member of a professional community engaging vision. Hubert Dreyfus (2001) discusses the differences between what he calls the proficient performer and the expert:

> The *proficient performer*, immersed in the world of his skilful activity, *sees* what needs to be done, but has to *decide* how to do it. The expert not only sees what needs to achieved; thanks to his vast repertoire of situational discriminations, he also sees immediately how to achieve his goal. Thus, the ability make more subtle and refined discriminations is what distinguished the expert form the proficient performer. (Dreyfus, 2001: 41)

The difference between the two categories of knowledgeable agents is that the former first sees and then decides upon an adequate action while the latter is "immediately" responding. The proficient performer is skilled but not sufficiently experienced; the expert is capable of bridging seeing and decision (or action more generally) into one single procedure. For instance, sport commentators reviewing, for instance, gymnastics, ice dancing, or any other discipline based on the trained judgment of the referees are swiftly moving between their observation work and their articulation of the events and their verdict regarding performance. In, for instance, gymnastics, the different routines being accomplished by the athletes are given specific names that tend to sound rather exotic, for the neophyte and the skilled sport commentator are capable of both identifying these routines, naming them correctly, and passing some judgment whether the routine was satisfyingly executed or not in a nick of time, in one single moment. The professional vision of the sport commentator has accomplished a certain proximity between seeing and saying and only a thin membrane is separating the two. Being able to understand and study such skills, ethnographic methods, or even more detailed ethnomethodological approaches are applicable. A number of researchers have both applied and advocated ethnographic approaches in organization studies (Linstead, 1997; Schwartzman, 1993; Van Maanen, 1979), suggesting that ethnographies are providing detailed insights that enable an understanding of how a particular practice is being undertaken and organized. An ethnomethodological approach is even more focused on the narrow details of how an actual practice is accomplished and established over time, and eventually modified to suit new needs and demands (Atkinson, 1988). "Ethnomethodology can be described briefly as *a way to investigate the genealogical relationship between social practices and accounts of those practices,*" Lynch (1993: 1; emphasis in the original) suggests. That is, ethnomethodological approaches underline the relationship between the "doings" and the "sayings"; people engage in activities in organizations and they account for those activities, seeking to make sense out of the stream of practices they have been part of. The ethnomethodological approach was developed by Harold Garfinkel in the 1960s (Garfinkel, 1967, 1988; Garfinkel and Sacks, 1970) and has been advocated by, for instance, Michael Lynch (1993) in the field of science and technology studies (Lynch, Livingston, and Garfinkel, 1983). Quite recently, Rawls (2008) has suggested that ethnomethodology is applicable in workplace studies more broadly. Livingston's (1986) ethnomethodological study of mathematicians' work is a fine example of the insight potentially provided by this approach. Atkinson (1988) points at Livingston's contribution:

> By taking the reader through a proof of Goedel's theorem, Livingston attempts to demonstrate that mathematical rigor resides in the *local sequence* of actions produced by mathematicians. Here is the most radical exemplar of all ethnomethodological studies of work: matters which are classically treated as context free and independent of human agency are here represented in terms of their detailed real-world enactment. Livingston's blow-by-blow recapitulation of a mathematical proof is a vivid example of the analysis of quiddity in occupational and scientific work. (Atkinson, 1988: 446)

Livingston (1986) thus manages to demonstrate that even mathematics, perhaps the most deductive of all sciences and consequently allegedly removed from local concerns and traditions, is in fact what is a form of enactment, a collective engagement in defining what counts as a proper mathematical proof and what does not.[5] This leaves us at the point where knowledge is in the first place local and contingent on the context, a form of knowledge that is "domain specific" (in Jerome Bruner's [1991] phrase):

> Knowledge and skill . . . are domain specific and, consequently uneven in their accretion. Principles and procedures learned in one domain do not automatically transfer to other domains . . . If the acquisition of knowledge and of mental powers is indeed domain specific and not automatically transferable, this surely implies that a domain, so called, is a set of principles and procedures, rather like a prosthetic device, that permits intelligence to be used in certain ways, but not in others. Each particular way of using intelligence develops an integrity of its own—a kind of knowledge-plus-tool integrity—that fits to a particular range of applicability. (Bruner, 1991: 2)

The ethnomethodological approach is helpful in unraveling how knowledge and expertise are enacted in such specific domains.

No matter if an ethnographic method or an ethnomethodological approach is favoured, what is important for the understanding of vision and visuality is that a detailed understanding of how and under what circumstances specific ways of seeing are regarded legitimate and credible. Rather than expecting that professional vision is a neatly structured and overtly transparent activity, the student of vision and visuality in organizations may observe social practices that comprise a range of resources, technologies, artefacts, and so forth: "Judging from existing studies in ethnomethodology and the sociology of science," Lynch (1993: 299) says, "different configurations of skills, purposes, instruments, texts, materials, routines, and modes of agency are likely to be discovered in a highly dispersed and discontinuous field of practices." Besides the cognitive complexity the researcher has to deal with, there is a challenge in terms of choice and selection of what aspect of the rich set of data generated to pay attention to. Here ethnographers tend to navigate between two end positions: on the one hand, there are accounts of ethnographic work where nothing particularly interesting is happening (e.g., in Lévi-Strauss's *Tristes Tropiques*) and where the ethnographer is left with a sense of insufficiency, boredom, and *ennui*, unable to find anything exciting to report. John Law (1994: 43–44) is here talking about "the ethnographer's anxiety" derived from the sense of wasting one's time and ultimately one's academic career. Drawing on his own experiences from an ethnographic study of a British corporation, Law (1994: 45) contends that "where the ethnographer is, the Action is not." John van Maanen (1979: 543) is providing an equally down-to-earth but less depressing image of practical research work: "Fieldwork, despite the best intentions of the researcher, almost always boils down to series of endless conversations intersected by a few major events and a host of less formidable ones." On the other hand, the ethnographer is facing a world so saturated with interesting practices, intriguing plots, and eventful acquaintances. The skilled ethnographer is here capable of carving out what is of significance from the broader social fabric and isolate and theorize the particularities as being universals. In Rabinow's (1996b) elegant formulation:

> Every situation is historically and culturally overdetermined, part of the work of fieldwork is to identify the particularities and generalities of the situation, of the contingent and less contingent—and to be concerned with both sides of these pairs. The ethical work is concerned less with being vigilant and more an attentiveness, a reserved and reflected curiosity about what form of life is being made. It is through fieldwork, through experimental experimentation, that one establishes 'partial connections,' reflects on them, given then an appropriate form. (Rabinow, 1996b: 21)

Rabinow here emphasizes attentiveness as an ethnographer's virtue of specific importance for the activities. Using once again Clifford Geertz's (1973) elaboration on Gilbert Ryle's (1949) concept of "thick descriptions," such attentiveness is helping the ethnographer to outline the broader social setting wherein a particular visual practice is located and executed. Such thick descriptions are normally based on actors' accounts of their own practices. Given a series of epistemological and methodological concerns, such descriptions are never wholly accurate, Howard Becker (1996) argues, but the descriptions should add some value or insight into the very practice:

> [W]e *always* describe how they [people studied] interpret the events they participate in, so the only question is not whether we should, but how accurately we do it. We can find out, not with perfect accuracy. But better than zero, what people think they are doing, what meanings they give to the objects and events and people in their lives and experience. We do that by talking to them, in formal and informal interviews, in quick exchanges while we participate and observe their ordinary activities, and by watching and listening as they go about their business; we can even do it by giving them questionnaires which let them say what their meanings are or choose between meanings we give them as possibilities. To anticipate a later point, the nearer we get to the conditions in which they actually do attribute meanings to objects and events, the more accurate our descriptions of those meanings are likely to be. (Becker, 1996: 58)

Ethnographers may occasionally find themselves in situations where nothing particularly interesting is happening, while in other cases being overwhelmed by a mind-boggling variety of intriguing events and practices. Depending on the social situation and the actual practice examined, the seasoned ethnographer knows approximately what to expect when encountering the social milieu subject to analysis. However, as Becker (1992) points out, social theorists and ethnographers are skilled in identifying things they think may be worthy of a proper analysis even in the most meager of empirical soils: "Imaginative, well-read social scientists can go a long way with a little fact," Becker (1992: 211) says. Being able to report something when returning to the office desk is part of the skills being trained when engaging with empirical research over time.

Studying vision and visuality in organizations is a theoretical and empirical pursuit that demands a reasonably detailed understanding of specific thought collectives, communities sharing modes of perception. In fact, being able to see the right things on a photographic plate, a photography, or in a piece of garment, is what ultimately determining the membership to the professional group. Following Ian Hacking's (1983) vocabulary, the ethnographer of visual practices in organizations must be skilled in both "representing" (i.e., theorizing) visual practices and "intervening" in the field (i.e., engage in empirical studies of visual practices in specific thought collectives). Just like professional vision per se is determined by the relationship between seeing and saying—embedded in the capacity to alter between first and second-order observation in Luhmann's (2000) terms— the study of professional vision must relate proper theories and analytical frameworks and detailed empirical studies of visual practices. Taken together, what students of visual practices are providing are thick descriptions of how professional vision *qua* the professional gaze accompanied by operative vocabularies are used in social settings and are employed to accomplish social effects.

SUMMARY AND CONCLUSION

The history of vision demonstrates a long trajectory from being the uncomplicated reception of sense impression in the *camera obscura* model to a most complex biological process including the sensory mechanisms of the human eye, the neural network, the capacity of memory and imagination, and the integration of the technologically mediated lifeworlds of both practicing scientists, architects, and other professionals as well as the "man on the street" and his or her everyday perception. Vision (or seeing, to use the more mundane term) is far from uncomplicated and deserves its proper study in the field of the social sciences. In organization and management studies and the discipline of organization theory, vision has not been subject to much practical research work. In order to find adequate studies of visual practices and the use of visual representations, one needs to move to the neighbouring disciplines, to sociology (i.e., science and technology studies), anthropology, and the humanities. However, while there are beautiful and well-articulated theories about visuality and practices of vision in, for instance, film studies and art history, these disciplines are primarily preoccupied with understanding the act of seeing as interpretation, that is, how a particular piece of art is being appropriated and accommodated by the spectator. In organization theory, a more adequate question is that which Daston (2008) talks about as a Fleckian view of vision (in opposition to the Kantian tradition operating on the basis of the dichotomy subjective/objective), that is, how vision is constituted as a collective and joint accomplishment for the sake of practical utility. For instance, how does a group of scientists manage to move the research project forward through shared interpretative procedures in their laboratory work, or how do a group of architects co-align their individual creative ideas and ambitions into one coherent model of the forthcoming building, integrating all the need and demands of the clients and end users? These are two perfectly relevant questions in the pharmaceutical industry and the construction industry. However, at times, organization and management studies would shortcut the meta-theoretical or theoretical layer of any practice and the level of practical or operative theories. What has been called "epistemologies of the eye," the theoretical body of text addressing the philosophical and scientific theories of what vision is and how it can be used to formulate knowledge claims, and the "practices of vision," that is, the actual practices and day-to-day engagements with visual representations and ways of seeing, need to be integrated and combined. The act of looking, of staring, of glancing, of glaring, and so forth, is never a trivial matter but is a combination of intricate biological processes and socially enacted customs and scripted behaviours. The capacity to fully understand how specific forms of vision are being used, what roles they play, and how they can be used—at the bottom line—to constitute economic or social value demands a theoretical grounding in the field of epistemology. If nothing else, this book encourages more such theoretical groundwork while at the same time more inspiring and intriguing studies of the use of professional visions in the workplace are called for. There are numerous domains where the practice of seeing serves a very central role and continuing to explore these organization activities would be very helpful for making organization and management studies a dynamic field of research.

Notes

NOTES TO CHAPTER 1

1. Roth and Bowen (2003) suggest that the use of graphs and other visual representations using lines and other "continuous images" are capable of capturing the experience of the duration of time in real life more effectively than texts, cutting up any entity of analysis to components: "The lines encode continuous change and are therefore suited to represent the dynamic nature of physical phenomena. Linguistic representations, on the other hand, divide the world into objects and classes of objects: Verbal representations is typological in character . . . Graphs, consisting of combinations of topological and typological features, have specificity (what they cannot leave unsaid about the observed situation) that aids in their use for constructing logical arguments" (Roth and Bowen, 2003: 430). The Gantt charts studied by Yakura (2002) are thus not only tools in the hands of project managers but are also "rhetorical devices" imposing an image of continuation and stability.

NOTES TO CHAPTER 2

1. In Foucault's *Birth of the Clinic* (1973: 145), this passage is given as follows: "Life is the totality of functions that resists the absence of life." In more recent research in the life sciences, a systems biology perspective on the body is emphasizing this idea of interrelated system collaboratively constituting life. Contrary to genomics research, conceiving of the body as being constituted from the bottom up "piece by piece," from the amino acids of the proteins produced by the DNA to the higher systems entities such as cells, tissue, and organs, systems biology is concerned with "[c]omponents and processes, and their potential perturbations" (Thacker, 2004: 162). That is, systems biology does not assume that the body could be understood on the basis of reductionist epistemologies, through piecemeal studies of isolated biological processes, but on the systems level. Thacker (2002: 170) illustrates this view with reference to the various processes of the cell: "The living system is a network in that it involves more than one process, which itself involves more than one component. In the cell, this is illustrated by the various processes of metabolism (themselves composed of disassembly, assembly, and energy-releasing processes), gene expression (involving structural, regulatory, operator, and other genes) and communication (including processes of cell signaling, membrane transport, protein synthesis)." Thus, Bichat's systems view of he body is, *mutatis mutandis*, still an adequate operative model for the life sciences.

2. As Davies (1982) points out, Taylor and his followers entertained the belief that a person was "[e]ndowed with certain 'natural' capabilities that automatically suited him or her to a certain type of work" (Davies, 1982: 122). As a consequence, "the ideal office workforce would be one in which the 'natural' differences between the employees determined their clerical niches." Adhering to such essentialist credo, it is little wonder that attentiveness was seen as an endowed skill rather than, as for instance Taylor's contemporary Hermann von Helmholtz and William James thought, a capacity to be acquired through training. Needless to say, Frederick W. Taylor was not a salient proponent of workplace learning and investment in costly training and education.

3. In his postcolonial masterpiece *Black Skin, White Masks*, Franz Fanon (1986: 191) is emphasizing that commonsense thinking is anchored in a shared culture inhibiting complementary thinking: "The collective unconsciousness is not dependent on cerebral heredity; it is the result of what I shall call the *unreflected imposition of culture*." For Fanon, however, such "collective unconsciousness" is the key to the understanding of racism and xenophobia and is therefore not by any means an unproblematic mechanism in human societies.

4. A plausible explanation for this rejection of scientific work that fails to adhere to prescribed formal procedures is the long tradition of exclusion of subjectivity in modern and Western science. As both Stengers (1997) and Rheinberger (2003) notice, subjectivity is not part of the operational vocabulary of scientists: "All of the phenomena that we know of are overloaded with multiple meanings, capable of authorizing an indefinite multiplicity of readings and interpretations, that is, of being utilized as evidence in the most diverse situations, and thus also of being disqualified as evidence. The whole situation is thus, for the scientist, to produce testimony that cannot be disqualified by being attributed to his or her own 'subjectivity,' to his biased reading, a testimony that others must accept, a testimony for which he or she will be recognized as a faithful representative and that will not betray him or her to the first colleague who come along" (Stengers, 1997: 86). Rheinberger also remarked that the linguistic marker "I" is more or less absent from scientific texts published after around 1900. For Rheinberger (2003: 311), this is indicative of the commitment to objectivity: "The supposed commitment to objectivity is build right into the language in which the scientists is allowed to speak to his or her fellows and to a wider audience. Therefore, and in a certain sense, authorship as a warrant to speak appears to be, in scientific writing, always already crossed out." Instead, the use of "an active voice" is present in the outer fringes of the sciences, in commemorations, keynote addresses, historical reflections and autobiographies, and other genres where anecdotes can be tolerated and are regarded as having a value. "Here," Rheinberger (2003: 311) says, "the scientist may take the freedom to expose his or her personal view, something that has no place in the regular canon of scientific writing."

NOTES TO CHAPTER 3

1. In the study of technology, it is commonplace to distinguish between "internalist" and "externalist" or "contextualist" perspectives on technology (Gitelman, 1999: 8; Nye, 2006: 61) wherein the former perspective assumes that technologies have intrinsic qualities that makes them more successful than competing technologies and the latter postulate that technologies are

always enacted by communities and are therefore not to be examined in terms of being good or bad but how well they have been received by social actors. "[A]n artefact does not suddenly appear as the result of a singular act of heroic invention; instead it is gradually constructed in the social interactions between and within relevant social groups," Bijker, (1995: 270) suggests (see also Pinch and Bijker, 1987). To take new reproductive technologies as what is "a force unto itself" as suggested by Franklin and Roberts (2006) would be to adhere to an externalist perspective. The internalist view of technology is, its critics contend, a form of "whig-history" portraying historical processes as being more or less programmed to lead up to the fortunate situation of today's society and where past events can be explained on the basis of what we know today. MacKenzie is warning against such a perspective on technology: "Hindsight often makes it appear that the successful technology is simply intrinsically superior, but hindsight—here and elsewhere—can be a misleading form of vision. Historians and sociologists of technology would do well to avoid explaining the success of technology by its assumed intrinsic technical superiority to its rivals. Instead, they should seek, even-handedly, to understand how its actual superiority came into being, while suspending judgment as to whether it is intrinsic" (MacKenzie, 1995: 7). That is, technology is society made durable—in Latour's (1991) condensed phrase—only as long as "society" (i.e., its various actors and communities of agents) is managing to collectively enact a technology as useful.

2. MacKenzie and Millo's (2003) study of the adoption of the Black-Scholes option pricing model in option trading in the Chicago Board Options Exchange in the 1970s and 1980s is one illustrative example of the normative role of mathematics and the procedures of mathematization. While the Black-Scholes model is at times put forth as the "crown jewel" of economic theory, ultimately supporting the authority of the entire discipline, MacKenzie and Millo (2003) suggest that the model was primarily "theoretical" rather than "empirical" and that it originally could only approximately predict option prices. Only after significant changes in the procedures involved in option trading and after the model was used by the traders—despite its apparent limitations—its pricing predictions converged towards the actual prices. "Gradually," MacKenzie and Millo (2003: 127) say, " 'reality' (in this case, empirical prices) was performatively reshaped in conformance with the theory." However, as pointed out by one option trader, the model helped legitimating this specific derivative financial instrument by imposing a seemingly solid mathematical foundation for the instrument: "Black-Scholes was really what enabled the exchange to thrive . . . It gave a lot of legitimacy to the whole notion of hedging and efficient pricing, whereas we were faced, in the late 60s-early 70s with the issue of gambling . . . It wasn't speculation or gambling, it was efficient pricing . . . I never heard the word 'gambling' again in relation to options" (Option trader, cited in MacKenzie and Millo, 2003: 121). A strong belief in mathematical formulae may indeed change the world.

3. The connection between religiosity and scientific endeavours has gradually loosened over the course of centuries. Not until the great French mathematician Pierre-Simon Laplace rejected the presence of God in his system with the famed statement "Sire, je n'ai pas eu besoin de cette hypothèse" ("Sir, I don't have any use for such an hypothesis") (cited by Koyré, 1959: 276) when responding to Napoleon's inquiries on the matter, God was for the first time left out from scientific activities. However, still today, in largely secular times, theological issues are at times debated when, for instance, the topic of what formerly was known as "creationism" and what is at present named "intelligent design" is discussed.

4. It is here possible to see the connections between Simondon's (1980) thinking and the neo-vitalist philosophy of Teilhard de Chardin (1965) and followers such as Deleuze and Guattari (1988) and De Landa (1991, 1992, 2006), speaking about the *phylum* as the "the individuation of the species," as "phylogenesis" or "ontogenesis" (Teilhard de Chardin, 1965: 113) or, more specifically, of the *machinic phylum* as "nonlinear flows of matter and energy spontaneously generate machinelike assemblages when internal or external pressures reach a critical level, which only a very few abstract mechanisms can account for" (DeLanda, 1992: 136). These diverse thinkers share the view that neither technological artefacts nor biological organisms are given *en bloc* but are gradually stabilized over time.

5. In opposition to the doctrine centring conscious to the brain, Timothy Lenoir (2007: 199) addresses recent research in the neuroscience and cognition sciences rejecting such a "simple location": "Rejecting Cartesian assumptions of a disembodied mind, Antonio Damasio, Francesco Varela, and other neuroscientists and cognitive scientists have shown that human consciousness is not localized in a set of neural connections in the brain alone but is highly dependent on the material substrate of the biological body, with emotions and other dimensions as supportive structure." That is, in this view, consciousness is relational and distributed rather than isolated within a limited set of biological mechanisms and processes in the brain. "[C]onsciousness apparently produces its own content, i.e., the world," Stafford (2009: 281) says.

6. What is called the tissue economy includes a variety of domains and practices including egg agencies and sperm banks, organ donations, and blood donation (Calvert, 2007; Hogle, 1995; Parry and Gere, 2006; Tober, 2001). It is an "economy" in the broadest sense of the term (in the sense of *oikonomikos*, "householding"), blending both what Richard Titmuss (1970) called "the gift relationship" in the case of blood donations and more strictly juridical and financial agreements. As Almeling (2007) shows in her study of egg agencies and sperm banks, egg agencies "[s]tructure the exchange not only as a legalistic economic transaction, but also the beginning of a caring gift cycle, which the staff foster by expressing appreciation to the donors, both on behalf of the agency and the agency's clients" (Almeling, 2007: 333). This gift economy is strongly gendered and racial and suggests that "[w]omen are perceived as more closely connected to their eggs than men are to their sperm" (Almeling, 2007: 328) and consequently the male sperm donors are not regarded as being as "caring" and "helpful" as the female egg donors. In addition, the egg donors are expected to be either "highly educated and physically attractive or caring and motherly with children of their own," whereas the sperm donors need to be "tall" and "college educated." The "reproduction industry" (see Clarke, 1998; Franklin and Roberts, 2006; Thompson, 2005), a substantial part of the tissue economy since it is estimated that about 10% of the American population is suffering from infertility problems, is thus demonstrating an intriguing mixture of commerce and philanthropy. This delicate balance between "the passions and the interests" (in Hirschman's [1977] here most apt phrase) is complicated to uphold and may easily be violated. For instance, women who aim at "making a career" as an egg donor "provoke disgust among staff" because they are threatening "the altruistic framing of donation" in terms of being too concerned about the financial compensation (Almeling, 2007: 334).

7. Wiener's theories about the use of cybernetics in the life sciences were eventually adopted by leading researchers in the field. For instance, the Nobel Prize laureates François Jacob and Jacques Monod individually addressed their joint work in cybernetic terms. For Monod, the organism is nothing but "a cybernetic system governing and controlling the chemical activity at numerous points"

(Jacques Monod, *Chance and Necessity*, 1970, cited in Kay, 2000: 17), and Jacob argued in the end of the 1970s that "heredity functions like a memory of a computer . . . Organs, cells and molecules are thus united by a communication network" (François Jacob, *The logic of life*, 1979, cited in Kay, 2000: 17). In addition, Wiener's cybernetics program has been influential in a wide range of scientific projects, including the field of nanotechnology and nanomachines (Jones, 2004; Thomas and Acuña-Narvaez, 2006), opening up, its proponents hope, possibilities for "posthuman engineering" and new forms of therapies on the nano or (more likely) the micro-scale (Milburn, 2004).

8. Bowker (2005: 73) here speaks about an "information mythology" wherein "information" can "[t]ravel anywhere and be made of anything, sequences in a gene, energy level in an atom, zeroes and ones in a machine, and signals from a satellite are all 'information.' " As opposed to this view, (Bowker, 2005: 73) suggests, "the global statement that 'everything is information' is not a preordained fact about the world, it becomes a fact when we make it so." Bowker (2005) thus suggests that one must not think of information in transcendental but in empiricist terms, namely as what is both informational and material at the same time.

9. Thacker (2005: 130) makes reference to Georges Bataille's (1988) concept of *the general economy* (as opposed to *the restricted economy*), suggesting that Bataille's ideas about the squandering of excessive resources—what Bataille calls the "accursed share"—is a defining mark of all higher cultures (see Styhre [2002] for an introduction), applicable when understanding the functioning of the hereditary material. Such a point is of course speculative but also indicative of the idea of abundance of information in the human genome.

10. Since it has been estimated that, in theory, two-thirds of the American population has "[a] phenotype that is associated with a susceptibility to depression" (Shostak and Conrad, 2008: S306), there were no specific ethnic, religious, or "lifestyle" groups being targeted in the process of geneticization and medicalization of depression, possibly allowing for such an event.

11. One of Shostak's (2005) interviewees, a researcher in the field of toxicogenomics, addressed this feeling of being overwhelmed by data and not knowing how to sort it out and interpret it: "What does the data mean? That's the big question. There is so much data. It's like being given the Encyclopaedia Britannica and ten seconds to find an answer . . . You know the answer is out there somewhere, but you have to learn the rules or what volume to go to, and you have to learn the rule within that volume. Where do you look it up? And you have to learn the rules for not only reading what's there, but understanding and interpreting" (Toxicogenomics researcher, cited in Shostak, 2005: 384).

12. In a study of a microbiology and bioengineering department in a major research university, one of the Ph.D. candidates interviewed demonstrated her individually constructed and immensely complex flowchart over the metabolic processes in the fungi cells she had studied for the last three years. She admitted that she used general software packages such as Illustrator or Matlab but also thought that 3D visualizations would be helpful in the research work: "It [3D images] would have been very helpful for some areas such as protein docking, drug target identification . . . the structure of enzymes" (Ph.D. candidate, Systems Biology University Department).

NOTES TO CHAPTER 4

1. The shift from "the knowledge society" to "the knowledge economy" is a curious shift in perspective, operating on basis of what literature theorists

calls *synecdoche*, letting the part represent the whole (e.g., Washington representing the whole of USA or speaking of "heads" when addressing individuals). In this Thatcherist trope, society is no longer what is of interest but the economy is taking its place as the proper object of analysis. The assumption is also that the operating mechanisms of the economy are also of relevance for society at large. We do indeed live in "economy-centric" times where society apparently is, with Derrida's term *sous rature*, "under erasure."

2. In her study of cattle breeders in Italy, Christina Grasseni (2004) reports that such "reference photos" are circulating in breeders community in a manner similar to that of the community of architects: "Dedicated breeders eagerly acquire, collect and exchange . . . visual materials as magazines, posters, prize photographs or videos of cattle fairs. Often also available on specialist websites, these mediate and propagate the training of the eye, constituting a common idiom, a shared ideology or professional practice" (Grasseni, 2004: 41).

NOTES TO CHAPTER 5

1. Complementing Flusser's (2000, 2002) thinking, Camille (1985: 27), an art historian, suggests that in the medieval period images are representations of speech rather than being an idiosyncratic form of visuality adhering to its own principles: "[M]uch of the visual art of the twelfth century was not so much an expression of the visible world, as of the spoken word in a still predominantly oral society." The medieval period in Europe was not in the first place a "visual culture" but an oral culture and reading was primarily a matter of hearing and speaking, not of seeing. However, as the codex—the form of the book we are still using today—started to replace the roll, the reader could increasingly "[r]ecapitulate, skim, check texts against picture and refer forwards in ways not possible with the roll." While the roll, just like speech, is linear and unidirectional—in medieval art, Camille (1985) says, scrolls held by talkers in images signified speech—the codex enabled new forms of visuality, a moving back and forth between documents and resources. Camille (1985) suggests that the complicated relationship between the "intellectual techniques" of speech, text, and image is highly contingent and dependent on technological innovations.

2. Starbuck (2006) offers an illustration of how the medieval scholar was guided by a corpus of major works that ultimately set the boundaries for what could be practically studies: "During the thirteenth century, professors at the university of Paris decided to find out whether oil would congeal if left outdoors on a cold night. They launched a research project to investigate this question. To them, research meant searching through the works of Aristotle. After much effort, they found that nothing Aristotle had written answered their question, so they declared the question unanswerable. The essential truth of the anecdote is that the Parisian professors were right: their question was unanswerable within the research tradition to which they confirmed" (Starbuck, 2006: 1).

3. Manovich (2009: 319–320), speaking about *Internet 2.0* as the shift from being, in the 1900s, *an information medium*, to a *communication medium* dominated by content produced by "nonprofessional users," reports that today the site MySpace has 300,000,000 users and Cyworld, a South Korean community site similar to Facebook, represents 90% of the South Korean population in their twenties and 25% of the entire population. In addition, Facebook has 14,000,000 photo uploads daily and 65,000 new videos are uploaded every 24 hours to YouTube (as of July 2006) (Manovich, 2009: 320). Even though much of the information provided on the Internet is in the form of

written texts (in, e.g., weblogs, "blogs"), it is fundamentally a mixed medium radically different from the conventional linear written text of the book.

4. Grasseni's (2004) study of cattle breeder fairs in Italy reveals a similar emphasis on professional vision and the negotiated order between participants and various authorities (i.e., cattle competition judges) and the truth claims and knowledge claims authorities advance as part of their alleged expertise: "Breeders often belong to geographically dispersed communities of practice which treat the next cattle fair as an appointment to discuss preceding feasts, champions and judges' performances: cattle fairs are often the objects of comment, complaints and gossip for months afterwards. Establishing one's judgement as authoritative is largely a question of trust and socially recognized skills" (Grasseni, 2004: 50). Similar to the London Fashion Week, the breeder fairs provide grist for the mill for months of discussions and gossiping, all forms of communication helping to reproduce what Entwhistle and Racamora (2006) call "fashion capital" and what Grasseni (2004) speaks of more loosely as "breeding aesthetics."

5. Another way to discuss Livingston's (1986) contribution is to point at the components of commonsense thinking in mathematics and indeed all sciences (as Dewey [1949] does), namely that of even strictly deductive systems relying on joint agreement on what rules to follow. Dewey (1949) is thus sceptical regarding the value of separating common sense into a domain of practical undertakings and scientific work as a field of pure theoretical interest: "The concerns of common sense knowing is 'practical,' that of scientific doing is 'theoretical.' But *practical* in the first case is not limited to utilitarian in the sense in which the word is disparagingly used. It includes all matters of direct enjoyment that occur in the course of living because of transformation wrought by the fine arts, by friendship, by recreation, by civic affair, etc. And 'theoretical' in the second instance is far away form the *theoria* of pure contemplation of the Aristotelian tradition, and from any sense of the word that excludes elaborate and exclusive doings and makings. Scientific knowing is that *particular* form of practical human activity which is concerned with the advancement of *knowing* apart from concerns with *other* practical affairs" (Dewey, 1949: 282). What ethnomethodological studies show, in this context, are that there is always a certain proximity between commonsense thinking and advanced theoretical work.

Bibliography

Abbott, Andrew, (1988), *The system of professions: An essay on the division of expert labor*, Chicago & London: Chicago University Press.

Adams, Annmarie, & Tancred, Peta, (2000), *'Designing women': Gender and the architectural profession*, Toronto, Buffalo, & London: The University of Toronto Press.

Agamben, Giorgio, (1998), *Homo Sacer: Sovereign power and bare life*, trans. by Daniel Heller-Roazen, Stanford, CA: Stanford University Press.

Alac, Morana,(2008), Working with brain scans: Digital images and gestural interaction in FMRI laboratory, *Social Studies of Science*, 38(4): 483–508.

Alexander, Amir R., (2002), *The voyages of discovery and the transformation of mathematical practice*, Stanford, CA: Stanford University Press.

Almeling, Renee, (2007), Selling genes, selling gender: Egg agencies, sperm banks, and the medical market in genetic material, *American Sociological Review*, 73(3): 319–340.

Althusser, Louis, (1984), *Essays on ideology*, London & New York: Verso.

Alvesson, M., (1994), Talking in organizations: Managing identity and impression in an advertising agency, *Organization Studies*, 15(4): 535–563.

Alvesson, Mats, (2001), Knowledge work: Ambiguity, image and identity, *Human Relations*, 54(7): 863–886.

Alvesson, Mats, (2004), *Knowledge work and knowledge-intensive firms*, Oxford & New York: Oxford University Press.

Alvesson, Mats, & Kärreman, Dan, (2000), Taking the linguistic turn in organizational research: Challenges, responses, consequences, *Journal of Applied Behavioral Science*, 36(2): 136–158.

Alvesson, Mats, & Kärreman, Dan, (2001), Odd couple: Making sense of the curious concept of knowledge management, *Journal of Management Studies*, 38(7): 995–1018.

Alvesson, Mats, & Willmott, Hugh, (1996), *Making sense of management: A critical introduction*, London, Thousand Oaks, CA, & New Delhi: Sage.

Amin, Ash, & Cohendet, Patrick, (2004), *Architecture of knowledge: Firms, capabilities, and communities*, Oxford & New York: Oxford University Press.

Angell, Marcia, (2004). *The truth about the drug companies: How they deceive us and what to do about it*, New York: Random House.

Ankrah, N. A., & Langford, D. A., (2005), Architects and contractors: A comparative study of organizational cultures, *Construction Management and Economics*, 23: 595–607.

Aragon, Louis, (1928/1991), *Treatise on style*, trans. by Alyson Waters, Lincoln & London: University of Nebraska Press.

Archimbaud, Michel, (1993), *Francis Bacon: In conversation with Michel Archibaud*, London. Phaidon Press.

Argyris, C., & Schön, D.A., (1978), *Organizational learning: A theory of action perspective*, Reading, MA: Addison-Wesley.

Arnoldi, Jakob, (2006), Frames and screens: The reduction of uncertainty in electronic derivatives trading, *Economy and Society*, 35(3): 381–399.

Atkinson, Paul, (1988), Ethnomethodology: A critical review, *Annual Review of Sociology*, 14: 441–465.

Atlan, H., (1974), On a formal definition of organization, *Journal of Theoretical Biology*, 45: 295–304.

Attewell, Paul, (1990), What is a skill?, *Work and Occupations*, 17(4): 422–448.

Babbage, Charles, (1833), *On the economy of machinery and manufactures*, London: Charles Knight.

Bachelard, G., (1934/1984), *The New Scientific Spirit*, Beacon Press, Boston.

Barad, Karen, (2003), Posthumanist performativity: Towards an understanding of how matter comes to matter, *Signs: Journal of Women in Culture and Society*, 28(3): 801–831.

Barley, Steven S., & Kunda; Gideon, (2004), *Gurus, warm bodies and hired guns: Itinerant experts in the knowledge economy*, Princeton, NJ: Princeton University Press.

Barley, Stephen R., & Kunda, Gideon, (2006), Contracting: A new form of professional practice, *Academy of Management Perspectives*, 20(1): 45–66.

Barry, Andrew, (2005), Pharmaceutical matters: The invention of informed materials, *Theory, Culture & Society*, 22(1): 51–69.

Barry, Ann Marie Seward, (1997), *Visual intelligence: Perception, image and manipulation in visual communication*, Albany: State University of New York Press.

Barthes, R., (1983), *The fashion system*, London: Jonathan Cope.

Bataille, Georges, (1988), *The accursed share: An essay on general economy*, New York: Zone Books.

Beaulieu, Anne, (2002), Images are not the (only) truth: Brain mapping, visual knowledge and iconoclasm, *Science, Technology and Human Values*, 27: 53–86.

Bechky, Beth A., (2003), Object lessons: Workplace artifacts as representations of occupational jurisdiction, *American Journal of Sociology*, 109(3): 720-752.

Becker, Howard S., (1992), Cases, causes, conjunctures, stories, and imagery, in Ragin, Charles C., & Becker, Howard S., eds., *What is a case?: Reexploring the foundations of social inquiry*, Cambridge: Cambridge University Press.

Becker, Howard S., (1996), The epistemology of qualitative research, in Jessor, Richard, Colby, Anne, & Shweder, Richard A., (1996), *Ethnography and human development; Context and meaning in social inquiry*, Chicago & London: University of Chicago Press., pp. 53–71.

Beistegui, Miguel de, (2005), From Merleau-Ponty's "Reduction" to Simondon's "Transduction," *Angelaki: Journal of Theoretical Humanities*, 10(3): 109–122.

Belfiore, Eleonora, (2002), Art as a means of alleviating social exclusion: Does it really work? A critique of instrumental policies and social impact studies in the UK, *International Journal of Cultural Policy*, 8(1): 91–106.

Beller, Jonathan, (2006), *The cinematic mode of production: Attention economy and the society of the spectacle,* Hanover, NH: Dartmouth College Press.

Bellow, Saul, (1982), *The dean's December*, London: Secker & Warburg.

Benjamin, Walter, (1999), *The arcades project*, trans. by Howard Eiland & Kevin McLaughlin, Cambridge: The Belknap Press.

Benschop, Yvonne, & Heihuizen, Hanne E., (2000), Keeping up gendered appearances: Representations of gender in financial annual reports, *Accounting, Organization and Society*, 27: 611–636.

Bentham, Jeremy, (1995), *The panopticon writings*, London: Verso.

Bergson, H., (1910/1988), *Matter and memory,* New York: Zone Books.

Berkeley, George, (1709/2004), From *An enssay towards a new theory of vision,* in Schwatz, Robert, ed. (2004), Perception, Oxford & Malden: Blackwell, pp. 18–23.

Bijker, Wiebe E., (1995), *Of bicycles, bakelites, and bulbs: Toward a theory of sociotechnical change,* Cambridge & London: MIT Press.

Blau, Judith R., (1984), Architects and firms: A sociological perspective on architectural practice, Cambridge. MIT Press.

Blau, Judith R., & William McKinley, (1979), Ideas, complexity and innovation, *Administrative Science Quarterly,* 24: 200–219.

Blech, Jörg, (2006), *Inventing disease and pushing pills: Pharmaceutical companies and the medicalization of normal life,* trans. by Gisela Wallor Hajjar, London & New York: Routledge.

Bloomfield, Brian P., & Vurdubakis, Theodore, (1997), Vision of organization and organization of vision: The representational practices of information systems development, *Accounting, Organization and Society,* 639–668.

Blumenberg, Hans, (1993), Light as a metaphor for truth: At the preliminary stage of philosophical concept formation, in Levin, David Michael, ed., *Modernity and the hegemony of vision,* Berkeley, Los Angeles, & London: University of California Press, pp. 30–62.

Böhme, Gernot, (2003), Contribution to the critique of the aesthetic economy, *Thesis Eleven,* 73: 72–82.

Boland, Richard J., Lyytinen, Kalle & Yoo, Youngjin, (2007), Wakes of innovation in project networks: The case of digital 3-D representation in architecture, engineering, and construction, *Organization Science,* 18(4): 631–647.

Bolter, David Jay, (1996), Virtual reality and the redefinition of self, in Strate, Lance, Jacobson, Ronald, Gibson, Stephanie, B., eds., (1996), *Communication and cyberspace: Social interaction in an electronic environment,* Cresskill, NJ: Hampton Press, pp. 105–119.

Borges, Jorge Luis, (1999), The postulation of reality, in Borges, Jorge Luis, *Selected non-fiction,* Weinberger, Eliot, ed., London: Penguin, pp. 59–64.

Bourdieu, Pierre, (1993), *The field of cultural production: Essays on art and literature,* ed. by Randall Johnson, Cambridge: Polity Press.

Bourdieu, Pierre, (2005), *The economic structures of society,* Cambridge: Polity Press.

Bowker, Geoffrey, (2005), *Memory practices of the sciences,* Cambridge & London: MIT Press.

Braidotti, Rosi, (2002), *Metamorphosis: Toward a materialist theory of becoming,* Cambridge: Polity Press.

Braidotti, Rosi, (2006); *Transpositions: On nomadic ethics,* Cambridge, MA, & Malden, MA: Polity Press.

Braidotti, Rosi, (2008), In spite of the times: The postsecular turn in feminism, *Theory, Culture & Society,* 25(6): 1–24.

Briscoe, Forrest, (2007), From iron cage to iron shield? How bureaucracy enables temporal flexibility for professional service workers, *Organization Science,* 18(2): 297–314.

Brown, Nik, & Kraft, Alison, (2006), Blood ties: Banking the stem cell promise, *Technology Analysis & Strategic Management,* 18(3): 313–327.

Bruner, Jerome, (1986), *Actual minds, possible worlds,* Cambridge, MA: Harvard University Press.

Bruner, Jerome, (1991), The narrative construction of reality, *Critical Inquiry,* 18(1): 1–21.

Bryson, Norman, (1988), The gaze in the expanded field, in Foster, Hal, ed., (1988), *Vision and visuality,* New York: The New Press, pp. 86–113.

Burawoy, M., (1979), *Manufacturing consent: Changes in the labour process under monopoly capitalism*, Chicago: University of Chicago Press.

Burrell, Gibson, (1988), Modernism, postmodernism and organizational analysis 2: The contribution of Michel Foucault, *Organization Studies*, 9(1): 91–112.

Burri, Regula Valérie, (2008), Doing distinctions: Boundary work and symbolic capital in radiology, *Social Studies of Science*, 38: 35–62.

Burri, Regula Valérie & Dumit, Joseph, (2008), Social studies of scientific imaging and visualization, in Hackett, Edward J., Amsterdamska, Olga, Lynch, Michael, & Wajcman, Judy, eds., *Handbook of science and technology studies*, 3rd. ed., Cambridge & London: MIT Press, pp. 297–317.

Butterfield, H., (1962), *The origins of modern science, 1300–1800*, London: G. Bell and Sons.

Cache, Bernard, (1995), *Earth moves: The furnishing of territories*, trans. B Anne Boyman, Cambridge, MA: MIT Press.

Caldwell, John Thornton, (2008), *Production culture: Industrial reflexivity and critical practice in film and television*, Durham, NC, & London: Duke University Press.

Calvert, Jane, (2007), Patenting genomic objects: Genes, genomes, function and information, *Science as Culture*, 16(2): 207–223.

Camille, Michael, (1985), Seeing and reading: Some visual implications of medieval literacy and illiteracy, *Art History*, 8(19): 26–49.

Canguilhem, Georges, (1991), *The normal and the pathological*, New York: Zone Books.

Carr, Adrian, & Downs, Alexis, (2004), Transitional and quasi-objects in organization studies: Viewing Enron from the object relations world of Winnicott and Serres, *Journal of Organization Change Management*, 17(4): 352–364.

Carr, Adrian & Hancock, Philip, eds., (2003), *Art and aesthetics at work*, Basingstoke, UK, & New York: Palgrave.

Carr-Saunders, A. M., & Wilson, P. A. (1933), *The professions*, Oxford: Clarendon Press.

Cartwright, Lisa, (1995), *Screening the body: Tracing medicine's visual culture*, Minneapolis & London: University of Minnesota Press.

Case, Peter, & Piñeiro, Erik, (2006), Aesthetic, performativity and resistance in the narrative of computer programming community, *Human Relations*, 59(6): 753–782.

Caves, Richard E., (2000), *Creative industries*, Cambridge & London: Harvard University Press.

Christopherson, Susan, (2008), Beyond the self-expressive creative worker: An industry perspective on entertainment media, *Theory, Culture and Society*, 25(7–8):73–95.

Cicmil, Svetlana, & Hogson, Damian, (2006), Making projects critical: An introduction, in Hodgson, Damian, & Cicmil, Svetlana, eds., *Making projects critical*, Basingstoke & New York: Palgrave, pp. 1–25.

Clarke, Adele E., (1998), *Disciplining reproduction: Modernity, American life sciences, and the problem of sex*, Berkeley: University of California Press.

Clarke, Adele E., Mamo, Laura, Fishman, Jennifer R., Shim, Janet K., & Fosket, Jennifer Ruth, (2003), Biomedicalization: Technoscientific transformations of health, illness, and U.S. biomedicine, *American Sociological Review*, 68: 161–194.

Clough, Patricia T., (2008), The affective turn: Political economy, biomedia and bodies, *Theory, Culture and Society*, 25(1): 1–22.

Cock, Jacklyn, (1989), *Maids and madams: Domestic work under apartheid*, London: The Women's Press.

Cohn, Laurie, Wilkinson, Adrian, Arnold, John, & Finn, Rachael, (2005), Remember I'm the bloody architect! Architects, organizations and discourses of professions, *Work, Employment and Society*, 19(4): 775–796.

Cohn, Simon, (2004), Increasing resolution, intensifying ambiguity: An ethnographic account of seeing life in brain scans, *Economy and Society*, 33(1): 52–76.

Collins, Randall, (1979), *The credential society*, New York: Academic Press.

Cook, Scott D., & Yanow, Dvora, (1993), Culture and organizational learning, *Journal of Management Inquiry*, 2(4): 373–390.

Cooper, Melinda, (2008), *Life as surplus: Biotechnology and capitalism in the neoliberal era*, Seattle & London: The University of Washington Press.

Cooren, François, (2004), The communicative achievement of collective minding: Analysis of Board meeting excerpts, *Management Communication Quarterly*, 17(4): 517–551.

Conrad, Peter, (2007), *The medicalization of society*: Baltimore: Johns Hopkins University Press.

Constable, Nicole, (1997), *Maid to order in Hong Kong: Stories of Filipina workers*, Ithaca, NY, & London: Cornell University Press.

Coulter, Jeff, & Parsons, E. D. (1991), The praxiology of perception: Visual orientations and practical action, *Inquiry*, 33(3): 251–272.

Crary, Jonathan, (1990), *Techniques of the observer: On vision and modernity in the nineteenth century*, Cambridge, MA, & London: MIT Press.

Crary, Jonathan, (1995), Unbinding vision: Manet and the attentive observer in the late nineteenth century, in Carney, Leo, & Schwartz, Vanessa R., eds., *Cinema and the invention of modern life*, Berkeley: University of California Press, pp. 46–71.

Crary, Jonathan, (1999), *Suspensions of perception: Attention, spectacle, and modern culture*, Cambridge, MA, & London: MIT Press.

Croce, Benedetto, ([1913] 1995), *Guide to aesthetics*, trans. by Patrick Romanell, Indianapolis & Cambridge: Hackett.

Cuff, Dana, (1991), *Architecture: The story of practice*, Cambridge, MA: MIT Press.

Czarniawska, Barbara, (1997), *Narrating the organization: Dramas of institutional identity*, Chicago & London: The University of Chicago Press.

Czarniawska, Barbara, (2001), Having hope in paralogy, *Human Relations*, 54(1): 13–21.

Czarniawska, Barbara, (2004), *Narratives in social science research*, London, Thousand Oaks & New Delhi: Sage.

Czarniawska-Joerges, B., (1993), *The Three-Dimensional Organization,* Lund: Studentlitteratur.

Daemmrich, Arthur, (1998), The evidence does not speak for itself: Expert witnesses and the organization of DNA-typing companies, *Social Studies of Science*, 28: 741–772.

Dalton, Melville, (1959), *Men who manage: Fusion of feeling and theory in administration*, New York: Wiley.

Daston, Lorraine, (2008), On scientific observation, *Isis*, 99: 97–110.

Daston, Loraine, & Galison, Peter, (2007), *Objectivity*, New York: Zone Books.

Davenport, Thomas, & Beck, John, (2001), *The attention economy.* Cambridge, MA: Harvard Business School Press.

Davies, Margery W., (1982), *Woman's place is at the typewriter: Office work and office workers 1870–1930*, Philadelphia: Temple University Press.

Deetz, S. A., (1992), *Democracy in an Age of Corporate Colonialization*, Albany: State University of New York Press.

De Landa, Manuel, (1991), *War in the age of intelligent machines*, New York: Zone Books.

De Landa, Manuel, (1992), Nonorganic life, in Crary, Jonathan, & Kwinter, Sanford, eds., *Incorporations*, New York: Zone Books, pp. 129–167.

De Landa, Manuel, (2006), A new philosophy of society: Assemblage theory and social complexity, London & New York: Continuum.

Deleuze, G., (1988a), *Foucault*, Minneapolis & London: University of Minnesota Press.

Deleuze, G., (1988b), *Bergsonism*, New York: Zone Books.

Deleuze, Gilles, (2006), *Two regimes of madness: Texts and interviews 1975–1995*, trans. by Hodges, Ames, & Taormina, Mike, New York & Los Angeles: Semiotext(e).

Deleuze, Gilles, & Guattari, Félix, (1988), *A thousand plateaus: Capitalism and schizophrenia*, Minneapolis & London: University of Minnesota Press.

Dempsey, A. M., (2006), Managing uncertainty in creative industries: Lessons from *Jerry Springer the Opera*, *Creativity and Innovation Management*, 15(3): 224–232.

Derrida, Jacques, (2007), *Learning to live finally: An interview with Jean Birmbaum*, trans. by Pascale-Anne Brault & Michael Naas, Hoboken; Melville House.

Dewey, John (1949), Common sense and science, in Dewey, J., & Bentley, A. F, *Knowing and the known*, Boston: Beacon press, pp. 270–286.

Dodge, Martin, & Kitchin, Rob, (2005), Code and the transduction of space, *Annals of the American Geographers*, 95(1): 162–180.

Dreyfus, Hubert L., (2001), *On the Internet*, London & New York: Routledge.

Drucker, Peter F., (1955), *The practice of management*, Melbourne, London & Toronto: Heineman.

Dubois, Anna, & Gadde, Lars-Erik, (2002), The construction industry as a loosely coupled system: Implications for productivity and innovation, *Construction Management and Economics*, 20: 621–631.

Dumit, Joseph, (2004), *Picturing personhood: Brain scans and biomedical identity*, Princeton, NJ: Princeton University Press.

Dumochel, Paul, (1995), Gilbert Simondon's plea for a philosophy of technology, in Feenberg, Andrew, & Hannay, Alastair, eds., *The politics of knowledge*, Bloomington & Indianapolis: Indiana University Press, pp. 255–271.

Edenius, Mats, & Yakhlef, A., (2007), Space, vision, and organizational learning: The interplay of incorporating and inscribing practices, *Management Learning*, 38(2): 193–210.

Eisenberg, Susan, (1998), *We'll call you if we need you: Experiences of women working construction*, Ithaca, NY, & London: Cornell University Press.

Eisenstein, E., (1983), *The printing revolution in early modern Europe*, Cambridge: Cambridge University Press.

Elkins, James, (1996), *The object stares back: On the nature of seeing*, New York: Simon & Schuster.

Elsbach, Kimberly D., (2006), *Organizational perception management*, Mahwah, NJ: Lawrence Erlbaum Associates.

Elsbach, Kimberly D., (2009), Identity affirmation through signature style: A study of toy car designers, *Human Relations,* 62(7): 1041–1072.

Empson, Laura, (2001), Fear of exploitation and fear of contamination: Impediments to knowledge transfer in mergers between professional service firms, *Human Relations*, 54(7): 839–862.

Enriques, J., & Goldberg, R. A., (2000), Transforming life, transforming business: The life-science revolution, *Harvard Business Review*, 78(2): 94–104.

Enthwistle, Joanna, & Racamora, Agnès, (2006), The field of fashion materialized: A study of London Fashion Week, *Sociology*, 40(4): 735–751.

Epstein, S. R., (1998), Craft guilds, apprenticeship, and technological change in preindustrial Europe, *Journal of Economic History*, 53(4): 684–718.

Eribon, Didier, (1991), *Michel Foucault*, Stehag: Symposion.

Erickson, Carolly, (1976), *The medieval vision: Essays in history and perception*, New York.

Esposito, Roberto, (2008), *Bíos: Biopolitics and philosophy*, trans. by Timothy Campbell, Minneapolis & London: University of Minnesota Press.

Ewenstein, Boris, & Whyte, Jennifer, (2007), Beyond words: Aesthetic knowledge and knowing in organizations, *Organization Studies*, 28(5): 689–708.

Fanon, Franz, (1986), *Black Skin, White Masks,* London: Pluto Press.

Fauchart, Emmanuelle, & von Hippen, Eric, (2008), Norm-based intellectual property systems: The case of French chefs, *Organization Science*, 19(2): 187–201.

Febvre, Lucien, & Martin, Henri-Jean, ([1958]1997), *The coming of the book: The impact of printing 1450–1800*, trans. by David Gerard, London & New York: Verso.

Fine, Gary Alan, (1996), *Kitchens: The culture of restaurant work*, Berkeley, Los Angeles, & London: University of California Press.

Fine, Gary Alan, (2007), *Authors of the storm: Meteorologists and the culture of prediction*, Chicago & London: University of Chicago Press.

Fleck, Ludwik, (1979), *Genesis and development of a scientific fact*, Chicago & London: University of Chicago Press.

Fleming, Peter, & Spicer, André, (2007), *Contesting the corporation: Struggle, power and resistance in organizations*, Cambridge: Cambridge University Press.

Flusser, Vilém, (2000), *Towards a philosophy of photography,* London. Reaktion Books.

Flusser, Vilém, (2002), *Writings*, Edited by Andreas Ströhl, trans. By Erik Eisel, Minneapolis & London: The University of Minnesota Press.

Foster, Hal, ed., (1988), *Vision and visuality*, New York: The New Press.

Foucault, M., (1967), *Madness and civilization*, London: Routledge.

Foucault, M., (1970), *The order of things*, London: Routledge.

Foucault, M., (1973), *The Birth of the Clinic*, London: Routledge.

Foucault, M., (1977), *Discipline and punish,* New York: Pantheon.

Foucault, M., (2000), Truth and juridical forms, in *Power: Essential works of Michel Foucault, Vol. 3*, Faubion, James D., ed., New York: The New Press, pp. 1–84

Foucault, Michel, (2006), *Psychiatric power: Lectures at the Collège de France, 1973–1974*, ed. by Jacques Lagrange, trans. by Graham Burchell, Basingstoke, UK: Palgrave.

Fournier, Valérie, & Grey, Chris, (2000), At the critical moment: Conditions and prospects for critical management studies, *Human Relations*, 53(1): 7–32.

Fowler, Bridget, & Wilson, Fiona, (2004), Women architects and their discontents, *Sociology*, 38(1): 101–119.

Franklin, Sarah, (2001), Culturing biology: Cell lines for the second millennium, *Health*, 5(3): 335–354.

Franklin, Sarah, (2005), Stem Cell R Us: Emergent life forms and the global biological, In Ong, Aihwa, & Collier, Stephen J., eds., (2008), *Global Assemblages: Technology, Politics, and Ethics as Anthropological Problems*, Malden, MA, & Oxford: Blackwell, pp. 59–78.

Franklin Sarah, (2007), *Dolly mixtures: The remaking of genealogy*, Durham, NC: Duke University Press.

Franklin, Sarah, & Roberts, Celia, (2006), *Born and made: An ethnography of preimplantation genetic diagnosis*, Princeton, NJ, & London: Princeton University Press.

Friedman, Andrew Lloyd, (2004), Strawmanning and labour process analysis, *Sociology*, 38(3): 573–591.

Freidson, Eliot, (1986), *Professional powers: A study of the institutionalization of formal knowledge*, Chicago & London: The University of Chicago Press.

Fry, Roger, (1920), *Vision and design*, London: Chatto and Windus.

Fujimura, Joan H. (1996), *Crafting science: A sociohistory of the quest for the genetics of cancer*, Cambridge, MA: Harvard University Press.

Gabriel, Yannis, & Willman, Paul, (2005), For dialogue rather than integration, *Human Relations*, 58(4): 423–427.

Galison, Peter, (1990) Aufbau/Bauhaus: Logical positivism and architectural modernism, *Critical Inquiry*, 16 (Summer): 709–752.

Galison, Peter, (2004), Images of self, in Daston, Lorraine, *Things That Talk: Object Lessons from Art and Science*, New York: Zone Books, pp. 257–294.

Galloway, Alexander R., (2006), Language wants to be overlooked: On software and ideology, *Journal of Visual Studies*, 5(3): 315–331.

Galloway, Alexander R., (2004), *Protocol: How power controls after decentralization*, Cambridge: MIT Press.

Galloway, Alexander R., & Thacker, Eugene, (2007), *The exploit: A theory of networks*, Minneapolis & London. University of Minnesota Press.

García, Baetriz, (2004), Urban regeneration, arts programming, and major events: Glasgow 1990, Sydney 2000, and Barcelona 2004, *International Journal of Cultural Policy*, 10(1): 103–118.

Garfinkel, H., (1967), *Studies in ethnomethodology*, Englewood Cliffs, NJ: Prentice Hall.

Garfinkel, Harold, (1988), Evidence for locally produced, naturally accountable, phenomena of order, logic, reason, meaning, method, etc. in and as of the essential quiddity of immortal ordinary society (I of IV): An announcement of studies, *Sociological Theory*, 6: 103–109.

Garfinkel, Harold, & Sacks, Harvey, (1970), On formal structure and practical action, in McKinney, John C., & Tiryakian, Edward A., *Theoretical sociology*, New York, pp. 337–366.

Garland-Thomson, Rosemarie, (2006), Ways of staring, *Journal of Visual Studies*, 5(2): 173–192.

Gassmann, Oliver, & Reepmeyer, Gerrit, (2005), Organizing pharmaceutical innovation: From science-based knowledge creators to drug-oriented knowledge brokers, *Creativity and Innovation Management*, 14(3): 233–245.

Geertz, C., (1973), *The interpretation of cultures*, New York: Basic Books.

Gherardi, Silvia, (1995), *Gender, symbolism, and organizational cultures*, London, Thousand Oaks, CA, & New Delhi: Sage.

Gherardi, Silvia, & Nicolini, Davide, (2001), The sociological foundations of organizational learning, in Dierkes, Meinolf, Berthon, Ariane, Child, John, & Nonaka, Ikujiro, eds., (2001), *Handbook of organizational learning & knowledge*, Oxford: Oxford University Press.

Gibson, Lisanne, (2002), Managing the people: Art programs in the American depression, *Journal of Arts Management, Law, and Society*, 31(4): 279–291.

Gieryn, Thomas F., (1983), Boundary-work and the demarcation of science from non-science: Strains and interest in professional ideologies of scientists, *American Sociological Review*, 48(6): 781–795.

Gieryn, Thomas F., (1999), *Cultural boundaries of science*, Chicago & London: University of Chicago Press.

Gill, Rosalind, & Pratt, Andy, (2008), In the social factory?: Immaterial labour, precariousness and cultural work, *Theory, Culture and Society*, 25(7–8): 1–30.

Gitelman, Lisa, (1999), *Scripts, grooves, and writing machines. Representing technology in the Edison era*, Stanford, CA. Stanford University Press.

Gitelman, Lisa, & Pingree, Geoffrey B., eds., (2003), *New media, 1740–1915*, Cambridge & London: MIT Press.

Golan , Tal, (2004), The emergence of the silent witness: The legal and medical reception of X-ray in the USA, *Social Studies of Science*, 34: 469–499.

Gombrich, E. H., (1960), *Art and illusion: A study in the psychology of pictorial representation*, London : Phaidon.
Goodwin, C., (1994), Professional vision, *American Anthropologist*, 96(3): 606–633.
Goodwin, Charles, (1995), Seeing in depth, *Social Studies of Science*, 25: 237–274.
Goody, Jack, (1997), *Representations and contradictions: Ambivalences towards images, theatre, fiction, relics and sexuality*, Oxford & Malden, MA: Blackwell.
Gouldner, Alvin W., (1954), *Patterns of industrial democracy*, Glencoe, IL: The Free Press.
Graham, L., (1995), *On the line at Subaru-Isuzu: The Japanese model and the American worker*, Ithaca, NY: ILR Press.
Grasseni, Cristina, (2004), Skilled vision: An apprenticeship in breeding aesthetics, *Social Anthropology*, 12(1): 41–55.
Greenberg, Daniel S., (1999), *The politics of pure science*, 2nd. ed., Chicago & London. University of Chicago Press.
Gregory, Richard Langton, ed., (2004a), Visual system: Organization, *The Oxford companion to the mind*, 2nd ed., Oxford & New York: Oxford University Press, pp. 931–937.
Gregory, Richard Langton, ed., (2004b), Perception, *The Oxford companion to the mind*, 2nd ed., Oxford & New York: Oxford University Press, pp. 707–710.
Grey, Christopher, (2004), Reinventing business schools: The contribution of critical management studies, *Academy of Management Learning and Education*, 3(2): 178–186.
Grosz, Elizabeth, (1994), *Volatile bodies: Toward a corporeal feminism*, Bloomington & Indianapolis: Indiana University Press.
Grosz, Elizabeth, (2001), *Architecture from the outside: Essays on virtual and real spaces*, Cambridge, MA. MIT Press.
Grosz, Elizabeth, (2008), *Chaos, territory, art: Deleuze and the framing of the earth*, New York: Columbia University Press.
Guillén, M. F., (1997), Scientific management's lost aesthetic: Architecture, organization, and the Taylorized beauty of the mechanical, *Administrative Science Quarterly*, 42, pp. 682–715.
Guillet de Monthoux, Pierre, (2004), *The art firm: Aesthetic management and metaphysical marketing from Wagner to Wilson*, Stanford, CA: Stanford University Press.
Guillet de Monthoux, Pierre, Gustafsson, Claes, and Sjöstrand, Sven-Erik, eds., (2007), *Aesthetic leadership: Managing fields of flow in art and business*, Basingstoke, UK: Palgrave Macmillan.
Gurevich, Aron, (1988), *Medieval popular culture: Problems of belief and perception*, Cambridge: Cambridge University Press.
Gunning, Tom, (1995), Tracing the individual body: Photography, detectives, and early cinema, in Carney, Leo, & Schwartz, Vanessa R., eds., *Cinema and the invention of modern life*, Berkeley: University of California Press, pp. 15–45.
Gustavsson, Eva, & Czarniawska, Barbara, (2004), Web woman: The on-line construction of corporate and gender images, *Organization*, 11(5): 651–670.
Gutman, Robert, (1988), *Architectural practice: A critical view*, Princeton, NJ: Princeton Architectural Press.
Guve, Bertil Gonzàlez, (2007), Aesthetics of financial judgments: On risk capitalists' confidence, in Guillet de Monthoux, Pierre, Gustafsson, Claes, and Sjöstrand, Sven-Erik, eds., *Aesthetic leadership: Managing fields of flow in art and business*, Basingstoke, UK: Palgrave Macmillan, pp. 128–140.
Habermas, Jürgen, (2003), *The future of human nature*, Cambridge: Polity Press.
Hacking, Ian (2006), Genetics, biosocial groups, and the future of identity, *Daedalus*, Fall: 81–96.

Hackman, W. D., (1989), Scientific instruments: Models of brass and aids to discovery, in Gooding, David, Pinch, Trevor, & Schaffer, Simon, (eds.), (1989), *The uses of experiments: Studies in the natural sciences*, Cambridge, New York, & Melbourne: Cambridge University Press, pp. 31–65.

Haigh, Elizabeth, (1984), *Xavier Bichat and the medical theory of the eighteenth century*, London: The Wellcome Institute for the History of Medicine.

Hallyn, Fernand, ([1987] 1990), The *poetic structure of the world: Copernicus and Kepler*, New York: Zone Books.

Hammer, Michael, & Champy, James, (1993), *Reengineering the corporation*, New York: Harper Business.

Hansen, Mark B. N., (2006), Media theory, *Theory, Culture & Society*, 23(2–3): 297–306.

Hanson, Norwood Russell, (1958), *Patterns of discovery: An inquiry into the conceptual foundations of science*, Cambridge: Cambridge University Press.

Hara, Takuji, (2003), *Innovation in the pharmaceutical industry: The process of drug discovery development*, Cheltenham & Northampton, UK: Edward Elgar.

Haraway, Donna J., (2000), *How like a leaf: An interview with Thyrza Nichols Goodeve*, New York & London: Routledge.

Harper, D., (1987), *Working knowledge: Skill and community in a small shop*, Chicago: University of Chicago Press.

Harter, Lynn M., Leeman, Mark, Norander, Stephanie, Young, Stephanie L., & Rawlins, William K., (2008), The intermingling of aesthetic sensibilities and instrumental rationalities in a collaborative arts studio, *Management Communication Quarterly*, 21(4): 423–453.

Hassard, John, & Rowlinson, Michael, (2002), Researching Foucault's research: Organization and control in Joseph Lancaster's monitorial schools, *Organization*, 9(4): 615–639.

Hassoun, Jean-Pierre, (2005), Emotions on the trading floor: Social and symbolic expressions, Knorr Cetina Karin, & Preda, Alex, eds., (2005), *The sociology of financial markets*, Oxford & New York: Oxford University Press, pp. 102–120.

Hayek, F. A., (1978), The two types of mind, in *New studies in philosophy, politics, economics, and the history of ideas*, London & Henley: Routledge and Kegan Paul.

Hayles, N. Katherine, (1999), *How we became posthuman: Virtual bodies in cybernetics, literature, and informatics*, Chicago & London: University of Chicago Press.

Hayles, N. Katherine, (2005), *My mother was a computer: Digital subjects and literary texts*, Chicago & London: University of Chicago Press.

Hayles, N. Katherine, (2006), Traumas of code, *Critical Inquiry*, 33 (Autumn): 136–157.

Hedgecoe, Adam & Martin, Paul, (2003), The drug don't work: Expectations and the shaping of pharmcogenetics, *Social Studies of Science*, 33(3): 327-364

Heidegger, Martin, (1966), *Discourse on thinking*, New York: Harper Torchbooks.

Heidegger, M., (1968), *What is called thinking?*, New York: Harper & Row.

Heidegger, Martin, (1977), *The question concerning technology and other essays*, New York: Harper & Row.

Helmholtz, Hermann von, (2004), From *Treatise on physiological optics*, in Schwatz, Robert, ed., *Perception*, Oxford & Malden, MA: Blackwell, pp. 42–49.

Helmholtz, Herman von, (1968), *Helmholtz on perception: Its physiology and development*, ed. by Warren, Richard M., & Warren, Roslyn P.,, New York: John Wiley.

Henderson, Kathryn, (1999), *On line and on paper: Visual representations, visual culture, and computer graphics in design engineering*, Cambridge & London: The MIT Press.

Hesmondhalgh, David, & Baker, Sarah, (2008), Creative work and emotional labour in the television industry, *Theory, Culture and Society*, 25(7–8): 97–118.

Hirschauer, Stefan, (1991), The manufacture of human bodies in surgery, *Social Studies of Science*, 21(2): 279–319.

Hirschman, A. O., (1977), *The passions and the interests*, Princeton, NJ: Princeton University Press.

Hitt, Michael, Bierman, Lonard, Shimzu, Katsuhiko, & Kochhar, Gahul, (2001), Direct and moderating effects of human capital on strategy and performance in professional service firms: A resource-based perspective, *Academy of Management Journal*, 44(1): 13–28.

Hogle, Linda, (1995), Standardization across non-standard domains: The case of organ procurement, *Science, Technology & Human Values*, 20: 480–500.

Holquist, Michael, (2003), Dialogism and aesthetics, in Gardiner, Michael E., ed., *Mikhail Bakhtin*, Vol. 1, London , Thousand Oaks, & New Delhi: Sage, pp. 367–385.

Hopkins, Michael M., Martin, Paul A., Nightingale, Paul, Kraft, Alison, & Mahdi, Surya, (2007), The myth of a biotech revolution: An assessment of technological, clinical and organizational change, *Research Policy*, 36(4): 566–589.

Hopper, Trevor, & Macintosh, Norman, (1998), Management accounting numbers: Freedom or prison—Geneen versus Foucault, in McKinlay, Alan, & Starkey, Ken, eds., *Foucault, management and organization theory*, London, Thousand Oaks, & New Delhi: Sage.

hooks, bell, (2000), *Where we stand: Class matters*, London & New York: Routledge.

Hochschild, Arlie R, (1983), *The Managed Heart*, Berkeley: University of California Press.

Howard, Ian P., (1996), Alhazen's neglected discoveries of visual phenomena, *Perception*, 25: 1203–1217.

Husserl, Edmund, (1970), *The crisis of the European sciences and transcendental philosophy*, Evanston, IL: Northwestern University Press.

Ihde, Don, (1995), Image technologies and traditional culture, in Feenberg, Andrew, & Hannay, Alastair, eds., *The politics of knowledge*, Bloomington & Indianapolis: Indiana University Press, pp. 147–158.

Ihde, Don, (2002), *Bodies in technology*, Minneapolis & London: University of Minnesota Press.

Illich, Ivan, (1977), *Disabling professions*, London: Marion Boyars.

Ingold, T. (2000) *The perception of the environment*, London: Routledge.

Ivory, Chris, (2004), Client, user, and architect interactions in construction: Implications for analyzing innovative outcomes from user-producer interactions in projects, *Technology Analysis & Strategic Management*, 16(4): 495–508.

Jackall, Robert, (1988), *Moral mazes: The world of corporate managers*, Oxford & New York: Oxford University Press.

James, William, ([1890] 1950), *Principles of psychology*, Vol. 1, New York: Dover.

James, William, (1975), *Pragmatism & the meaning of truth*, Cambridge, MA: Harvard University Press.

Jaques, Elliott, (1951), *The changing culture of a factory*, London: Tavistock Publications.

Jay, Martin, (1988), Scopic regimes of modernity, in Foster, Hal, ed., *Vision and visuality*, New York: The New Press, pp. 3–23.

Jay, Martin, (1996), Vision in context: Reflection and refractions, in Brennan, Teresa, & Jay, Martin, eds., *Vision in context: Historical and contemporary perspectives on sight*, New York & London: Routledge, pp. 1–12.

Jay, Martin (2002a), That visual turn, *Journal of Visual Culture*, 1(1): 87–92.

Jay, Martin, (2002b), Cultural relativism and the visual turn, *Journal of Visual Culture*, 1(3): 267–278.

Jeffcut, Paul, (2000), Management and the creative industries, *Studies in Cultures, Organizations and Societies*, 6: 123–127.

Jermier, John M., Slocum, John W. Jr., Fry, Louis W., & Gaines, Jeannie, (1992), Organizational subcultures in a soft bureaucracy: Resistance behind the myth and façade of an official culture, *Organization Science*, 2(2): 170–194.

Johnson, Ericka, (2007), Surgical simulations and simulated surgeons: Reconstituting medical practices and practitioners in simulations, *Social Studies of Science*, 37: 585–608.

Johnson, Ericka, (2008), Simulating medical patients and practices: Bodies and the construction of valid medical simulators, *Body & Society*, 14(3): 105–128.

Johnston, John, (1999), Machinic vision, *Critical Inquiry*, 26: 27–48.

Jones, Richard A. L., (2004), *Soft machines: Nanotechnology and life*, Oxford & New York: Oxford University Press.

Jong, Simcha, (2006), How organizational structures in science shape spin-off firms: The biochemistry departments of Berkeley, Stanford, and UCSF and the birth of biotech industry, *Industrial and Corporate Change*, 15(2): 251–283.

Jordanova, Ludmilla, (1989), *Sexual visions: Images of gender in science and medicine between the eighteenth and twentieth centuries*, London: Harvester Wheatsheaf.

Joyce, Kelly E., (2006), From numbers to pictures: The development of magnetic resonance imaging and the visual turn in medicine, *Science as Culture*, 15(1): 1–22.

Kahn, Jonathan, (2008), Exploiting race in new drug development; BiDil's interim model of pharmacogenomics, *Social Studies of Science*, 38(5): 737–758.

Kamara, J. M., Augenbroe, G., & Carillo, P. M., (2002), Knowledge management in the architecture, engineering and construction industry, *Construction Innovation*, 2: 53–67.

Kantorowicz, Ernest H., (1957/1997), *The king's two bodies*, Princeton, NJ: Princeton University Press.

Kärreman, Dan, & Alvesson, Mats, (2004), Cages in tandem: Management control, social identity, and identification in a knowledge-intensive firm, *Organization*, 11(1): 149–175.

Kasson, John F., (1976), *Civilizing the machine: Technology and republican values in America, 1776–1900*, New York: Grossman.

Kay, Lily E., (2000),*Who wrote the book of life? A history of the genetic code*, Stanford, CA, & London: Stanford University Press.

Keller, Evelyn Fox, (1983), *A feeling for the organism: The life and work of Barbara McClintock*, New York & San Francisco: W. H. Freeman.

Klein, Norman M., (2004), *The Vatican to Vegas: A history of special effects*, New York & London: The New Press.

Kline, Morris, (1954), *Mathematics in Western culture*, London. George Allen & Unwin.

Kline, Morris, (1972), *Mathematical thought from ancient to modern times*, Vol. 3, New York & Oxford: Oxford University Press.

Knorr Cetina, Karin, (1995), Laboratory studies: The cultural approach to the study of science, in Jasanoff, Sheila, Markle, Gerald E., Peterman, James C., & Pinch, Trevor, eds., *Handbook of science and technology studies*, Thousand Oaks, CA, London, & New Delhi: Sage.

Knorr Cetina, Karin, & Bruegger, Urs, (2001), Transparency regimes and management by content in global organizations: The case of institutional currency trading, *Journal of Knowledge Management*, 5(2): 180–194.

Knorr Cetina, Karin, & Bruegger, Urs, (2002), Traders' engagement with markets: A postsocial relationship, *Theory, Culture and Society*, 19(5/6): 161–185.

Kofman, Sarah, (1999), *Camera obscura: Of ideology*, trans. by Straw, Will, Ithaca, NY: Cornell University Press.

Koolhaas, Rem, (1978), *Delirious New York,* New York: The Monticelli Press.

Koyré, Alexandre, (1959), *From the closed world to the infinite universe,* New York: Harper Torchbooks.

Koyré, Alexandre, ([1968] 1992), *Metaphysics and measurement,* Reading, UK: Gordon and Breach Science Publishers.

Kracauer, Siegfried, (1995), Photography, in *The mass ornament: Weimar essays,* Trans. by Thomas Y. Levin, Cambridge & London: Harvard University Press, pp. 47–64.

Krause, E. A., (1996), *Death of the guilds,* New Haven: Yale University Press.

Kristeva, Julia, (1980), *Desire in language: A semiotic approach to literature and art,* New York: Columbia University Press.

Kruse, Corinna, (2006), *The making of valid data: People and machines in genetic research practice,* Ph.D thesis, Linköing, Sweden: Linköping University.

Lacan, Jacques, ([1973] 1998), *The four fundamental concepts of psychoanalysis: The seminars of Jacques Lacan, Book XI,* trans. by Alan Sheridan, New York & London: W. W. Norton.

Lakoff, Andrew, (2006), *Pharmaceutical Reason: Knowledge and Value in Global Psychiatry,* Cambridge: Cambridge University Press.

Lakoff, Andrew, (2008), The right patients for the drug: Pharmaceutical circuits and the codification of illness, in Hackett, Edward J., Amsterdamska, Olga, Lynch, Michael, & Wajcman, Judy, eds., *Handbook of science and technology studies,* 3rd. ed., Cambridge & London: MIT Press, pp. 741–760.

Lamont, Michèle, & Molnár, Virág, (2002), The study of boundaries in social sciences, *Annual Review of Sociology,* 28: 167–195.

Landecker, Hannah, (2007), *Culturing life: How cells became technologies,* Cambridge, MA: Harvard University Press.

Lanham, Richard, (2006), *The economics of attention: Style and substance in the age of information,* Chicago & London: University of Chicago Press.

Larson, Magali Sarafatti, (1977), *The rise of professionalism: A sociological analysis,* Berkeley, Los Angeles, & London: University of California Press.

Latour, B., (1986), The power of association, in Law, J., ed., *Power, action, and belief: A new sociology of knowledge,* London: Routledge & Kegan Paul.

Latour, B., (1987), *Science in action,* Cambridge, MA: Harvard University Press.

Latour, Bruno, (1988), *The pasteurization of France,* trans. By Alan Sheridan & John Law, Cambridge & London: Harvard University Press.

Latour, Bruno, (1991), Technology is society made durable, in Law, John, ed., *A sociology of monsters: Essays on power, technology and domination,* London & New York: Routledge.

Latour, Bruno, (2008), A textbook case revisited—Knowledge as a mode of existence, in Hackett, Edward J., Amsterdamska, Olga, Lynch, Michael, & Wajcman, Judy, eds., *Handbook of science and technology studies,* 3rd. ed., Cambridge & London: MIT Press, pp. 83–112.

Law, John, (1994), *Organizing modernity,* Oxford & Cambridge: Blackwell.

Lazzarato, Maurizio, (2007), Machines to crystallize time: Bergson, *Theory, Culture and Society,* 24(6): 93–122.

Le Corbusier, (1946), *Towards a new architecture,* trans. by Frederick Etchell, London: The Architectural Press.

Le Goff, Jacques, ([1985]1993), *Intellectuals in the middle ages,* Oxford & Cambridge: Blackwell.

Leidner, Robin, (1993), *Fast food, fast talk: Service work and the routinization of everyday life,* Berkeley: University of California Press.

Lenoir, Timothy, (1997), *Instituting science. The cultural production of scientific disciplines,* Stanford, CA: Stanford University Press.

Lenoir, Timothy, (2004), Foreword, in Hansen, Mark B. N., *New philosophy for new media*, Cambridge & London: MIT Press.

Lenoir, Timothy, (2007), Techno-humanism: Requiem for the cyborg, in Riskin, Jessica, ed., *Genesis redux: Essays in the history and philosophy of artificial life*, Chicago & London: University of Chicago Press, pp. 196–220.

Leppert, Richard, (1996), *Art and the committed eye: The cultural foundations of imaginary*, Boulder, CO: Westview Press.

Leroi-Gourhan, André, (1993), *Gesture and speech*, Cambridge, MA, & London: MIT Press.

Levin, David Michael, ed., (1993), *Modernity and the hegemony of vision*, Berkeley, Los Angeles, & London: University of California Press.

Lindberg, Kajsa & Czarniawska, Barbara, (2006), Knotting the action et, organizing between organizations, *Scandinavian Journal of Management*, 22: 292–306.

Linstead, Stephen, (1997), The social anthropology of management, *British Journal of Management*, 8(1): 85–98.

Linstead, Stephen, & Höpfl, Heather, eds., (2000), *The aesthetics of organization*, London, Thousand Oaks, CA, and New Delhi: Sage.

Livingston, Eric, (1986), The *ethnomethodological foundations of mathematics*, London, Boston, & Henley: Routledge & Kegan Paul.

Lock, Margaret, (2001), *Twice Dead: Organ Transplants and the Reinvention of Death*, Berkeley. Los Angeles and London: University of California Press.

Locke, Karen, & Golden-Biddle, Karen, (1997), Constructing opportunities for contribution: Structuring intertextual coherence and 'problematizing' in organization studies, *Academy of Management Journal*, 40(5): 1023–1062.

Locke, Karen, & Golden-Biddle, Karen, & Feldman, Martha S., (2008), Making doubt generative: Rethinking the role of doubt in the research process, *Organization Science*, 19(6): 907–918.

Lotringer, Sylvère, (2001), Doing theory, in Lotringer, Sylvère, & Cohen, Sane, eds. *French theory in America*, New York & London: Routledge.

Løvendahl, Bente R., Revang, Øivind, & Fosstenløkken, Siw M., (2001), Knowledge and value creation in professional service firms: A framework for analysis, *Human Relations*, 54(7): 911–931.

Lymer, Gustav, (2009), Demonstrating professional vision: The work of critique in architectural education, *Mind, Culture and Activity*, 16: 145–171.

Lynch, M., (1985), Discipline and the material form of images: An analysis of scientific visibility, *Social Studies of Science*, 15: 37–66.

Lynch, Michael, (1988), The externalised retina: Selection and mathematization in the visual documentation of objects in the life sciences, in Lynch, Michael, & Woolgar, Steve, eds., *Representation in scientific practice*, Cambridge & London: MIT Press, pp. 153–186.

Lynch, Michael, (1993), *Scientific practice and ordinary action*, Cambridge: Cambridge University Press.

Lynch, Michael, Livingston, Eric, & Garfinkel, Harold, (1983), Temporal order in laboratory work, in Knorr Cetina, Karin D., & Mulkay, Michael, eds., Science observed: Perspectives on the social study of science, London, Beverly Hills, & New Delhi: Sage, pp. 115–140.

Luhmann, Niklas, (2000), *Art as a social system*, trans. by Eva M. Knodt, Stanford, CA: Stanford University Press.

MacKenzie, Donald, & Millo, Yuval, (2003), Constructing a market, performing a theory: A historical sociology of a financial market derivatives exchange, *American Journal of Sociology*, 109(1): 107–145.

Macnaughton, Jane, (2007), Art in hospital spaces: The role of hospitals in an aestheticised society, *International Journal of Cultural Policy*, 13(1): 86–101.

Manovich, Lev, (2001), *The language of new media*, Cambridge & London: MIT Press.

Manovich, Lev, (2009), The practice of everyday (media) life: From mass consumption to mass cultural production? *Critical Inquiry*, 35 (Winter): 319–331.

Martin, Patricia Yancey, (2002), Sensations, bodies, and 'the spirit of a place': Aesthetics in a residential organization for the elderly, *Human Relations*, 55(7): 861–885.

Massumi, Brian, (2002) *Parables of the virtual: Movement, affect, sensation*, Durham, NC, & London: Duke University Press.

Mauss, Marcel, (1934/1992), Techniques of the body, in Crary, Jonathan, & Kwinter, Sanford, eds., (1992), *Incorporations*, New York: Zone Books, pp. 455–477.

McLeod, Mary, (1983), Architecture and revolution: Taylorism, technocracy and social change, *Art Journal*, 43(2): 123–147.

Merleau-Ponty, Maurice, (1962), *Phenomenology of Perception*, London: Routledge.

Merleau-Ponty, Maurice, (1964), *The primacy of perception and other essays on phenomenological psychology, the philosophy of art, history and politics*, trans. by Edie, James M., Chicago: Northwestern University Press.

Metz, Christian, (1982), *Psychoanalysis and cinema: The maginary signifier*, trans. by Britton, Calia, Williams, Annwyl, Brewster, Ben, & Guzzetti, Alfred, London: Macmillan.

Meyer, John W., & Rowan, Brian, (1977), Institutionalizing organizations: Formal structure as myth and ceremony, *American Journal of Sociology*, 83(2): 340–363.

Milburn, Colin, (2004), Nanotechnology in the age of posthuman engineering: Science fiction as science, in Hayles, N. Katherine, ed., (2005), *Nanoculture: Implications of the new technoscience*, Bristol: Intellect Books, pp. 109–129.

Mitchell, W. J. T., (2005), There are no visual media, *Journal of Visual Studies*, 4(2): 257–266.

Miztroeff, Nicholas, (2006), On visuality, *Journal of Visual Studies*, 5(1): 53–79.

Mol, Annemarie, (2002), *The body multiple: Ontology in medical practice*, Durham, NC: Duke University Press,

Morris, Timothy, (2001), Asserting property rights: Knowledge codifications in the professional service firm, *Human Relations*, 54(7): 819–838.

Moxey, Keith, (2008), Visual studies and the iconic turn, *Journal of Visual Studies*, 7(2): 131–146.

Mulvey, Laura, (1989), Visual pleasures and narrative cinema, in *Visual and other pleasures*, London: Macmillan, pp. 14–26.

Murningham, J. Keith, & Conlon, Donald E., (1991), The dynamics of intense work groups: A study of British string quartets, *Administrative Science Quarterly*, 36: 165–186.

Myers, Natasha, (2008), Molecular embodiments and the body-work of modeling in protein crystallography, *Social Studies of Science*, 38: 163–199.

Nagel, Thomas, (1986), *The view from nowhere*, Oxford & New York: Oxford University Press.

Natharius, Davis, (2004), The more we know, the more we see: The role of visuality in media literacy, *American Behavioral Scientist*, 48(2): 238–247.

Neiva, Eduardo, (1999), *Mythologies of vision: Image, culture and visuality*, New York: Peter Lang.

Nelson, R. R., & Winter, S. G., (1982), *An evolutionary theory of the economic change*, Cambridge: Belknap.

Nicolini, Divide, (2007), Studying visual practices in construction, *Building Research and Information*, 35(5): 576–580

Nietzsche, F., (1974), *The gay science*, New York: Vintage.

Nightingale, Paul, (1998), A cognitive model of innovation, *Research Policy*, 27: 698–709.

Nishizaka, Aug, (2000), Seeing what one sees: Perception, emotion, and activity, *Mind, Culture and Activity*, 7(1–2); 105–123.

Novas, Carlos, & Rose, Nicolas, (2000), Genetic risk and the birth of the somatic individual, *Economy and Society*, 29: 485–513.

Nye, David E., (1994), *American technological sublime*, Cambridge & London. MIT Press.

Nye, David E., (2006), *Technology matters: Questions to live with*, Cambridge & London: MIT Press.

Obrist, Hans Ulrich, & Koolhaas, Rem, (2001), Relearning from Las Vegas: An interview with Denise Scott Brown and Robert Venturi, in Chung, Chuihua Judy, Inaba, Jeffrey, Koolhaas, Rem, & Leong, Sze Tsung, eds., *Harvard design school guide to shopping*, Köln, Germany: Taschen.

Ofori, George, & Kien, Ho Lay, (2004), Translating Singapore architects' environmental awareness into decision making, *Building Research and Information*, 32(1): 27–37.

Oliver, Richard W., (2000), *The coming biotech age: The business of biomaterials*, New York: McGraw-Hill.

Orlikowski, Wanda J., (2002), Knowing in practice: Enacting a collective capability in distributed organizing, *Organization Science*, 13(3): 249–273.

Orr, Julian E., (1996), *Talking about machines: An ethnography of a modern job*, Ithaca, NY, and London: Cornell University Press.

Pallasmaa, Juhani, (1996), *The eyes of the skin: Architecture and the senses*, London: Academic Press.

Parker, Martin, (2002), *Utopia and organization*, Oxford: Blackwell.

Parry, Bronwyn, & Gere, Cathy, (2006), Contested bodies: Property models and the communication of human biological artefacts, *Science as Culture*, 15(2): 139–158.

Paules, Greta Foff, (1991), *Dishing it out: Power and resistance among waitresses in a New Jersey restaurant*, Philadelphia: Temple University Press.

Pauwels, Luc, ed., (2006), *Visual cultures of science; Rethinking representational practices in knowledge building and science communications*, Hanover, NH: Dartmouth College Press.

Perrow, C., (1984), *Normal Accidents*, New York: Basic Books.

Perrow, Charles, (2007), *The next catastrophe: Reducing our vulnerabilities to natural, industrial and terrorist disasters*, Princeton, NJ: Princeton University Press.

Perrow Charles & Guillén Mauro F., (1990), *The AIDS disaster: The failure of organizations in New York and the nation*, New Haven: Yale University Press.

Péteri, György, (1989), Engineer utopia: On the position of technostructure in Hungary's war communism, 1919, *International Studies in Management & Organization*, 19(3): 82–102.

Peters, Thomas J. & Waterman, Robert H., (1982), *In Search of Excellence*, Harper & Row, New York.

Petryna, Adriana, (2006), Globalizing human subjects research, in Petryna, Adriana, Lakoff, Andrew, & Kleinman, Arthur, eds., *Global pharmaceuticals: Ethics, markets, practices*, Durham, NC, & London: Duke University Press, pp. 33–60.

Pfeffer, Jeffrey, (1993), Barriers to the advance of organizational science: Paradigm development as a dependent variable, *Academy of Management Review*, 18(4): 599–620.

Pfeffer, Jeffrey, (2008), What ever happened to pragmatism?, *Journal of Management Inquiry*, 17(1): 67–60.

Pfeffer, Jeffrey, & Fong, Christina T., (2002), The end of business schools: Less success than meets the eye, *Academy of Management Learning and Education*, 1(1): 78–95.

Pfeffer, Jeffrey & Salancik, Gerald R., (1978), *The External Control of Organizations: A Resource Dependence Perspective*, Harper and Row, New York.

Pfeffer, Jeffrey, & Sutton, Robert I.. (2006), *Hard facts, dangerous half-truths, and total nonsense: Profiting from evidence-based management*, Boston: Harvard Business School Press.

Piaget, Jean, (1950/2001), *The psychology of intelligence*, London & New York: Routledge.

Pickering, Andrew, (1995), *The mangle of practice: Time, agency, and science*, Chicago & London: University of Chicago Press.

Pinch, Trevor J., & Bijker, Wiebe E., (1987), The social construction of facts and artefacts: Or how the sociology of science and the sociology of technology might benefit one another, in Bijker, Wiebe E., Hughes, Thomas P., & Pinch, Trevor J., eds., *The social construction of technological systems: New directions in the sociology and history of technology*, Cambridge & London: MIT Press, pp. 17–50.

Piñeiro, Erik, (2007), Aesthetics at the heart of logic: On the role of beauty in computing innovation, Guillet de Monthoux, Pierre, Gustafsson, Claes, and Sjöstrand, Sven-Erik, eds., *Aesthetic leadership: Managing fields of flow in art and business*, Basingstoke, UK: Palgrave Macmillan, pp. 105–127.

Pinnington, Ashly, & Morris, Timothy, (2002), Transforming the architect. Ownership from the archetype change, *Organization Studies*, 23(2): 189–210.

Pisano, Gary O., (2006), *Science business: The promise, the reality and the future of biotech*, Boston: Harvard Business School Press.

Porter, Theodore M., (1995), *Trust in numbers: The pursuit of objectivity in science and public life*, Princeton, NJ: Princeton University Press.

Postrel, Virginia, (2003), *The substance of style;: How the rise of aesthetic value is remaking commerce, culture and consciousness*, New York: Perennial.

Powell, T. C., (1995), Total quality management as competitive advantage: A review and empirical study, *Strategic Management Journal*, 16: 15–37.

Powell, Walter W., & Snellman, Kaisa, (2004), The knowledge economy, *Annual Review of Sociology*, 30: 199–220.

Prasad, Amit, (2005), Making images/making bodies: Visibility and disciplining through magnetic resonance imaging (MRI), *Science, Technology and Human Values*, 30(2): 291–316.

Prentice, Rachel, (2005), The anatomy of surgical simulations: The mutual articulation of bodies in and through the machine, *Social Studies of Science*, 35(6): 837–866.

Rabinow, Paul, (1992), Artificiality and enlightenment: From sociobiology to biosociality, Crary, Jonathan, & Kwinter, Sanford, eds., *Incorporations*, New York: Zone Books, pp. 234–251.

Rabinow, Paul, (1996a), *Making PCR: A story of biotechnology*, Chicago & London: University of Chicago Press.

Rabinow, Paul, (1996b), *Essay on the anthropology of reason*, Princeton, NJ, & London: Princeton University Press.

Rabinow, Paul, (2008), *Marking time: On the anthropology of the contemporary*, Princeton, NJ, & Oxford: Princeton University Press.

Rabinow, Paul, & Dan-Cohen, Talia, (2005), *A machine to make a future: Biotech chronicles*, Princeton, NJ: Princeton University Press.

Rafaeli, Anat, Dutton, Jane, Harquail, Celia V., & Mackie-Lewis, Stephane, (1997), Navigating by attire: The use of dress by female administrative employees, *Academy of Management Journal*, 40(1): 9–45.

Rajan, Kaushik Sunder, (2006), *Biocapital: The Constitution of Postgenomic Life*, Durham, NC: Duke University Press.

Rajchman, J., (1991), Foucault's art of seeing, in *Philosophical events: Essays of the '80s*, New York: Columbia University Press, pp. 68–102.

Rajchman, John, (1998), *Constructions*, Cambridge & London: MIT Press.

Ratey, John J., (2002), *A user's guide to the brain: Perception, attention and the four theatres of the brain*, London: Vintage.

Rawls, Anne Warfield, (2008), Harold Garfinkel, ethnomethodology and workplace studies, *Organization Studies*, 29(5): 701–732.

Reed, Michael, (2005), Reflections on the realist turn in organization and management studies, *Journal of Management Studies*, 42(8): 1621–1644.

Rheinberger, Hans-Jörg, (1997), *Toward a history of epistemic things: Synthesizing proteins in the test tube*, Stanford, CA: Stanford University Press.

Rheinberger, Hans-Jörg, (2003), 'Discourses of circumstances': A note on the author in science, in Biagliolo, Mario, & Galison, Peter, eds., *Scientific authorship: Credit and intellectual property in science*, London & New York; Routledge, pp. 309–324.

Riegl, Alois, ([1928] 2004), The modern cult of monuments; The character and its origin, in Schwartz, Vanessa R., & Przyblyski, Jeannene M., eds., (2004), *The nineteenth-century visual culture reader*, London & New York: Routledge, pp. 56–59.

Rifkin, Jeremy, (1998), *The biotech century: Harnessing the gene and remaking the world*, New York: Penguin Putnam.

Robertson, Maxine, Scarbrough, Harry, & Jacky, Swan, (2003), Knowledge creation in professional service firms: Institutional effects, *Organization Studies*, 24(6): 831–857.

Ropo, Arja, & Parviainen, Jaana, (2001), Leadership and bodily knowledge in expert organizations: Epistemological rethinking, *Scandinavian Journal of Management*, 17: 1–18.

Rorty, Richard, (1992), Ten years after, in Rorty, Richard, ed., (1967/1992), *The linguistic turn: Essays in philosophical method*, Chicago & London: University of Chicago Press.

Rorty, Richard, (2006), *Take care of freedom and truth will take care of itself: Interviews with Richard Rorty*, ed., by Mendieta, Eduardo, Stanford, CA: Stanford University Press.

Rose, Nikolas S., (2007), *The politics of life itself: Biomedicine, power and subjectivity in the twenty-first century*, Princeton, NJ, & Oxford: Princeton University Press.

Rose, Nicholas, & Novas, Carlos, (2005), Biological citizenship, in Ong, Aihwa, & Collier, Stephen J., eds., (2008), *Global Assemblages: Technology, politics, and ethics as anthropological problems*, Malden, MA, & Oxford: Blackwell, pp. 439–463.

Rosen, Michael, (1985), Breakfast at Spiro's: Dramaturgy and dominance, *Journal of Management*, 11(2): 31–48.

Rosen, M., & Astley, W. G., (1988): Christmas time and control: An exploration in the social structure of formal organizations, *Research in the Sociology of Organizations*, 6: 159–182.

Roth, Wolff-Michael, (2003), *Toward an anthropology of graphing: Semiotic and activity-theoretic perspectives*, Dordrecht, Netherlands: Kluwer.

Roth, Wolff-Michael, (2009), Radical uncertainty in scientific discovery work, *Science, Technology & Human Values*, 34(3): 313–336.

Roth, Wolff-Michael, & Bowen, G. Michaal, (1999), Digitalizing lizards: The topology of 'vision' in ecological fieldwork, *Social Studies of Science*, 29(5): 719–764.

Roth, Wolff-Michael, & Bowen, Gervase Michael, (2003), When are graphs ten thousand words worth? An expert/expert study, *Cognition and Instruction*, 21(4): 429–473.

Roy, Donald, (1952), Quote restriction and goldbricking in a machine shop, *American Journal of Sociology*, 57(5): 427–442.

Rubin, Beatrix P., (2008), Therapeutic promise in the discourse of human embryonic stem cell research, *Science as Culture*, 17(1): 13–27.

Ryle, G., (1949), *The concept of mind*, Harmondsworth, UK: Penguin.

Salter, Brian, & Salter, Charlotte, (2007), Bioethics and the global moral economy: The cultural politics of human embryonic stem cell science, *Science, Technology and Human Values*, 32(5): 554–581.

Salzer-Mörling, Miriam, (2002), Changing corporate landscapes, in Holmberg, Ingagill, Salzer-Mörling, Miriam, & Strannegård, Lars, eds., *Stuck in the future: Tracing the 'new economy,'* Stockholm: Bookhouse Publishing.

Sang, Katherine J. C., Dainty, Andrew J., & Ison, Stephen G., (2007), Gender: A risk factor for occupational stress in the architectural profession?, *Construction Management and Economics*, 25: 1305–1317.

Schatzki, Theodore R., (2002), *The site of the social: A philosophical account of the constitution of social life and change*, University Park. The Pennsylvania State University Press.

Schatzki, Theodore R., Knorr Cetina, Karin, & Savigny, Eike von, eds., (2001), *The practice turn in contemporary theory*, London & New York: Routledge.

Schivelbusch, Wolfgang, (1986), *The railway journey: The industrialization and perception of time and space in the 19th century*, Leamington Spa, UK: Berg.

Schmidgen, Henning, (2004), Thinking technological and biological beings: Gilbert Simondon's philosophy of machines, manuscript presented at 4S-EASST, Annual Meeting, Paris, August 28, 2004, Available at: http://www.csi.ensmp. fr/WebCSI/4S/download_paper/download_paper.php?paper=schmidgen.pdf (accessed August 4, 2006).

Schopenhauer, Arthur, (1995), *The world as will and idea*, London: Everyman.

Schrödinger, Erwin, (1946), *What is life?: Physical aspects of the living cell*, Cambridge: Cambridge University Press.

Schultze, Ulrike & Stabell, Charles, (2004), Knowing what you don't know? Discourses and contradictions in knolwdge mangement research, *Journal of Management Studies*, 41(4): 549–573.

Schutz, A., (1962), *Collected papers, Vol. I: The problem of social reality*, The Hague: Martinus Nijhoff.

Schwartz, Vanessa R., & Przyblyski, Jeannene M., eds., (2004), *The nineteenth-century visual culture reader*, London & New York: Routledge.

Schwartzman, Helen B., (1993), *Ethnography in organization*, Newbury Park, CA, London, & New Delhi: Sage.

Scott, W. Richard, (2008), Lords of the dance: Professionals as institutional agents, *Organization Studies*, 29(2): 219–238.

Selznick, Philip, (1949), *TVA and the grassroots*, Berkeley: University of California Press.

Shah, Sonia, (2006), *The body hunters: Testing new drugs on the world's poorest patients*, London & New York: The New Press.

Shapin, Steven, (1994), *A social history of truth: Civility and science in seventeenth-century England*, Chicago & London: University of Chicago of Press.

Shapin, Steven, (2008), *The scientific life: A moral history of a late modern vocation*, Chicago & London: University of Chicago Press.

Shapin, Steven, & Schaffer, Simon, (1985), *Leviathan and the airpump*, Princeton, NJ: Princeton University Press.

Sharp, Lesley, (2000), The commodification of the body and its parts, *Annual Review of Anthropology*, 29: 287–328.

Shostak, Sara, (2005), The emergence of toxicogenomics: A case study of molecularization, *Social Studies of Science*, 35(3): 367–403.

Shostak, Sara, & Conrad, Peter, (2008), Sequencing and its consequences: Path dependence and the relationships between genetics and medicalization, *American Journal of Sociology*, 114: S287–S316.

Shusterman, Richard, (2006), Aesthetics, *Theory, Culture & Society*, 23(2–3): 237–252.

Simmel, G., (1978), *The philosophy of money*, London: Routledge & Kegan Paul.

Simondon, Gilbert, ([1958]1980), *On the mode of existence of technical objects*, trans. by Mallahphy, Ninian, London: University of Western Ontario.

Silverman, David, (1970), *The theory of organizations: A sociological framework*, London: Heineman.

Silverman, Kaja, (1994), Fassbinder and Lacan: A reconsideration of gaze, look and image, in Bryson, Norman, Holly, Michael Ann, & Moxey, Keith, eds., *Visual culture: Images and interpretations*, pp. 272–301.

Smith Hughes, Sally, (2001), Making dollars out of DNA: The first major patent in biotechnology and the commercialization of molecular biology, 1974–1980, *Isis*, 92(3): 541–575.

Sontag, Susan, (1973), *On photography*, New York: Farrar, Straus & Giroux.

Stafford, Barbara Maria, (2009), Thoughts not our own: Whatever happened to selective attention, *Theory, Culture & Society*, 26(2–3): 275–293.

Starbuck, William H., (1992), Learning by knowledge-intensive firms, *Journal of Management Studies*, 29(6): 713–740.

Starbuck, William H., (2006), *The production of knowledge: The challenge of social science research*, Oxford & New York: Oxford University Press.

Starkey, Ken, & Madan, Paula, (2001), Bridging the relevance gap: Aligning stakeholders in the future of management research, *British Journal of Management*, 12, Special Issue, S3–S26.

Stengers, Isabelle, (1997), *Power and invention: Situating science*, Minneapolis & London: Minnesota University Press.

Steuer, Jonathan, (1992), Defining virtual reality: Dimensions determining telepresence, *Journal of Communication*, 42(4), 73–93.

Stiegler, Bernard, (1998), *Technics and time, 1: The fault of Epimetheus*, trans. by Beardsworth, Richard, & Collins, George, Stanford, CA: Stanford University Press.

Stiegler, Bernard, (2009), *Technics and time, 2: Disorientation*, trans. by Barker, Stephen, Stanford, CA: Stanford University Press.

Stock, Brian, (1983), *The implications of literacy: Written language and models of interpretation in the eleventh and twelfth centuries*, Princeton, NJ: Princeton University Press.

Strati, Antonio, (1999), *Organization and aesthetics*, London, Thousand Oaks & New Delhi: Sage.

Strati, A., (2007), Sensible knowledge and practice-based learning, *Management Learning*, 38(1): 61–77.

Strauss, Anselm, Schatzman, Leonard, Bucher, Rue, Ehrlich, Danuta, & Sabshin, Melvin, (1964), *Psychiatric ideologies and institutions*, 2nd ed., New Brunswick & London: Transaction Books.

Styhre, Alexander, (2002), Information and communication technology and the excess(es) of information: An introduction to Georges Bataille's general economy, *Ephemera*, 2(1): 28–42.

Styhre, Alexander, (2009), The cinematic mode of organizing: Media and the problem of attention in organization theory, *Information and Organization*, 19: 47–58.

Suddaby, Roy, & Greenwood, Royston, (2001), Colonizing knowledge: Commodification as a dynamic of jurisdictional expansion in professional service firms, *Human Relations*, 54(7): 933–953.

Sutton, R. I., & Staw, B. M., (1995), What theory is *not*, *Administrative Science Quarterly*, 40: 371–384.

Symes, Martin, Eley, Joanna, & Seidel, Andrew D., (1995), *Architects and their practice*, London: Butterworth.

Tarde, Gabriel, (1969), *On communication and social influence: Selected papers*, Terry N. Clark, ed., Chicago & London: University of Chicago Press.

Taylor F.W. (1903), *Shop Management*, Harper & Brothers, New York.

Taylor, F. W., (1911), *The Principles of Scientific Management*, Harper & Brothers publishers, New York.

Taylor, Steven S., (2002), Overcoming aesthetic muteness: Researching organizational members' aesthetic experience, *Human Relations*, 55(7): 821–840.

Taylor, Steven S., & Hansen, Hans, (2005), Finding form: Looking at the field of organizational aesthetics, *Journal of Management Studies*, 42(6): 1211–1231.

Teilhard de Chardin, Pierre, ([1955], 1965), *The phenomenon of man*, 2nd ed., trans. by Wall, Bernard, London: Collins.

ten Bos, René, (2000), *Fashion and utopia in management thinking*, Amsterdam & Philadelphia: John Benjamins.

Terranova, Tatiana, (2004), *Network culture*, London: Pluto.

Thacker, Eugene, (1999), Performing the technoscientific body: Real video surgery and the anatomy theatre, *Body & Society*, 5(2–3): 117–136.

Thacker, Eugene, (2004), *Biomedia*, Minneapolis & London.: University of Minnesota Press.

Thacker, Eugene, (2005), *The Global Genome: Biotechnology, Politics and Culture*, Cambridge & London: MIT Press.

Thacker, Eugene, (2006), *The global genome: Biotechnology, politics and culture*, Cambridge & London: MIT Press.

Thomas, David C., (2006), Domain and development of cultural intelligence: The importance of mindfulness, *Group & Organization Management*, 31(1): 78–99.

Thomas, Tom C., & Acuña-Narvaez, Rachelle, (2006), The convergence of biotechnology and nanotechnology: Why here, why now?, *Journal of Commercial Biotechnology*, 12(2): 105–110.

Thompson, Chris, (2005), *Making parents: The ontological choreography of reproductive technologies*, Cambridge & London: MIT Press.

Thompson, J. D., (1967), *Organizations in Action*, New York: McGraw-Hill.

Timmermans, Stefan, (2008), Professions and their work: Do market shelters protect professional interests?, *Work and Occupations*, 35(2): 164–188.

Titmuss, Richard M., (1970), *The gift relationship: From human blood to social policy*, London: George Allen & Unwin.

Tober, Diane M., (2001), Semen as gift, semen as good: Reproductive workers and the market in altruism, *Body & Society*, 7(2–3): 137–160.

Townley, Barbara, Beech, Nic, & McKinlay, Alan, (2009), Managing the creative industries: Managing the motley crew, *Human Relations*, 62(7): 939–962.

Trethewey, A., (1999), Disciplined bodies: Women's embodied identities at work, *Organization Studies*, 20(3): 432–450.

Trumbo, Jean, (2006), Making science visible: Visual literacy in science communication, in Pauwels, Luc, ed., *Visual cultures of science; Rethinking representational practices in knowledge building and science communications*, Hanover, NH: Dartmouth College Press, pp. 266–283.

Tsoukas, Haridimos, (1996), The firm as distributed knowledge system: A constructionist approach, *Strategic Management Journal*, 17 (Winter special issue): 11–25.

Tsoukas, Haridimos, (2005), *Complex knowledge: Studies in organizational epistemology*, Oxford & New York: Oxford University Press.

Tsoukas, Haridimos, & Mylonopoloulos, Nikos, (2004), Introduction: Knowledge construction and creation in organizations, *British Journal of Management*, 15: S1–S8.

Tsoukas, Haridimos, & Vladimirou, Efi, (2001), What is organizational knowledge?, *Journal of Management Studies*, 38(7): 973–993.

Tyler, Melissa, & Abbott, Pamela, (1998), Chocs away: Weight watching in the contemporary airline industry, *Sociology*, 32(3): 433–450.

Tyler, Melissa, & Taylor, Steve, (1998), The exchange of aesthetics: Women's work and 'the gift,' *Gender, Work and Organization*, 5(3): 165–171.

Ullman , Ellen, (1997), *Close to the machine: Technophilia and its discontents*, San Francisco: City Lights Book.

Urry, John, (2005), The complexity turn, *Theory, Culture & Society*, 22(5): 1–14.

Van Maanen, John, (1975), Police socialization: A longitudinal examination of job attitudes in an urban police department, *Administrative Science Quarterly*, 20: 207–228.

Van Maanen, John, (1979), The fact of fiction in organizational ethnography, *Administrative Science Quarterly*, 24: 539–550.

Vattimo, G., (1992), *The end of modernity*, Cambridge: Polity Press.

Venturi, Robert, Brown, Denise Scott, & Izenour, Steven, (1977), *Learning from Las Vegas: The forgotten symbolism of architectural form*, Cambridge, MA MIT Press.

Vico, G., (1999), *New science,* London: Penguin.

Vidler, Anthony, (2000), *Warped space: Art, architecture, and anxiety in modern society*, Cambridge & London: The MIT Press.

Virilio, Paul, (1989), *War and cinema: The logistics of perception*, trans. by Camiller, Patrick, London & New York: Verso.

Virilio, Paul, (1994), *The vision machine*, Bloomington & Indianapolis: Indiana University Press.

Wajcman, Judy, (2007), From women and technology to gendered technoscience, *Information, Communication & Society*, 10(3): 287–298.

Waldby, Catherine, (2000), *The visible human project: Informatics bodies and posthuman medicine*, London & New York: Routledge.

Waldby, Catherine, (2002), Stem cells, tissue cultures, and the production of biovalue, *Health*, 6(3): 305–322.

Waldby, Cathy, & Mitchell, Robert, (2006), *Tissue economies: Blood, organs, and cell lines in late capitalism*, Durham, NC, & London. Duke University Press.

Wark, McKenzie, (2004), *A hacker manifesto*, Cambridge & London: Harvard University Press.

Warneke, Georgia, (1993), Ocularcentrism and social criticism, in Levin, David Michael, ed., *Modernity and the hegemony of vision*, Berkeley, Los Angeles, & London: University of California Press, pp. 287–308.

Warren, Samantha, (2008), Empirical challenges in organizational aesthetics: Towards a sensual methodology, *Organization Studies*, 29(4): 559–580.

Warwick, Andrew, (2005), X-ray as evidence in German orthopedic surgery, 1985–1900, *Isis*, 96: 1–24.

Watts, Jacqueline H., (2009), 'Allowed into a man's world' meanings of work-life balance: Perspectives on women civil engineers as 'minority' workers in construction, *Gender, Work and Organization*, 16(1): 37–57.

Weick, Karl E., (1979), *The Social Psychology of Organizing*, New York: McGraw-Hill.

Weick, Karl E., (1989), Theory construction as disciplined imagination, *Academy of Management Review*, 14(4): 516–553.

Weick, Karl E., (1999), Theory construction as disciplined reflexivity: Tradeoffs in the 90s, *Academy of Management Review*, 24(4): 797–806.

Weick, Karl E., (2005), The experience of theorizing: Sensemaking as topic and resource, in Smith, Ken G., & Hitt, Michael A., eds., *Great minds in management: The process of theory development*, Oxford & New York: Oxford University Press, pp. 394–413.

Whitehead, Alfred North, (1929), *The aims of education*, New York: Mentor Books.

Whitehead, A. N., (1925), *Science and the modern world*, Cambridge: Cambridge University Press.

Whyte, Jennifer K., Ewenstein, Boris, Hales, Michael & Tidd, Joe, (2007), Visual practices and the objects used in design, *Building Research and Information*, 35(1): 18–27.

Wiener, Norbert, (1950), *The human use of human beings*, London: Eyre & Spottiswoode.

Winch, Graham, & Schneider, Eric, (1993), Managing the knowledge-based organization: The case of architectural practice, *Journal of Management Studies*, 30(6): 923–937.

Wittgenstein, L., (1953), *Remarks in the foundations of mathematics*, ed. by von Wright, G. H., Rhees, R., & Anscombe, G. E. M., trans. by Anscombe, G. E. M., Oxford: Blackwell.

Witz, Anne, (2000), Whose body matters? Feminist sociology and the corporeal turn in sociology and feminism, *Body & Society*, 6(2): 1–24.

Wray-Bliss, Edward, (2002), Abstract ethics, embodied ethics: The strange marriage of Foucault and positivism in labour process theory, *Organization*, 9(1): 5–39.

Yakura, Elaine K., (2002), Charting time: Timelines as temporal boundary objects, *Academy of Management Journal*, 45(5): 956–970.

Yaneva, Albena (2005), Scaling up and down: Extraction trails in Architectureal design, *Social Studies of Science*, 35(6): 867–894.

Zackariasson, Peter, Styhre, Alexander, & Wilson, Tim, (2006), Phronesis and creativity: Knowledge work in video game development, *Creativity and Innovation Management*, 15(4): 419–429.

Zembylas, Tasos, (2004), Art and public conflict: Notes on the social negotiation of the concept of art, *Journal of Arts Management, Law, and Society*, 34(2): 119–131.

Zielinski, Siegfried, (2006), *Deep time of the media: Towards an archaeology of hearing and seeing by technical means*, Cambridge & London: MIT Press.

Žižek, Slavoj, (1992), *Looking awry: An introduction to Jacques Lacan through popular culture*, Cambridge & London: MIT Press.

Žižek, Slavoj, (1995), *The metastases of enjoyment*, London: Verso.

Index

For Product Safety Concerns and Information please contact our EU
representative GPSR@taylorandfrancis.com
Taylor & Francis Verlag GmbH, Kaufingerstraße 24, 80331 München, Germany